Repairs: tenants' rights

LAG Law and Practice Guide No 12 (revised)

Repairs: tenants' rights

second edition

Jan Luba, barrister

Published by the Legal Action Group
January 1991

Jan Luba is a barrister. He has worked at a law centre in south London and as legal officer to the Child Poverty Action Group. Presently he is on the staff of the National Housing Law Service. He has written extensively in *Legal Action* and other journals on housing and welfare law matters, and his publications include *The Owner Occupier Handbook* (Sphere), *The Disabled Person's Handbook* (Sphere) and *Defending Possession Proceedings* (Legal Action Group). He is well known for his training on housing matters for LAG, Shelter and other national groups.

British Library Cataloguing in Publication Data
Luba, Jan
Repairs: tenants' rights.—2nd ed.
1. England. Rented residences. Maintenance & repair.
Liability of landlords. Enforcement by tenants
I. Title
344.206434

ISBN 0–905099–27–3

LAG Law and Practice Guide No 12 (revised)

Phototypeset by Kerrypress Ltd, Luton, Beds
Printed by Biddles Ltd, Guildford, Surrey
ISSN 0955–1018
ISBN 0 905099 27 3

Acknowledgements

The author wishes to thank Ros O'Brien and the LAG staff for their work on the manuscript, index and tables.

LAG would like to thank the Controller of HMSO for permission to reproduce the legislation in Appendices One to Four.

The law is as stated for England and Wales at 30 November 1990. Where possible account has been taken of recent caselaw at proof stage. However, statutory references are to the housing legislation effective from 1 April 1990 and environmental protection legislation effective from 1 January 1991.

The material in this book may be updated by reference to Nic Madge and Jan Luba "Recent developments in housing law", a quarterly series in *Legal Action* (LAG, monthly).

Readers' comments on the text are warmly invited.

Cover picture courtesy of David Hoffman.

How to use this Guide

If the law concerned with tenants' rights to housing repairs were simple, straightforward and effective, this book need not have been written. Instead our repairs law is a messy, overlapping conglomeration of rules, rights, powers and duties derived from a host of statutes, cases and regulations. There is no easy way of sorting it out.

The best way of using this book is to pass quickly through it to note the structure and main headings. Test the contents list and index and then, as calls for its use arise in practice, dip into the most appropriate entry. It certainly assumes some basic familiarity with the legal framework and process in the United Kingdom and, if unable to supply an "answer" to the particular enquirer, will, it is hoped, refer the reader (through the extensive footnoting) to a more appropriate source.

The book is primarily concerned with the law of England and Wales although reference is made to provisions of Scottish law and to decisions of the Scottish courts where these may be helpful.

Foreword to the Second Edition

In the five years that have passed since the first edition of this work was prepared there have been major developments in repairs law and these are reflected in the revisions incorporated in this edition. Depressingly, however, the chapter requiring the least revision has been the opening one which describes the appalling repairs problem in Britain's housing stock that has hardly improved at all for a decade or more. The revisions in other chapters note both progress and setbacks.

Chapter 2 (contractual rights) now embraces the substantive extension of the Landlord and Tenant Act 1985 s11 made by the Housing Act 1988, as well as recording a wealth of recent caselaw. Chapter 3 notes the substantial progress in the law of negligence that has eroded all but the most fundamental immunities of the landlord from liability for disrepair in tort and records the interruption of that progress by the decisions in *Murphy v Brentwood DC* and *Department of Environment v Thomas Bates & Sons Ltd.* The chapter on civil remedies (chapter 4) has been revised to give more emphasis to the most important legal remedies for disrepair (mandatory orders and compensation). The revision of chapter 5 reflects the continued development by practitioners of Public Health Act 1936 s99 as a tool to help tenants, and deals with the recasting of that provision by the Environmental Protection Act 1990. The most extensive re-writing has been in chapter 6 which deals with Housing Act powers. The text now describes the wholly revised procedures operative from 1 April 1990. Chapters 7 and 8 have been revised to reflect developments in both law and practice and to note the implications of the Planning and Compensation Bill 1990.

In order to strengthen the book's usefulness to practitioners, two new appendices have been prepared. Appendix 6 contains a table of damages awards which will be of assistance in advising on compensation quantum in disrepair claims. Appendix 7 contains precedents for use with a variety of enforcement procedures.

Jan Luba
December 1990

Contents

	page
Table of Statutes	xv
Table of Cases	xxiii
Table of Rules and Regulations	xxxvi
One: The Repairs Problem	1
1 Introduction	1
2 The condition of the housing stock	1
3 One hundred years' worth of bad housing	3
(a) Victorian–1945	3
(b) Non-traditional housing: 1950s and 1960s	4
(c) System and industrialised building: 1960s and 1970s	4
(d) Timber frame: 1970s and 1980s	5
(e) The present day	6
4 Conclusion	6
Two: Contractual Rights	9
1 Introduction	9
(a) The contract of letting	9
(b) The principle of "caveat emptor"	9
2 Express terms	10
Interpreting express terms	11
3 Implied terms	12
(a) Fit to be lived in	12
(b) Obligation to repair common parts	16
(c) Basic repairs (LTA 1985 s11)	18
(d) An implied term on general stuctural repair?	28
Three: Landlords' Liability for Disrepair	34
1 Introduction	34
2 General liability for disrepair at common law	35
(a) Builders	35
(b) Developers	35

(c) Local authorities 35
(d) Architects, engineers etc 36
(e) Landlords 37
(f) Limitation 41
3 General liability for disrepair under statute 41
(a) Occupiers' Liability Act 1957 41
(b) Defective Premises Act 1972 42

Four: Civil Remedies for Disrepair 49
1 Introduction 49
Preparing for action 49
2 Direct action 50
(a) Using rent to pay for repairs 50
(b) Withholding rent and rent strikes 52
(c) Set-off against rent 52
(d) Reduction in rent 53
(e) Reduction in rates 54
(f) Appointing a receiver or manager 54
3 Court proceedings 55
(a) Preliminaries 55
(b) Interim injunctions 56
(c) Landlord's undertakings 58
(d) Specific performance 58
(e) Remedies for breach of orders 59
(f) Declarations 60
(g) Damages 60
4 Using the ombudsman 64

Five: Using the Public Health and Environmental Protection Acts 69
1 Introduction 69
2 Statutory nuisance 69
(a) Generally 69
(b) "Any premises in such a state as to be prejudicial to health or a nuisance" 70
3 Action by local authorities 73
(a) Abatement notices 73
(b) High Court actions 74
(c) Emergency procedure 75
(d) Recurring nuisances 75
4 Action by tenants and other occupiers 76
(a) Private sector 76
(b) Public sector 77
5 Section 82 proceedings 77
(a) Preparatory work 79

(b) Procedure 80
(c) Nuisance orders 81
(d) Penalties 84
(e) Compensation 84
(f) Appeals 85
(g) Costs and legal aid 85
6 Environmental Protection Act and the Housing Act 85

Six: Bad Housing and the Housing Act 1985 91
1 Introduction 91
2 Housing unfit for human habitation 92
(a) Identifying unfit property 92
(b) The meaning of "unfit" 92
(c) Selecting the appropriate action 95
(d) The repairs procedure 96
(e) The closure/demolition procedure 99
(f) Mobilising the local authority 100
(g) Tenants' rights to rehousing 102
(h) Implications for tenants 102
(i) Council tenants 103
3 Housing in need of substantial repair 104
4 Fit houses in disrepair 105
5 "Houses" 106
6 Conclusion 108

Seven: Housing Conditions 111
1 Area action 111
(a) Clearance areas 111
(b) Renewal areas 112
2 Asbestos 113
3 Condensation 114
(a) LTA 1985 s11 or DPA 1972 s4 114
(b) EPA 1990 s82 (formerly PHA 1936 s99) 115
(c) Ombudsmen 116
4 Dampness 117
5 Dangerous buildings 118
6 Dilapidated buildings 118
7 Drains and sewers 119
8 Fire precautions 119
9 Improvements 120
(a) Voluntary improvement 120
(b) Compulsory improvement 120
10 Multi-occupied property 121
11 Neighbouring property 122

12 Noise 123
13 Overcrowding 123
14 Refuse 124
15 Sanitary installations 124
16 Services (gas, water and electricity) 125
17 Vandalism 125
18 Vermin 126

Eight: Displaced Tenants 128
1 Introduction 128
2 Causes of displacement 128
(a) Landlord willing to repair where work cannot be done with tenant in occupation 128
(b) Landlord in breach of obligation to repair where work cannot be done with tenant in occupation 131
(c) Landlord needs vacant possession to carry out improvement works 131
3 Rehousing for displaced tenants 132
(a) Land Compensation Act 1973 s39 133
(b) Housing Act 1985 Pt III 134
4 Financial compensation 134
(a) Home loss payments 135
(b) Disturbance payments 138
(c) Discretionary home loss and disturbance payments 141
(d) Contractual payments 142
(e) Well maintained payments 142
(f) Removal expenses 142
(g) Compensation for displacement caused by repairs work 143
(h) Getting the rent/community charge reduced 143
5 Help from a solicitor 144
6 Help from an ombudsman 144
7 Further reading 144

Appendices
One: Defective Premises Act 1972 s4 147
Two: Housing Act 1985 s606 149
Three: Environmental Protection Act 1990 ss79–82 150
Four: Landlord and Tenant Act 1985 ss8 and 11–17 155
Five: Useful Addresses 160
Six: Tables of Damages Awards for Disrepair 161
1 Court of Appeal 161
2 High Court 164
3 County Courts 164
Seven: Precedents 170

I The civil action 171
1 Particulars of claim 171
2 The application for an injunction 174
3 The draft order 176
II The complaint 177
1 The complaint to the magistrate 177
2 Draft complaint by magistrate 178
III The EPA proceedings 179
1 The initial information 179
2 Further information laid in magistrates' court 180
3 Draft summons 181
Eight: Amount of Home Loss Payment 182

Index 183

Table of Statutes

page

Agricultural Holdings Act 1948 27
Building Act 1984 75
  ss21, 59 119
  s72 120
   76(1) .... 88[48]
    (3) .... 88[50]
    (12) .... 88[49]
  ss77–83 118
  s79 118
Control of Pollution Act 1974 .... 123, 124
  s59 123
Costs in Criminal Cases Act 1973 .... 90[123]
County Courts Act 1959
  s51(A) .... 66[38]
County Courts Act 1984
  s69 64
   76 59
Criminal Justice Act 1982
  s67 .... 90[109]
Criminal Justice Act 1988
  s104 .... 90[111]
   105 .... 90[112]
Defective Premises Act 1972 42–46
  s1 .... 42, 46[12, 15], 56, 114
    (3) 56
    (4) .... 47[55]
   2 42
   3 .... 38, 43
    (2)(a) .... 47[57]
   4 .... 29, 43, 44, 45, 46, 56, 59, 114, 147–8
    (1)–(3) 43
    (1) 43, 44

Defective Premises Act 1972—*contd*
s4(2) 44
(3) 44, 45
(4) 43, 44
(5) 43
(6) . . . . 47[58]
6(3) 46
Environmental Protection Act 1990
s13 84
Pt III 69
ss79–82 . . . . 69, 150–154
s79 . . . . 69, 70, 72, 88[26]
(1) 76
(a) 70, 71, 72, 179, 181
(e) 70
(7) . . . . 71, 87[2]
80(1) . . . . 88[30, 32, 51, 54]
(2)(b) . . . . 88[33]
(c) . . . . 88[36]
(3) . . . . 88[38]
(4) . . . . 88[41]
(5) . . . . 88[42]
81(1) . . . . 88[37]
(3) . . . . 88[43]
(4) . . . . 88[44]
(5) . . . . 88[45]
82 . . . . 77, 77–86, 115–116, 123, 127, 170, 179
(1) . . . . 84, 89[64], 180
(2) . . . . 84, 89[66], 181
(b) . . . . 89[67]
(3) 87, 136
(4) . . . . 89[65]
(b) 82
(5) . . . . 89[65]
(6) 79, 80
(8) 78, 83, 84, 180
(12) . . . . 90[119]
164(2) 69
Sch 3 para 1(2) . . . . 88[39]
(4) . . . . 88[40]
2 . . . . 88[28]
paras 2–3 84
para 4 . . . . 88[52]
15 para 4 70

Environmental Protection Act 1990—*contd*
Sch 15 para 24 .... 88[48]
Fire Precautions Act 1971
ss 1, 3 119
Health and Safety at Work etc Act 1974
s71 43
Housing Act 1961
s32 18
Housing Act 1969
s72 .... 109[64]
Housing Act 1974
s130 .... 145[28, 34]
Sch 13 .... 145[28, 34]
paras 38(2), 39(3) .... 146[62]
Housing Act 1985 .... 91, 133
s22 .... 110[78], 133
ss26, 30 .... 146[73]
Pt III 118, 133, 134
s58(2A) 134
70 .... 146[71]
84(2)(a) .... 65[13]
96 51
ss97–98 120
s104 53
(1) .... 30[14]
105 137
106(1), (2), (4) 133
Pt VI 92, 95, 103, 106, 107
s189 .... 96, 97, 101, 102, 105, 107, 110[76]
(1A) 97
(1B) 96
(2)(a) 97, 98
(3) 97
(4) .... 109[36]
(5) .... 109[31]
190 .... 104, 105, 106, 107, 108
(1)(a) 104
(b) 105
190(1A) 104
(b) 106
(1B), (1C), (2), (3) 104
(5) 105
190A 96, 101
191 .... 97, 98, 102, 105, 107, 109[69]

Housing Act 1985—*contd*
s191(1A) 105
(1B), (2) 98
(3) 97, 99
(3A)–(3C) 98
(3A) 105
191A 98
192 99
193 . . . . . 98, 107
(2), (2A) 98
194 98
196 122
198A 97, 99, 105
202 97
203(3) 86, 103
205 107
207 . . . . . 97, 105, 106, 109[65], 110[75]
Pt VII 121, 133
IX 106
s264 . . . . . 99, 107
(2) 99
265 . . . . . 99, 107
(2) 99
267(2) 100
268 (1), (2) 99
269, (2), (2A)(a), (3A) 100
ss270, 277 102
289–306 111–112
s289 107
(2A), (2B) 112
300 (1) 100, 102
302 15
(a),(c) 100
Pt X 123
s317 102
(2) . . . . . 109[54]
336 . . . . . 88[35]
345 106
ss352, 354–357 121
365–368 . . . . . 120, 121
369, 379–400 121
Pt XVII 112
s586 . . . . . 146[69]
604 . . . . . 94–5, 107

Housing Act 1985—*contd*
s604(1) 92
(2), (3), (4) 93
(5) .... 108[11]
604A 96, 99, 107, 112
605 .... 108[5], 112
606 .... 101, 149, 170
(1) 92
(2) 101, 103, 107
(b) 101
623 .... 108[7]
Sch 1 para 3 .... 109[39]
2 ground 10 .... 129, 131, 132, 136, 137, 141
10A 136, 137, 141
10 paras 1, 2, 4 .... 98, 107
6A 98
23 112
paras 1–3, 7, 8 .... 146[69]
24 112
Housing Act 1988 .... 91, 133
s11 143
16 .... 30, 47[59], 128
Pt III 104
65 104
ss270, 276 103
Sch 2 ground 6 .... 130, 132, 143
8 52
9 143
Housing (Consequential Provisions) Act 1985
Sch 2 para 24 .... 145[20, 23]
(4) .... 145[13]
Housing and Planning Act 1986
s9(3) .... 145[26]
(4) .... 146[67]
Justices of the Peace Act 1979
s64 .... 89[82]
Land Compensation Act 1973 132
ss29–39 .... 109[51]
s29 .... 135, 136
(1) .... 145[28]
(2) .... 146[67a]
(3A) .... 146[62]
(4) .... 145[21]
(6) .... 145[22]

Land Compensation Act 1973—*contd*
s29(7) .... 145[23]
(7A) .... 145[34]
30 .... 182[1]
(1) .... 182[4]
32(1) .... 136, 145[27]
(2) .... 145[29]
(3) .... 145[31]
(5) .... 145[32]
(6) .... 145[30]
(7) .... 145[27]
(7B) .... 146[67]
37(1) 141
(2), (b) 138
(3) 139
(3A) .... 146[62]
(5) .... 146[64]
(6) 140
(9) .... 145[48]
38(1) .... 145[46]
(3) .... 145[56]
(4) .... 145[47]
39 .... 102, 133–4
(1) 133
(3), (6) 134
(6A) 134
Landlord and Tenant Act 1985 93
s1 50
8 .... 11, 14, 15, 16, 30, 155
(2), (5) 15
(6) 14
10 15
ss11–16 .... 65[12]
11–17 156–9
s11 .... 11, 14, 18–28, 30, 33[132A], 52, 114, 125
(1)(a) 19, 24
(b) 24, 25, 125
(c) 24, 125
(1A) 17, 18, 24
(1B) 17, 24
(2) 27
(3) 25
(3A), (4), (6), ... 18
ss12–15 27

Landlord and Tenant Act 1985—*contd*
s12 (1)(a) 18
13 (1), (2) 27
14(4) 27
15 28
16(b) 22
17, (2) 59
32(2) 27
Landlord and Tenant Act 1987
Pt II 54
ss22, 24, (8), 52 54
Latent Damage Act 1986 56
Legal Aid Act 1988
ss8, 21 .... 90[122]
Limitation Act 1980 55
ss14A, (5), 14B 41
Local Government Act 1972
s101 .... 88[27], 109[56]
Local Government and Housing Act 1989 91
s165(2) 121
194 133
Sch 9 para 76 142
83 .... 108[6]
85 .... 108[5]
12 133
Pt II .... 145[24, 49]
Local Government (Miscellaneous Provisions) Act 1976 73
s8 .... 109[42]
16 .... 88[35]
33 125
Local Government and Planning Act 1980
s114 .... 145[27]
Magistrates' Courts Act 1980
s50 .... 88[63]
Occupiers' Liability Act 1957 41–2
s2 42
3(1) .... 47[53]
Planning and Compensation Bill 1990 .... 135, 146[67a]
clause 47 .... 145[19]
(9) .... 145[18]
Powers of Criminal Courts Act 1973
s35 .... 90[107], 99
Prevention of Damage by Pests Act 1949 126
Public Health Act 1936 .... 69, 74

Public Health Act 1936—*contd*
Pt II 126
s72 124
ss91–100 69
s94(2) 136
99 .... 77, 78, 80, 85, 88[58], 115–6
ss141, 259, 268 70
Public Health Act 1961
s17 119
Public Health (Recurring Nuisances) Act 1969 76
Rent Act 1977 .... 128, 133
s3(2) .... 33[152]
67(3) .... 146[75]
(a) .... 66[20]
98(1) .... 65[13]
116 132
148 .... 30, 47[59], 128
Supreme Court Act 1981
s37(1) 54
Unfair Contract Terms Act 1977 .... 11, 13, 42

Table of Cases

page

ACT Construction v Customs and Excise [1981] 1 WLR 1542, HL .... 32[107]
Abdullah and Ors v South Tyneside BC (1987) September *Legal Action* 12 .... 116[3], 167
Acrecrest v Hattrel (WS) & Partners [1983] 1 All ER 17 .... 46[14]
Adams v Tuer (1923) 22 LGR 88 .... 109[34]
Ahmed v GLC (1984) May *Legal Action* 53 .... 67[77]
Alexander v Mercouris [1979] 3 All ER 305 .... 47[56]
Al Hassani v Merrigan (1988) 20 HLR 238, CA .... 33[147], 52
Ali v LB Hackney (1985) December *Legal Action* 171 .... 83, 85, 89[90]
Allport v Securities Corp (1895) 64 LJ Ch 491; 39 SJ 362 57
American Cyanamid v Ethicon [1975] AC 396, HL .... 66[42]
Anns v Merton LBC [1977] 2 WLR 1024 .... 36, 37, 46[4, 14, 19]
Arden v Pullen (1842) 10 M & W 321 .... 30[6]
Armstrong v GLC (1980) November *LAG Bulletin* 269 .... 145[43]
Asco Developments & Newman v Lowes, Lewis and Gordon (1978) 248 EG 683 51
Astro Exito Navegacion SA v Southland Enterprise Co Ltd and Others [1982] QB 1248 57
Bacon v Grimsby Corp [1950] 1 KB 272 .... 108[25]
Ball v London CC [1949] 2 KB 159 .... 47[32]
Ball v Plummer (1879) *Times* 17 June, CA .... 33[114]
Barrett v Lounova (1982) Ltd (1988) 20 HLR 584, CA .... 33[135], 44, 60, 67[57]
Battersea Freehold and Leasehold Property Co Ltd v Norman (1990) October *Legal Action* 24 169
Batty v Metropolitan Property Realisations [1978] QB 554 .... 46[11], 47[28]
Beaney v Branchett (1987) 19 HLR 471, CA .... 109[55]
Bennett v Preston BC (1984) March/April *Roof* 18 .... 87[16]
Benson v Liverpool CC (1988) March *Legal Action* 22 .... 33[132]
Berg v Trafford BC (1988) 20 HLR 47, CA 120
Betts v Penge UDC [1942] 2 KB 154 .... 87[17]

Billings (AC) & Sons v Riden [1957] 3 All ER 1 ... 47[32]
Birchall v Wirral UDC (1953) 117 JP 384 ... 108[8]
Bird v Greville (1844) C & E 317 ... 30[31]
Birmingham DC v Kelly and Ors (1985) 17 HLR 572 ... 83, 89[85, 91, 92, 94, 99], 116
Birmingham DC v McMahon and Others (1987) 19 HLR 452 ... 87[5]
Bishop v Consolidated London Properties (1933) 102 LJKB 257 . 31[73]
Bishop Auckland Local Board v Bishop Auckland Iron and Steel Co Ltd (1883) 10 QBD 138 ... 87[22]
Black v Oliver [1978] 1 QB 870 ... 66[23], 146[76]
Blawdziewicz v Diodon Establishment (1988) 35 EG 83 ... 66[29]
Bond v Chief Constable of Kent [1983] 1 All ER 456 ... 90[106]
Booth v Thomas [1926] Ch 397 ... 31[70]
Borg v Southwark LBC (1987) June *Legal Action* 19, CA ... 146[68]
Boswell v Crucible Steel Co of America [1925] 1 KB 119 ... 33[113]
Bottomley v Bannister [1932] 1 KB 458 ... 46[3]
Bradley v Chorley BC (1985) 275 EG 801; 17 HLR 305, CA ... 32[82], 109[66], 162
Brent LBC v Roberts (1990) December *Legal Action* 16 ... 169
Brew Bros Ltd v Snax [1970] 1 QB 612 ... 32[79]
Brikom Investments v Seaford [1981] 1 WLR 863 ... 27
Bristol Corp v Sinnot [1918] 1 Ch 62 ... 88[32]
British Anzani v International Marine [1979] 2 All ER 1063 ... 53, 65[16]
Brown v Biggleswade Union (1879) 43 JP 554 ... 89[100]
Brown v Liverpool Corp [1969] 3 All ER 1345 ... 32[105]
Brunyee v Lambeth LBC (1982) January *Roof* 25 ... 83, 89[71]
Bulgar v Knowsley BC (1989) June *Legal Action* 25 ... 145[41, 45, 54]
Bunn v Harrison (1886) 3 TLR 146, CA ... 31[36, 40]
Buswell v Goodwin [1971] 1 WLR 92 ... 15, 110[79]
Bygraves v Southwark LBC (1990) December *Legal Action* 16 ... 169
Calabar Properties Ltd v Stitcher [1983] 3 All ER 759; (1984) 11 HLR 20, CA ... 33[127], 67[69, 71, 72, 75, 84, 85, 89, 92], 129, 146[74], 161
Calthorpe v McOscar [1924] 1 KB 716 ... 30[17, 19], 33[122]
Camden Nominees v Forcey [1940] Ch 352 ... 65[11]
Cameron v Glasgow DC (1984) January *Scolag* 9 ... 33[120]
Campden Hill Towers v Gardner [1977] QB 823; 1 All ER 739 ... 24, 33[115], 65[12]
Canadian Pacific Rly v Gaud [1949] 2 KB 239 ... 66[40]
Caplan v GLC (1980) 5 HLR 104, CA ... 145[42]
Cardiff CC v Cross (1982) 6 HLR 1, CA ... 88[57]
Casale v Islington LBC (1985) 18 HLR 146 ... 141
Castle v Northampton CC (1989) September *Legal Action* 24 ... 67[67]
Cavalier v Pope [1906] AC 428 ... 46[3]

Cedar Transport Group v First Wyvern Property Trustees Co (1981) 258 EG 1077 .... 46[16]
Celcrest Properties Ltd v Hastings BC (1979) 29 October, unreported, Ch D .... 88[47]
Charsley v Jones [1889] 5 TLR 412 .... 30[25]
Chester v Powell (1885) 52 LT 722 .... 31[33]
Chevron Petroleum (UK) Ltd v Post Office 1987 SLT 588 .... 31[72]
Chiodi *see* PRs of Chiodi v De Marney
Christou v Islington LBC (1980) 51 *Community Action* 10 83
Church v Ministry of Defence (1984) NLJ 623 114
Church of Our Lady of Hal v LB Camden (1980) 255 EG 991, CA .... 109[67]
City and Metropolitan Properties v Greycroft [1987] 3 All ER 839 .... 67[85]
Clarke v Taff Ely BC (1984) 10 HLR 44 44
Clarridge and Meerschwam v Swallow Securities (1986) January *Legal Action* 14 .... 66[49]
Clayhope Properties v Evans (1986) 18 HLR 361, CA .... 66[25, 30]
Cochrane v Chanctonbury RDC [1950] 2 All ER 1134 .... 109[37]
Cockburn v Smith [1924] 2 KB 119 .... 16, 31[61]
Cocker v Cardwell (1869) LR 5 QB 15 .... 88[29, 53]
Cohen v West Ham Corp [1933] Ch 814 .... 108[25]
Cole v Southwark LB (1979) 251 EG 477, Lands Tr .... 145[57]
Cole v Swansea CC (1988) 21 HLR 468, CA .... 108[25]
Coley v LB Camden (1983) 12 September, unreported, Bloomsbury and Marylebone County Court, noted at *Times* 13 September 126
Collins v Flynn [1963] 2 All ER 1068 .... 32[81]
Collins v Hopkins [1923] 2 KB 617 .... 31[31]
Cmmrs of Customs and Excise v Sutton Housing Trust [1983] STC 399; [1984] STC 352, CA .... 32[84], 33[108]
Cmmrs of Customs and Excise v Viva Gas Appliances Ltd [1983] 1 WLR 1445, HL .... 32[84]
Connell v Hackney LBC (1985) unreported, CAT 85/316, CA .... 67[56]
Consolidated Agricultural Suppliers v Rushmere (1976) 120 SJ 523 .... 66[53]
Cook v Southend BC (1989) 11 CL 323, CA .... 90[114]
Cophil v Blair (1978) January *LAG Bulletin* 14 .... 65[13]
Coventry CC v Cartwright [1975] 1 WLR 845; 2 All ER 99 . 87[14,22], 88[60]
Coventry CC v Doyle [1981] 2 All ER 184 .... 89[76, 86]
Crawford v Newton (1886) 2 TLR 877, CA .... 33[112]
Cruse v Mount [1933] Ch 278 .... 13, 30[5]
D & F Estates Ltd v Church Cmmrs for England [1989] AC 177, HL .... 47[22]

Daejan Properties Ltd v Elliott (1977) September *LAG Bulletin* 208 .... 67[77]
Daiches v Bluelake Investments Ltd (1985) 275 EG 462 .... 66[25]
Daly v Elstree RDC [1948] 2 All ER 13 .... 108[10]
Davies v Brenner [1986] CLY 1874; (1989) June *Legal Action* 24 .... 33[132A]
Davies v Peterson (1988) 21 HLR 63, CA .... 67[78], 163
Davis v Edinburgh DC (1984) June *Scolag* 86 .... 31[46]
Davis v Floors [1940] 1 KB 116 .... 46[3]
Day v Sheffield CC (1988) August *Legal Action* 19 .... 87[6], 90[121]
Dear v Newham LBC (1988) 20 HLR 348, CA 124
De Meza v Veribest Mfg (1952) 160 EG 364 .... 31[67]
Dennis v Charnwood BC [1982] 3 All ER 486, CA .... 46[14]
Department of Environment v Thomas Bates & Son [1990] 3 WLR 457, HL .... 47[22]
Department of Transport v Egoroff (1986) 18 HLR 326, CA .... 33[130]
De Rosario v Dewing (1982) August *LAG Bulletin* 91 .... 67[77]
Dinefwr BC v Jones (1987) 19 HLR 445, CA .... 29, 33[141]
DPP v Carrick (1985) 31 *Housing Aid* 5 124
Dodd Properties (Kent) Ltd v Canterbury CC [1980] 1 All ER 928, CA .... 67[68]
Donaghue v Stevenson [1932] AC 562 .... 46[2]
Douglas-Scott v Scorgie [1984] 1 All ER 1086 .... 33[116]
Dover DC v Farrar (1982) 2 HLR 32 .... 90[123], 115, 116[6]
Downie v Lambeth LBC (1986) June *Legal Action* 95 165
Duke of Westminster v Guild [1984] 3 WLR 630 .... 31[62]
Duncan v Brent LBC (1989) June *Legal Action* 18 123
Dunster v Hollis [1918] 2 KB 795 .... 16, 31[55]
Dutton v Bognor Regis UDC [1972] 1 QB 373 .... 46[14]
Eames London Estates v North Hertfordshire DC (1981) 259 EG 491 .... 46[17]
Edwards v Etherington (1825) Ry & M 268 .... 31[32]
Edwards v Upton (1980) 253 EG 818 .... 30[5]
Elite Investments Ltd v TI Bainbridge Silencers Ltd (1986) 280 EG 1001; 12 CL 148 20
Elite Investments Ltd v TI Bainbridge Silencers Ltd (No 2) (1987) 283 EG 747 .... 67[91]
Elliott v Brighton BC (1981) 79 LGR 506 .... 109[33]
Elmcroft Development v Tankersley-Sawyer (1984) 270 EG 140 .... 20, 22
Esso Petroleum v Marden [1976] 1 QB 801 .... 46[13]
Estate & Trust Co v Singapore Improvement Trust [1937] 3 All ER 324, PC .... 108[22]
Evans v Clayhope Properties (1988) 20 HLR 176, CA .... 54, 66[28]
FFF Estates Ltd v Hackney LBC [1981] QB 503 121
re Falmouth Clearance Order [1937] 3 All ER 308 .... 109[36]

Felix v Karachristos (1987) August *Legal Action* 17 166
Finch v Manchester CC (1986) December *Legal Action* 167...... 164
Fisher v Walters [1926] 2 KB 315 .... 31[53]
Fitzpatrick v Dawnray (1976) May *Roof* 92 .... 116[5]
Fletcher v Ilkeston Corp (1931) 96 JPLGR 7 .... 109[38]
Follows v The Peabody Trust (1983) 10 HLR 65, CA .... 145[38, 44]
Foster v Day (1968) 208 EG 495.............................. 33[133]
Francis v Cowliffe Ltd (1976) 239 EG 977; 33 P&CR 368 59
Fraser v Hopewood Properties (1986) 1 CL 217; June *Legal Action* 81 165
Fulham Vestry v London CC [1897] 2 QB 76 .... 87[3]
Gallagher v McDowell Ltd [1961] NI 26....................... 46[10]
Gandolfo v Gandolfo (Standard Chartered Bank, Garnishee) [1980] 1 All ER 833, CA .... 66[55]
Glasgow Corp v Anderson 1976 SLT 225 .... 145[55]
Gordon v Selico Co Ltd (1986) 18 HLR 219, CA .. 16, 31[61,62,70], 32[74], 67[86]
Goss v Paddington Churches Housing Association (1981) 261 EG 373 .... 146[58]
Gott v Gandy (1853) 2 E & B 845 .... 30[4]
Gould v Times Square Estates Ltd (1975) September *LAG Bulletin* 247 78
Gozra v Hackney LBC (1988) 21 HLR 1; 46 EG 87, CA........ 146[66]
Graddage v Haringey LBC [1975] 1 All ER 224 .... 109[36]
Granada Theatres v Freehold Investment (Leytonstone) [1959] 1 WLR 570 .... 33[111, 151], 144[2]
Gravesham BC v Secretary of State for the Environment (1984) 47 P&CR 142 .... 32[101]
Great Western Rly v Bishop (1872) LR 7 QB 550 .... 87[22]
GLC v Feroushos (1982) March, unreported, Inner London Crown Court .... 89[78]
GLC v Holmes (1985) 18 HLR 131, CA .... 145[25,40]
Green v Eales (1841) 2 QB 225 .... 32[104], 144[5]
Griffen v Pillet [1926] 1 KB 117 .... 33[146]
Griffiths v Swansea CC (1984) March/April *Roof* 18 .... 116[1]
Guinan v Enfield LBC (1990) June *Legal Action* 16 123
Gunn v NCB 1982 SLT 526.................................... 31[46]
Hall v Howard (1988) 20 HLR 566, CA 29
Hall v Manchester Corp (1915) 84 LJ Ch 732 .... 108[13]
Halliard Property Co Ltd v Nicholas Clarke Investments Ltd (1984) 269 EG 1257 .... 32[86]
Hamilton v Martell Securities (1984) 48 P&CR 69.............. 47[60]
Hammersmith and Fulham LBC v Gamble (1989) March *Legal Action* 24 122

Hammersmith and Fulham LBC v Gill, Same v Abrahams (1989) June *Legal Action* 24 122
LB Hammersmith and Fulham and RB Kensington and Chelsea v Ward (1984) May/June *Roof* 18 .... 89[101]
Hammersmith LBC v Magnum Automated Forecourts [1977] 1 All ER 401, CA .... 90[117]
Harrison v Malet [1886] 3 TLR 58 .... 30[27, 30], 31[45]
Hart v Emelkirk Ltd [1983] 3 All ER 15 54
Hart v Windsor (1844) 12 M & W 68 .... 30[5, 22]
Harvey v Crawley DC [1957] 1 QB 485 .... 146[61]
Hatfield v Moss (1988) 40 EG 112 .... 33[116]
Hastie v City of Edinburgh 1981 SLT 61 .... 33[114]
Hermitage Court Owners Association v Clyftville Properties (1979) 18 May, unreported, CAT 79/304, CA 55
Hewitt v Rowlands (1924) 93 LJKB 729, 1080 .... 67[73]
Hillbank Properties v Hackney LBC [1978] 3 WLR 260; (1982) 3 HLR 73 .... 107, 108[4], 109[69]
Hilton v Hopwood (1899) 44 SJ 96 .... 89[70]
Hodgson v Sunderland Corp (1937) LJNCCR 187 .... 109[34]
Holiday Fellowship v Hereford [1959] 1 WLR 211 .... 33[113]
Holland v Yates Building Co Ltd (1989) 45 LS Gaz 36 .... 47[49]
Hone v Benson (1978) 248 EG 1013 38
Hooper v Rogers [1974] 3 All ER 417 .... 66[44]
Hopwood v Cannock Chase DC [1975] 1 WLR 373 .... 32[106]
Horrex v Pidwell [1958] CLY 1461 .... 31[54], 67[77]
Hubble v Lambeth LBC (1986) April *Legal Action* 50 165
Hudson v RB Kensington and Chelsea (1985) December *Legal Action* 171 .... 47[33], 126
Hughes v Liverpool CC (1988) *Times* 30 March, CA .... 33[148]
Ideal Film Renting Co v Nielsen [1921] 1 Ch 575 .... 67[66]
Inworth Property Co Ltd v Presslee (1990) October *Legal Action* 24 169
Ion v Liverpool CC (1987) 10 June, unreported, QBD 40
Ireland v Sheffield CC (1987) December *Legal Action* 16 167
Issitt v LB Tower Hamlets (1983) 6 December, Ub Transcript 1115, unreported, CA 45
Jackson v Horizon Holidays Ltd [1975] 3 All ER 92, CA .... 67[88]
Jarvis v Swans Tours [1973] 1 All ER 71, CA .... 67[74]
Jeune v Queens Cross Properties [1974] Ch 97 .... 67[58]
Jones v Public Trustee (1988) September *Legal Action* 21 .... 89[73]
Jordan v Archara (1988) 20 HLR 607, CA .... 47[52]
Josiah v Thames Housing Association (1989) December *Legal Action* 16 .... 90[114]
Joyce v LB Hackney (1976) September *LAG Bulletin* 211 .... 87[25], 123

Kearns v Liverpool CC (1985) 22 February, unreported, Liverpool County Court .... 68[96], 164
Kenny v Kingston upon Thames LBC (1985) 274 EG 395; 17 HLR 344 .... 110[72]
Ketteman v Hansel Properties [1984] 1 WLR 1274 .... 47[47], 66[35]
Kinch v LB Lambeth (1988) June *Legal Action* 20............. 65[2], 167
Kind v Cox (Valuation Officer) LVC/265/1984 noted at (1986) LS Gaz 2914.. 66[23]
King v Liverpool CC [1986] 3 All ER 544; 1 WLR 890; (1986) 18 HLR 307, CA.. 40, 126
Kirkpatrick v Watson [1943] Ir Jur Rep 4 .... 31[47]
Kotecha v Manchester CC (1983) March *LAG Bulletin* 35 .... 66[54]
Lal v Nakum (1982) 1 HLR 50, CA.......................... 65[13]
Lamb v LB Camden [1981] QB 625 126
Lambert Flat Management v Lomas [1981] 1 WLR 898......... 123
Lambeth LBC v Stubbs (1980) 255 EG 789; 78 LGR 650 ...... 87[4], 89[76]
Law v Hillingdon LBC (1989) December *Legal Action* 16 .... 116[9]
Lawton v East Devon DC (1982) July/August *Roof* 28 .... 116[8]
Lee-Parker v Izzet [1971] 1 WLR 1688 50
Lewisham LBC v All-Aziz (1990) June *Legal Action* 16 168
Lister v Lane [1893] 2 QB 212, CA .... 30[18], 32[95]
Little v Glasgow DC 1988 SCLR 482 .... 67[89]
Liverpool Corp v Irwin [1977] AC 239, HL .... 16, 31[69], 32[102]
Locabail International Finance Ltd v Agroexport [1986] 1 All ER 901.. 66[41]
London Congregational Union v Harriss [1988] 1 All ER 15, CA .... 47[48]
London Housing and Commercial Properties v Cowan [1977] QB 148 .... 66[21]
Longrigg, Burrough and Trounson v Smith (1979) 251 EG 847 .. 30[3]
Loria v Hammer [1989] EGCS 126 .... 31[73], 164
Lubren v LB Lambeth (1988) 20 HLR 165, CA............. 67[83,95], 162
Lurcott v Wakeley [1911] 1 KB 905 .... 19, 32[80]
Luxmore v Robson (1818) B & Ald 584 .... 32[75]
Lyons v Booth (F W) (Contractors) and Maidstone BC (1982) 262 EG 981.. 46[14]
McCarrick v Liverpool Corp [1947] AC 219.................. 16, 33[138]
Maclean v Currie (1884) Cab & El 361 .... 31[34]
McClean v Liverpool CC (1988) 20 HLR 25, CA 26
McCorley v Birmingham DC (1984) 12 January, unreported, DC 89[80]
McCoy v Clarke (1982) 13 HLR 89 .... 67[76]
McDermott v Southwark LBC (1986) December *Legal Action* 167; (1987) June *Legal Action* 21......................... 166
McDougall v Easington DC (1989) 21 HLR 310, CA........... 21

McGourlick v Renfrew DC (1982) 30 September, unreported, Paisley Sheriff Court .... 116[8]
McGreal v Wake (1984) 13 HLR 107; 269 EG 1254, CA .... 32[82], 33[144], 67[90], 109[66], 129, 144[3], 161
McKay v Norwell (1983) March *LAG Bulletin* 35 .... 33[114]
McManus v Landfarm Properties Ltd (1990) December *Legal Action* 17 168
McNerney v LB Lambeth (1988) 21 HLR 188, CA .. 31[42], 38, 39, 48[68], 116[4]
McPhail v Islington LBC [1970] 2 WLR 583, CA .... 88[53]
Makin v Watkinson (1870) LR 6 Ex 25 .... 33[136]
Malik v Politi [1964] CLY 1703 .... 109[54]
Malton Urban Sanitary Authority v Malton Farmers Manure Co (1879) 4 Ex D 302 .... 87[10]
Manchester Bonded Warehouse Co v Carr (1880) 5 CPD 507 .... 30[7]
Manprop v O'Dell [1969] 2 Ch 378 .... 32[76]
Marsden v LB Havering (1983) 11 March, unreported, CA 45
Mattis v Islington LBC (1987) March *Legal Action* 20 41
May v Pooles Park Neighbourhood Co-operative (1984) May *Legal Action* 54 .... 67[77]
Meah v Tower Hamlets LBC [1987] CLY 1127; (1986) October *Legal Action* 135 165
Melles & Co v Holme [1918] 2 KB 100 .... 31[73]
Melville v Grapelodge Developments (1978) 39 P&CR 179 .... 65[17]
Metropolitan Asylum District Managers v Hill (1881) 6 App Cas 193 .... 87[3]
Middleton v Hall (1913) 108 LT 804 .... 30[8], 46[1]
Millard v Wastall [1898] 1 QB 342 .... 87[31]
Miller v Cannon Hill Estates [1931] 2 KB 113 .... 47[27]
Miller v Emcer Products [1956] Ch 304 16
Miller v Hancock [1893] 2 QB 177 .... 31[68]
Minchburn v Peck (1987) 20 HLR 392, CA .... 30[20], 67[93], 162
Mint v Good [1951] 1 KB 517 .... 33[134]
Mira v Aylmer Square Investments Ltd [1988] EGCS 172; (1989) 21 HLR 284 .... 31[71], 67[84], 164
Mitchell v LB Brent (1984) May *Legal Action* 53 .... 67[77], 116[1]
Moodie v Hackney LBC (1987) June *Legal Action* 21 166
Morcom v Campbell-Johnson [1956] 1 QB 106 .... 32[78]
Morgan v Liverpool Corp [1927] 2 KB 131 .... 31[57], 33[137], 95
Morris v Liverpool CC (1987) 20 HLR 498, CA .... 33[128,129], 40
Morris-Thomas v Petticoat Lane Rentals Ltd (1987) 53 P&CR 238, CA .... 31[37]
Mortimer v Wilson (1883) 33 WR 927 .... 66[55]
Murphy v Brentwood DC [1990] 3 WLR 414, HL .... 36, 46[9, 14, 18], 47[25]
Murray v Birmingham CC (1988) 20 HLR 39, CA 20

NCB v Neath BC [1976] 2 All ER 478; 1 WLR 543 72
NCB v Thorne [1976] 1 WLR 543 .... 87[20]
Newey v Liverpool CC (1982) 14 HLR 73.................... 139, 145[50]
Nolan v Sheffield MDC (1979) 38 P&CR 741, Lands Tr 140
Northern Ireland Trailers v Preston CB [1972] 1 All ER 260 .. 88[62], 90[115]
Nottingham Corp v Newton [1974] 2 All ER 760 .... 89[93]
O'Brien v Robinson [1973] AC 912 .... 33[139, 145]
Office Overload v Gunn [1977] FSR 39, CA .... 66[43]
O'Grady v Westminster CC (1983) 266 EG 227, Lands Tr 140
Oliver v Islington LBC (1987) September *Legal Action* 12 .... 90[110]
Palmer v Sandwell MB (1988) 20 HLR 74, CA .... 11, 33[110]
Parker v LB Camden [1985] 2 All ER 141 .... 59, 66[27, 51]
Patel v Mehtab (1982) 5 HLR 78 .... 89[79], 116[6]
Patel v LB Newham [1979] JPL 303.......................... 25, 33[110]
Peabody Donation Fund Governors v Sir Lindsay Parkinson & Co Ltd [1985] AC 210, HL .... 46[20]
Pearlman v Harrow School [1979] 1 All ER 365 .... 32[103]
Pembery v Lamdin [1940] 2 All ER 434, CA .... 30[18], 32[107]
Peninsular Maritime v Padseal (1981) 259 EG 860, CA 57
Perestrello e Companhia Limitada v United Paint Co [1969] 3 All ER 479, CA .... 67[87]
Perl (Exporters) Ltd v LB Camden [1984] QB 342 126
Perry v Phillips (Sidney) & Son [1982] 3 All ER 705, CA .... 65[7]
Perry v Sharon Development Co [1937] 4 All ER 390 .... 47[27]
PRs of Chiodi v De Marney (1988) 21 HLR 6; 41 EG 80, CA..67[81, 82], 163
Pickering v Phillimore (1976) 10 May, unreported.............. 32[103]
Piper v GLC (1977) July *Roof* 122 .... 116[5]
Pirelli General Cable Works Ltd v Faber (Oscar) & Partners [1983] 1 All ER 65.......................................47[47], 66[35]
Plough Investments Ltd v Manchester CC [1989] EGCS 1 ...... 32[86]
Pocklington v Melksham UDC [1964] 2 All ER 862............ 109[43]
Pollway Nominees Ltd v Croydon BC (1986) 18 HLR 443, HL .... 109[30,36], 110[76]
Pollway Nominees Ltd v LB Havering (1989) 21 HLR 462 ..... 87[9], 88[34]
Porter v Jones [1942] 2 All ER 570 .... 65[7]
Portsmouth v Treleavan (1976) January *Roof* 21 .... 116[5]
Post Office v Aquarius Properties Ltd [1987] 1 All ER 1055, CA.. 32[88, 93]
Proudfoot v Hart (1890) 25 QBD 42 .... 25, 30[19], 32[75]
Pursey v Acrochoice Investments Ltd (1988) December *Legal Action* 18 168
Quick v Taff Ely BC [1985] 3 All ER 321, CA... 22, 31[49], 32[83,94], 116[2], 117
R v Amey [1983] 1 All ER 865, CA .... 90[109]
R v Birmingham City DC ex p Sale (1983) 9 HLR 33; (1984) 48 P&CR 270 .... 109[40]

R v Bristol Corp ex p Hendy [1974] 1 All ER 1047, CA ... 109[52, 53], 134
R v Camberwell Green Magistrates' Court ex p Healey (1985) December *Legal Action* 171 .... 89[88]
R v Camden LBC ex p Rowton (Camden Town) [1984] LGR 614 110[75]
R v Cardiff CC ex p Cross (1983) 6 HLR 1, CA .... 109[61], 136, 145[39]
R v Chappell [1984] Crim LR 574, CA .... 90[108]
R v Cooper [1982] Crim LR 308, CA .... 90[105]
R v Corby DC ex p McLean [1975] 2 All ER 568 .... 145[38a]
R v Dorton [1988] Crim LR 254, CA .... 90[104]
R v LB Ealing ex p Richardson (1982) 4 HLR 125, CA ...... 108[27], 109[44]
R v East Hertfordshire DC ex p Smith (1990) *Independent* 4 April, CA .... 145[15]
R v Epping (Waltham Abbey) JJ ex p Burlinson [1947] 2 All ER 537; [1948] 1 KB 79 .... 88[59]
R v Epsom and Ewell Corp ex p R B Property Investments (Eastern) [1964] 2 All ER 832 .... 109[41]
R v Fenny Stratford JJ ex p Watney Mann [1976] 2 All ER 888 . 89[77]
R v Forest of Dean DC ex p Trigg (1989) 12 CL 254; *Times* 9 November .... 109[27]
R v Horrocks ex p Boustead (1900) 69 LJQB 688 .... 89[89]
R v Horsham JJ ex p Richards [1985] 2 All ER 1114 .... 90[109]
R v Inner London Crown Court ex p Bentham (1988) 21 HLR 171 .... 90[122]
R v Islington LBC ex p Knight [1984] 1 All ER 154 .... 145[53]
R v Kerrier DC ex p Guppys (Bridport) (1976) 32 P&CR 411, CA .... 90[126], 107, 109[28, 49]
R v Leominster DC ex p Legg (1985) unreported, CA, noted at (1986) 9 *IEHO Housing Law Newsletter* 2 .... 108[27]
R v Mabbot (1987) *Times* 4 August, CA 119
R v Maldon DC ex p Fisher (1986) 18 HLR 197 .... 109[27]
R v Neill (1826) 2 Car & P 485 .... 87[21]
R v Newham East JJ ex p Hunt [1976] 1 All ER 839; 1 WLR 420 88[63]
R v Parlby (1889) 22 QBD 520 .... 87[7]
R v Secretary of State for the Environment ex p Ward [1984] 2 All ER 556 .... 87[6]
R v Smethwick JJ ex p Hands (1980) *Times* 4 December .... 89[83]
R v Thamesdown BC ex p Pritchard (1988) 20 HLR 633 .... 7[25]
R v Vivian [1979] 1 All ER 48, CA .... 90[107]
R v Wells Street Magistrates' Court ex p Morrissey (1989) 18 July, unreported, QBD .... 90[116]
R v Wheatley (1885) 16 QBD 34 .... 88[31]
R v White and Ward (1757) 1 Burr 333 .... 87[21]
Rainbow v Lambeth LBC (1986) January *Legal Action* 14 .... 67[60]
Rapid Results College v Angell (1986) 277 EG 856, CA .... 33[116]

Ravenseft Properties Ltd v Davstone (Holdings) Ltd [1980] QB 12 20
Redland Bricks Ltd v Morris [1970] AC 652, HL .... 66[45]
Rees v Davies (1987) September *Legal Action* 12 167
Regan & Blackburn Ltd v Rogers [1985] 2 All ER 180 .... 67[64]
Regional Properties Ltd v City of London Real Property Co (1980) 257 EG 64 122
Rich Investments Ltd v Camgate Litho [1988] EGCS 132 .... 32[86]
Rimmer v Liverpool CC [1984] 1 All ER 930, CA..37, 38, 46[21], 47[36, 50], 56
Robbins v Jones (1863) 15 CB (NS) 221 .... 30[1]
Roberts v GLC (1975) 3 LTC case 6 .... 145[57]
Rose v Laskington (1989) 139 NLJ 973 60
Rossall v Southwark LBC (1985) unreported, noted at 8 *IEHO Housing Law Newsletter* 7 123
Rousou v Photi [1940] 2 KB 379 .... 31[48]
Ryall v Cubitt Heath [1922] 1 KB 275 .... 109[32]
Ryall v Kidwell & Son [1914] 3 KB 135 .... 30[8], 46[1]
Ryan v LB Camden (1982) 8 HLR 75, CA 45
Salford CC v McNally [1975] 3 WLR 87, HL .... 87[12, 18], 89[94], 90[127]
Salisbury Corp v Roles [1948] WN 412; 92 SJ 618 .... 90[125]
Sandwell MBC v Bujok (1989) 22 HLR 87 .... 90[118]
Saner v Bilton (1878) 7 Ch D 815 .... 30, 32[75], 144[1]
Sarson v Roberts [1895] 2 QB 395 .... 30[26], 31[39]
Saunders v Edwards [1987] 1 WLR 1116 .... 67[78]
Saunders v Maltby (1976) 19 Rydes Rating Cases 33; 239 EG 205 .... 66[22]
Savage and Savage v Harscott Ltd (1987) September *Legal Action* 12 .... 32[88], 33[110], 166
Savizon v Lambeth LBC (1986) June *Legal Action* 81 .... 90[102]
Savory v Southwark LBC (1987) March *Legal Action* 19 165
Seal v LB Greenwich (1981) October *LAG Bulletin* 237 .... 67[77]
Sella House Ltd v Mears (1989) 12 EG 67, CA 163
Sharpe v Manchester MDC (1982) 5 HLR 71 .... 47[33]
Sheldon v West Bromwich Corp (1973) 25 P&CR 360; 13 HLR 23, CA .... 33[117, 140]
Sillitoe v Liverpool CC (1988) 29 November, unreported, Liverpool County Court 124
Sim v Aberdeen CDC (1981) 258 EG 451; (1984) P&CR 278 .... 146[61]
Siney v Dublin Corp [1980] IR 400 .... 30[9], 31[41], 47[29]
Sleafer v Lambeth BC [1960] 1 QB 43, CA .... 30[4]
Smedley v Chumley & Hawkes Ltd (1982) 44 P&CR 50 .... 20, 32[107]
Smith v Bradford MC (1982) 44 P&CR 171, CA .... 44, 144[4]
Smith v Marrable (1843) 11 M & W 5 .... 30[24, 28]
Smith v Nottinghamshire CC (1981) *Times* 13 November, CA .... 31[37]

Smith v Peters (1875) 20 LR Eq 511 .... 66[48]
Ex p Sonola (1980) November, unreported, HC .... 146[60]
LB Southwark v Ince (1989) 21 HLR 504 .... 87[8], 89[94], 123
Springett v Harold [1954] 1 All ER 568 .... 87[13]
Stanton v Southwick [1920] 2 KB 642 .... 31[56]
Staves v Leeds CC (1990) December *Legal Action* 17 168
Steel v Newham LBC (1985) 2 June, unreported; noted at 34 *Housing Aid* 11; (1985) December *Legal Action* 171 and (1986) April *Legal Action* 49, Bow County Court .... 116[1]
Steele v Minister of Housing and Local Government and West Ham County BC (1956) 168 EG 37, CA .... 108[23]
Stent v Monmouth DC (1987) 19 HLR 269, CA .... 22, 32[93, 99]
Stevenson (Westminster) v Mock [1954] JPL 275 .... 109[57]
Stockley v Knowsley MBC (1986) 279 EG 677, CA 40
Straudley Investments v Barpress Ltd (1987) 282 EG 1124, CA .. 33[116]
Sturolson & Co v Mauroux (1988) 20 HLR 332, CA... 66[33], 67[79,80,94], 162
Summers v Salford Corp [1943] AC 283 .... 31[51,57], 95
Sutton v Temple (1843) 12 M & W 52 .... 30[23]
Sylvester v Solon Housing Association (1979) 6 LTC 27; (1978) 246 EG 665, Lands Tr .... 145[57]
Taylor v Beal (1591) Cro Eliz (1) 222 .... 65[3]
Taylor v Knowsley BC (1985) 17 HLR 376, CA 162
Taylor v Liverpool Corp [1939] 3 All ER 329 .... 47[39]
Taylor v Webb [1937] 2 KB 283 .... 33[109]
Tennant Radiant Heat Ltd v Warrington Development Corp (1988) 11 EG 71, CA .... 47[38]
Thompson v Birmingham CC (1990) December *Legal Action* 17 .. 168
Tower Hamlets LBC v GLC (1983) 15 HLR 54 115
Travers v Gloucester Corp [1947] KB 71 .... 46[3]
Tusting v RB Kensington and Chelsea (1975) 3 January, unreported; noted at 27 NILQ 16 and *Municipal Journal* 17 January, Inner London Crown Court 83
Udechuko v Lambeth LB (1982) Rating Appeals 291; 262 EG 1309; [1983] JPL 124, Lands Tr .... 66[23], 146[76]
Victoria Square Property Co v LB Southwark [1978] 2 All ER 281; 1 WLR 463 .... 109[40]
Wainwright v Leeds CC (1984) 13 HLR 117, CA 26
Walker v Hatton (1842) 10 M & W 249 .... 30[19]
Walker v Hobbs & Co (1889) 23 QBD 458 .... 31[52, 59]
Wandsworth LBC v Orakpo (1986) *Independent* 29 October, CA . 122
Wandsworth LBC v Sparling (1987) 20 HLR 169 122
Wansbeck DC v Morley (1987) 20 HLR 247, CA .... 144[11]
Ward v Cannock Chase DC [1985] 3 All ER 537 126
Warner v LB Lambeth (1984) 15 HLR 42, DC .... 89[72]

Warwick RDC v Miller-Mead [1962] 2 WLR 284, CA 75
Waters v Weigall (1795) 2 Anstr 757 .... 65[3]
Webb v Ipswich BC (1989) 21 HLR 325, CA 122
Weigall v Waters (1796) 6 Term Rep 488 .... 65[3]
Weller v Lewisham LBC (1988) September *Legal Action* 15...... 167
Wettern Electric Ltd v Welsh Development Agency [1983] 2 All ER 629... 31[37]
Whatling v Rees (1914) 84 LJKB 1122......................... 88[31]
Whitcombe v Pollock [1956] 106 LJ 554 .... 31[47]
White v LB Barnet (1989) 21 HLR 346, CA .... 109[65]
White v Hackney LBC (1989) March *Legal Action* 24........... 127
Whittaker v Derby Urban SA (1885) 55 (ns) LJ MC 8 .... 89[101]
Whittington v Liverpool CC (1985) 18 February, unreported, Liverpool County Court .... 66[52]
Williams v Khan (1981) 258 EG 554, CA .... 109[59]
Williamson v Kirklees DC (1979) 44 *Community Action* 10 ...... 90[128]
Wilson v Finch-Hatton (1877) 2 Ex D 336 .... 30[29], 31[44]
Wimpey Construction Co v Poole (1984) *Times* 3 May; 128 SJ 969 .... 47[24]
Worldwide Dryers Ltd v Warner Howard Ltd (1982) *Times* 9 December .... 66[50]
Wright v Lawson (1903) 19 TLR 510......................... 32[95]
Wycombe AHA v Barnet (1982) 264 EG 619 25
Wyse (EA) v Secretary of State for the Environment and Borough of Newcastle-under-Lyme [1984] JPL 256........... 108[12]
Yorston v Crewfield Ltd and Ors (1985) 11 July, unreported, Clerkenwell County Court .... 66[26]
Yorston and Yorston v Crewfield Ltd and Festal International Ltd (1985) July *Legal Action* 102.......................... 165
Zenca and Ors v Pouyiouros (1989) September *Legal Action* 24 .. 120
Zone Properties Ltd v Painter (1987) June *Legal Action* 21 166

Table of Rules and Regulations

page

Collection and Disposal of Waste Regulations 1988 SI No 819 124
Control of Pollution Act 1974 (Commencement No 19) Order 1988
SI No 818 124
County Court Rules 1981 SI No 1687
Ord 13 r1 .... 66[39], 67[65]
8 .... 66[37]
Home Loss Payments Order 1989 SI No 24 182
Housing Benefits Regulations 1987 SI No 1971
regs 88(1), 95 51
Legal Advice and Assistance (Scope) Regulations 1989 SI No 550
regs 7, 8 .... 89[81]
Local Government and Housing Act (Commencement No 5) Order
1990 SI No 431 92
Local Government Finance (Repeals, Savings and Consequential Amendments) Order 1990 SI No 776
Sch 3 para 19 182
Rules of the Supreme Court 1965 SI No 1776
Ord 29 60
45 r8 59
Secure Tenancies (Right to Repair Scheme) Regulations 1985
SI No 1493 51

Chapter One

The Repairs Problem

1 Introduction

The state of Britain's housing stock is nothing short of a national scandal. The scale of unfitness and serious disrepair in the homes of this country is now such that present housing policies are completely unable to halt the continuing rapid decline in standards. On the contrary, capital spending on housing has for the past decade and more borne a substantial part of overall reductions in public expenditure. Current programmes of demolition, rehabilitation and improvement are unable to do more than scratch the surface of the problem and local housing authorities are starved of the financial resources with which to improve them.

Even a standstill position would be preferable to the present decline. However our ability simply to maintain the present status quo is seriously undermined by both the continuing structural failures of "replacement" dwellings built in the past 20-30 years and the difficulties of raising current standards in house building and renewal. Against such a depressing background, the Department of Environment has been able to find only very limited additional resources for financing of remedial works on housing in recent years. Relatively small amounts are distributed through the Estate Action programme to deal with the worst conditions in council housing.[1] This has obvious implications for the ability of housing authorities to respond to what is needed.

These are not issues of interest only to those academically or politically concerned with the physical quality of Britain's housing. They are indicative of the massive personal and social cost borne by the country's tenants and occupiers in all sectors. In this chapter, attention is given to the objective evidence of the scale of the problems in the housing stock. Each main form of housing provision will then be examined in turn.

2 The condition of the housing stock

The latest survey of national housing conditions was undertaken in 1985/

86. It embraced all housing tenures by sample but focused mainly on older housing rather than new-build. The results published in the *English House Condition Survey 1986*[2] confirm a dire state of disrepair in the housing stock with virtually no improvement achieved since the earlier survey conducted in 1982, although the results are difficult to compare with earlier periods due to changes in the survey systems adopted.[3]

The figures reveal:

(a) 5% of the total housing stock is unfit for human habitation;
(b) a further 2.4 million dwellings are in poor repair;
(c) 15% of the total housing stock is in poor condition; and
(d) 543,000 dwellings lack basic amenities.

The scale of disrepair disclosed by the survey affects all tenure sectors although, as usual, the condition in the private rented sector is worse than elsewhere; for example, one in six dwellings in the private sector was found to be unfit for human habitation.

The scale and extent of such disrepair is borne out by other similar surveys. In Wales, a survey report concludes that "the overall state of repair of the Welsh housing stock has deteriorated" in the five years, with the number of houses which, although "fit", need repair, increasing from 31,000 to 46,000.[4]

In London, figures collected by the London Research Centre with the help of the London boroughs revealed not only the rapid decay of inner city housing as suggested by the national survey, but also the extent to which chronic disrepair is now prevalent even in suburban areas. In London as a whole, 370,000 houses are seriously unsatisfactory (many of them "unfit").[5] In outer London 200,000 homes required repairs costing more than £4,200 in each case.[6]

Using the figures from the earlier 1976 and 1981 surveys it has been calculated that properties are deteriorating into a serious state of disrepair at the rate of 75,000 per year and that the annual number of houses becoming unfit for human habitation is running at 40,000.[7] Converting this sort of projection into figures for the amount of necessary new-build and rehabilitation is not an exact science. However, it has been suggested that on the present basis it would take 46 years to clear the backlog in housing disrepair.[8] To eradicate the problem by replacement with good housing stock will take "anything between 500 and 1,000 years."[9] 200,000 houses will be needed each year to the end of the century simply to satisfy new demand and replace demolished properties.[10] However, present new-build and rehabilitation programmes offer no prospect of meeting this need. Indeed, at the current rate of clearance it will take more than 100 years just to replace the properties today classified as "unfit".[11]

The vast majority of the housing covered by these figures is *occupied*. Hundreds of thousands of people in Britain are living in conditions which are either officially "unfit for human habitation" or in acute disrepair.

In addition, millions live in housing subject to some form of dampness or condensation problem[12] and many more experience the difficulties caused by minor disrepair and inadequate maintenance. The very existence of these conditions is a major indictment of both our present laws to secure compulsory repairs and our application of them.

Before turning to examine, in the ensuing chapters of this book, the existing legal rights of tenants to secure repairs, the following pages offer a short summary of the main problems experienced with different component parts of our present housing stock.

3 One hundred years' worth of bad housing

(a) Victorian - 1945

Some occupiers of modern housing may look back with fond memories to the sturdy housing built with solid walls around the turn of the century. However, property built in that era is now truly coming to the end of its useful life even though it still represents a substantial proportion of our housing stock. One distinguished correspondent draws justified attention to the fact that "a major crisis is looming as the houses constructed in the building boom of the 1880s and 1890s reach their hundredth anniversary."[13]

If one moves on to consider all the housing built prior to 1914, the picture becomes considerably bleaker. Such housing accounts for one-third of the present housing stock. If these houses have been improved then their period of useful life can obviously be extended. However it has been suggested that unimproved housing built before 1914 will require substantial repair work to keep it in use, even if conversion to a higher standard is not contemplated. Such works will include: main roof and drain repairs, damp proofing, guttering, pipes, woodworks and stabilisation. Houses built in the Victorian era are particularly prone to problems with defective bay windows and differential floor levels.[14]

In the inter-war years, the vast majority of house building was of the solid, traditional type. Such housing would probably simply require upgrading to modern standards. However, with official encouragement, non-traditional house building was started and between 1919 and 1945 some 52,000 dwellings of the new type were constructed. It is possibly these properties which will require greater attention in years to come.

Some considerable problems are already starting to emerge from properties built in the inter-war years using a cavity wall method of construction. The need for extensive repair arises when the "ties" holding the inner and outer sections of the wall corrode - this becomes noticeable as horizontal cracks appear and the outer wall bulges or collapses. It has been suggested that difficulties are most acute in properties in the north, East Anglia and on the south coast.[15] In the city of Birmingham alone, out of 42,000 pre-war dwellings, 25,000 need modernisation. At current renewal rates the programme will take 600 years.[16] England's local authorities have a stock of 450,000 unmodernised pre-war dwellings.

(b) Non-traditional housing: 1950s and 1960s

The house-building boom in the post-war years led developers and architects to experiment with newer forms of domestic house construction. Generally, this involved the use of prefabricated reinforced concrete (PRC) in the major structural components of the dwelling. In recent years, widespread concern has been expressed about the early failure in some parts of the structure of these dwellings. The Building Research Establishment (address in Appendix 5) has carried out evaluations of each of the main types used in construction.[17] In the Spring of 1981 the Department of the Environment notified local authorities of potential defects in the "Airey" system.[18] These defects were most clearly identified from local authority returns since the majority were (and are) occupied by council tenants.[19] In the Autumn of 1982 a scheme of compensation was introduced for private owner occupiers of Airey homes.[20] This was accompanied by further information to local authorities advising that potential defects had been found in "Orlit" type homes constructed by roughly the same technique.[21] In July 1983 the Association of Metropolitan Authorities (AMA) published a major survey on "non-traditional" dwellings built in the 1940s and 1950s[22] suggesting that the cost of repairing or replacing homes built with these methods (the vast majority of them for local authorities) would cost £5,000 million.

In the Autumn of 1983 the Government gave a commitment to introduce legislation to assist owner occupiers of PRC housing,[23] and the 1984 Housing Defects Act (now Housing Act 1985 Pt XVI) introduced rights for the owners of specified types of PRC houses and other designated categories of defective dwellings who purchased from public sector landlords to call for at least 90 per cent grant aid for repairs or, where repairs are impracticable, to require the local authority to purchase at 95 per cent of the defect-free value.[24] The legislation offers nothing to local authority tenants of PRC housing or their municipal landlords and is proving difficult to operate in practice.[25] In any event, the present designation categories are limited to PRC constructed dwellings and do not extend, for example, to defective steel frame and cladding houses.[26]

(c) System and industrialised building: 1960s and 1970s

Conditions of acute disrepair, dampness and poor design are rarely so commonly encountered as in the defective mass-produced housing erected during the past 30 years. Housing estates built by assembling factory-produced components into high density, high rise structures with a projected life of 60 years are being demolished all over the country. The vast majority were constructed for municipal landlords, who will continue to be liable to pay interest charges for monies borrowed to finance initial construction long after the dwellings are razed. Problems concerning infestation of vermin, chronic condensation and penetrating dampness were consistently reported by local authority tenants of such property and their associations throughout the 1970s.[27] But these problems received little attention from the media until the early 1980s, when visible signs of decay and shoddy workmanship were revealed as huge concrete panels and slabs began to fall away from high rise blocks.[28] The extent of the acute problems caused by this deficient form of house building is now more widely recognised, although solutions other than complete demolition (now known as "decommissioning"[29]) or total rehabilitation have been rare.[30] An extensive survey by the AMA suggested that the cost of repairing or replacing the defective housing of the era would be in the region of £5,000 million.[31]

Many local authorities have tried to respond to defective design and construction by traditional legal means. Thus legal proceedings have been taken to fix architects, developers, construction companies and others with financial liability for the fiasco.[32] These proceedings have not always been successful, either because the responsible companies cannot be traced or are in liquidation or because court decisions have placed restrictions on the limitation period after which those responsible achieve immunity from legal suit.[33]

Those suffering most from the dire consequences of botched design and construction have been the tenants. However, notwithstanding the apparently insurmountable scale of the problems, tenants' groups have achieved considerable success in their attempts to get system and industrialised buildings demolished or reconstructed.[34] This has been particularly true of defective housing in the form of high-rise tower blocks.[35]

(d) Timber frame: 1970s and 1980s

Although less housing has been constructed over the last 15 years, and much of it has been in the traditional form, a new technique has been applied in a large proportion of recently-constructed property. This involves the erection of pre-assembled timber frames to give a house structure, with an external skin of brick built around the erected frame. By the 1980s 25 per cent of all new housing (including some built for local authorities) was constructed using this technique.

In the summer of 1983 critical media coverage[36] suggested that a combination of inadequate design and inadequate supervision of on-site erection might give rise to future repairing problems and danger to occupiers. The construction industry responded with a defence of the timber frame method,[37] and the BRE published its own report.[38] Recognising the concern of municipal developers of timber frame housing for rent, the AMA published a cautionary note in late 1983.[39] Although the debate as to the quality and safety of timber frame continues, another period of uncertainty as to the extent that occupiers can rely on the structure of their homes is now under way. Already, more information is becoming available about the potential fire risk posed by some poorly constructed timber-framed houses.[40]

(e) The present day

Municipal housebuilding and renovation programmes are currently at their lowest levels since the 1920s.[41] This should provide an incentive for those who are in fact building to produce high quality, long-life, sound dwellings with which to replace the legacy of shoddy housing described above. There is however, serious concern about the continuing low standards of workmanship in construction.[42] A summary of recent work conducted by the BRE and NBA of on-site standards of design and construction identifies an "ongoing problem of an unnecessarily and unreasonably high level of defects in new built housing" concentrated mainly in "structural faults upon which the highest remedial cost will have to be incurred."[43] The problems with construction are simply compounded by the continually lowered space and design standards in new-build and rehabilitated property.[44]

The construction industry appears to have achieved a 50 per cent reduction in instances of major structural failure since 1974,[45] but this can lead only to even deeper suspicion and concern about the quality of early 1970s housing and continuing concern about present day standards.[46]

4 Conclusion

Britain faces a major crisis in the quality of its housing stock. As early as 1979 it was suggested that £200 million would be the minimum needed to bring poor housing up to standard.[47] By the early 1980s the figure of £3,000 million was widely accepted. More recently the AMA puts a figure of £10,000 million on repairing or replacing 1940s-1970s non-traditional buildings.[48] If the total cost of repair just for defective *council* housing is put at £18,000 million on Government figures, it gives some indication of the scale of the problem faced.[49] The figures put forward by the Confederation of Building Employers (£30,000 million) and the AMA (£50,000 million) perhaps represent the upper limit of the current range,[50] but even the rather more conservative thinking RIBA puts the figure for Manchester (105,000 council houses) at £600 million, Edinburgh at £800 million and Glasgow at £1.6 billion.[51] In terms of individual properties (at 1988 costings), the RIBA estimate is that 10 per cent of houses require repairs costing more than £2,500 and 5 per cent need more than £4,000 worth of repairs each. The latest projection from the Association of District Councils is that £38,000 million is required for repairs to dilapidated buildings with £50,000 million needed, in all, to tackle disrepair.[52]

It is not the intention of this author to address the major political options available to deal with this problem.[53] Rather, the following chapters of this book will consider in turn each of the legal remedies available to the tenants of unrepaired housing who are personally seeking relief from the consequences of this all-embracing crisis.

1 C Nevitt "How to help the four million" *Times* 17 June 1987.
2 *English house condition survey* 1986 HMSO,1988.
3 P Walentowicz "Lies, damned lies and house condition statistics" Mar/Apr 1989 *Roof* 13 and see HC Written Answers col 725, 7 March 1990.
4 Feld "Welsh house condition survey: increase in private sector unfitness" Jan/Feb 1983 *Roof 4*; and see Committee on Welsh Affairs *Second report on the condition and repair of privately owned housing 1986/87* HC 230-I, HMSO.
5 *London housing survey 1986-87* London Research Centre, 1989.
6 D Walker "Suburban homes in disrepair" *Times* 7 May 1984; and see *Capital decay* SHAC, 2nd edn, 1985.
7 D McCulloch "Rehab and redevelopment debate re-opened" 13 January 1984 *Municipal Journal.*
8 C McKean "Why the home front is heading for collapse" *Times* 15 December 1983.
9 J Peart, chair RTPI housing working party, letter to *Times* 20 October 1983.
10 C Warman "Housing in crisis: 1" *Times* 22 April 1985.
11 *A time to take stock* Association of District Councils, 1989.
12 *Report of Scottish Grand Committee 1984* HC 206, HMSO paras 16-20.
13 J Peart n9.
14 H Smith "Not what it used to be" *Sunday Times* 29 June 1986.
15 B Phillips "Millions of homes at risk from hidden fault that weakens outer walls" *Times* 16 May 1983.
16 C Warman "Housing in crisis: 2" *Times* 23 April 1985.
17 See for example *The structural condition of Cornish unit houses* BRE, 1983.
18 DoE letter to local authorities 14 May 1981: Airey houses.
19 *Airey houses: technical information and guidance* BRE, April 1982.
20 DoE Circ 6/83, HMSO.
21 DoE letter to local authorities 2 September 1982: Orlit dwellings.
22 *Defects in housing – Part 1: Non-traditional dwellings of the 1940s and 1950s* AMA, July 1983.
23 Ian Gow, minister of housing, HC Debs col 422, 10 November 1983.
24 DoE Circ 14/86.
25 See the adjournment debates on the operation of the Act (Kevin Barron) HC Debs col 598, 6 December 1985; (Gerald Haworth) HC Debs col 1265, 22 October 1986; (Oonagh McDonald) HC Debs col 244, 24 February 1987. See also T Pettigrew "Homes that turn to straw" *Sunday Times* 19 October 1986 and *R v Thamesdown BC ex p Pritchard* (1988) 20 HLR 633, QBD.
26 B Hill "People who live in tin houses shouldn't own homes" *Guardian* 22 March 1989; and R Critchley "Battle on defective homes heats up" July/August 1989 *Roof* 9.
27 See, eg, *Slums on the drawing board* Benwell CDP, 1978.
28 D Sudjic "Council housing – a national scandal" *Sunday Times* 30 August 1981; J Young

"Tenants told to beware low-flying concrete" *Times* 20 October 1981; three articles by M Wallace in the *Sunday Times* – "Scandal of model slums forces demolition" 11 April 1982, "More council blocks are doomed" 18 April 1982, and "Concrete follies to tumble" 9 May 1982; J Drury and C Tighe "Crash! A 3-ton brick drops on Whitehall" *Sunday Times* 1 August 1982; C McKean "Built for speed without stability" *Times* 28 March 1983; M Davie "Great UK housing disaster" *Observer* 28 August 1983; and G Stamp "Homes that were never fit to live in" *Independent* 6 March 1989.

29 I Williams "The subtle art of destruction" *Independent* 11 April 1988.

30 For a summary of the most common construction problems see D Connett "The faults that built up into disasters" *Sunday Times* 7 July 1985; and *Cracks in concrete* SCAT, 1985. For solutions see *The structural adequacy and durability of large panel system dwellings* BRE, 1987; and C Counsell "Rebuilding blocks into homes on a human scale" *Independent* 14 May 1988.

31 *Defects in housing - Part 2: Industrialised and system built dwellings of the 1960s and 1970s* AMA, March 1984.

32 See, eg, "Council sues over defects in estate" *Times* 4 October 1982; and see "Sheffield issues housing writ" 29 July 1983 *Municipal Journal* 1103.

33 See below p41.

34 See, in particular, *High and dry* SCAT, 1984.

35 See *National Tower Blocks Directory* (Community Links, 1988); F Clarke "A lift to high society" *Guardian* 2 March 1988; C Pepinster "High hopes" *Guardian* 13 September 1989.

36 *World in action* 27 June 1983; T Cunnew "Ongoing row situation" (1983) 267 EG 926; B Phillips "Timber frame homes not inferior" *Times* 31 August 1983; "Warning on timber houses" *Times* 2 September 1983; M Brown "Calming fears about timber frame" *Times* 14 September 1983; A Haigh "Study clears timber homes, builders say" *Times* 23 September 1983.

37 *Timber frame dwellings* NHBC Practice Note 5, 1982, revised May 1983; and see *The timber and brick homes handbook* Timber and Brick Homes Information Council, 1985.

38 *Timber-framed housing – a technical appraisal* BRE, 1983.

39 *Timber frame housing – a cautionary note* AMA, September 1983; see also "Trusting in timber" *Sunday Times* 10 November 1985.

40 J Joyce "Fire risk fear strikes 25,000 home owners" *Sunday Times* 29 November 1989.

41 *Managing the crisis in council housing* Audit Commission, 1986.

42 See C McGhie "When your dreams fall through the floor" *Sunday Times* 18 September 1983.

43 R Pontin "Basic lessons from current experience" March/April 1983 *Housing Review* 63.

44 *Housing in crisis: a policy statement* RIBA, 1989.

45 G Graham, London director, NHBC, letter to *Times* 6 April 1983.

46 See Prof Kennaway "Call for a new building structure" letter to *Times* 5 September 1983; and K Gosling "Building neglect is costing billions" *Times* 20 January 1984.

47 *Building design* 5 January 1979.

48 See nn22 and 31 above and *The case for local housing* AMA, 1986.

49 *An inquiry into the condition of local authority housing stock in England* DoE, 1985.

50 C Warman "Housing in crisis: 3" *Times* 24 April 1985.

51 "The drive to stop the decay" *Times* 31 October 1985; and "Glasgow needs 1.6 bn" *Times* 28 November 1985.

52 See n11 above.

53 See *Cracking up! Building faults in council homes: proposals for a new deal* NCC, 1982.

Chapter Two

Contractual Rights

1 Introduction

> "Fraud apart, there is no law against letting a tumble-down house, and the tenant's remedy is upon his contract, if any".[1]

Although this broad declaration must now be read subject to much statutory and judicial development,[2] it remains an important directive that in most repairs disputes a useful starting point will be an examination of the terms of the tenancy.

(a) The contract of letting

A tenant occupies premises under the terms of a contract of letting. This contract may be made orally or in writing or may even be inferred from the circumstances (for example where a person occupies premises and the landlord accepts money as rent[3]).

The terms of the contract or "tenancy agreement" may be:

(a) *expressly* incorporated into the agreement either orally or in writing; or

(b) *implied* into the tenancy agreement either by statute or by the operation of common law.

Whether express or implied, these terms may impose an obligation upon the landlord to carry out repairs, which s/he is then contractually bound to perform.

(b) The principle of "caveat emptor": a cautionary note

The common law (ie the judge-made law developed by the system of precedent) concerning rights to repair, which was formulated in the 18th and 19th centuries and which underpins present-day "repairs law", rested upon the fundamental principle of *caveat emptor*, ie let the buyer beware the bargain. In dealings with land and houses (as with other property) the onus was placed on the person intending to take them to have inspected the premises, satisfied him/herself as to the quality of the property, and then to have freely negotiated an appropriate contract accordingly.

It followed from the application of this principle that once property had been accepted by the tenant, the landlord had a virtual immunity from repairing obligations other than those imposed by the contract. Thus the courts were able to develop numerous shields to help landlords avoid liability for repairs. For example, at common law:

(a) the landlord is under no obligation to do *any* repairs unless such an obligation is contained in the express or implied terms of the tenancy agreement or is imposed by legislation;[4]
(b) the landlord is under no general obligation to ensure that an *unfurnished* house or flat is fit for human occupation or habitation;[5]
(c) in letting any property, a landlord does *not* undertake by implication that the premises are sufficiently structurally sound to last the duration of the tenancy[6] or fit for the purposes for which they are let;[7]
(d) redress for breach of an express or implied repairing obligation is confined to the tenant, so that persons other than the tenant do not have a contractual remedy for the landlord's failure to repair.[8]

Clearly, a strict application of the principle *caveat emptor* in today's society is wholly inappropriate and artificial, since the landlord and incoming tenant no longer (if they ever did in the past) bargain as equals over the letting of property. In another jurisdiction it has been said that "Today the application of such a rule, in a society which is becoming more and more urbanised and in which the building and sale of houses has become a major industry, may appear somewhat harsh and inappropriate".[9]

Even in this country, continued application of the principle has been identified as a source of great injustice.[10] However, since the principle of "no liability apart from contract" still operates (albeit less harshly today) in the English courts, any examination of a landlord's repairing obligations must start with reference to any rights contained in the contract of letting.

2 Express terms

Precisely because tenants so seldom bargain with landlords as equal parties, the most common express contractual repairing obligations are those imposing responsibilities on tenants (such express obligations are known as "covenants"). Indeed, until recently, the examination of repairing responsibilities in the relevant legal textbooks was concerned almost exclusively with the interpretation of the *tenants'* contractual duties to repair. Today, landlords remain relatively free to impose repairing obligations on tenants through the contract of letting. Intervention has come not from the common law but from statute.

Where repairing obligations are now imposed by law on landlords (for example by the Landlord and Tenant Act 1985 s11,[11] or s8[12]), the statutes generally provide that these cannot be transferred to tenants by way of express contractual terms.

Similarly, the Unfair Contract Terms Act 1977 assists tenants by preventing landlords from including unreasonable contractual terms by which they might seek to qualify or undermine their own repairing obligations. The 1977 Act provides that where the landlord is in the business of letting and the tenant deals as consumer, the landlord is not entitled to exclude his/her own liability for breach of a repairing covenant by insertion of a term in the contract, unless it is reasonable to do so. The landlord could not claim to be entitled to rely on a clause exonerating him/her from carrying out any repairing obligation, unless such a clause were reasonable.[13]

Interpreting express terms

If the tenancy agreement does contain an express term imposing a repairing obligation on the landlord, it should clearly be considered whether this covers the disrepair in question. The express terms relating to *secure* tenants can easily be checked since local authorities and housing associations are required to have copies available on demand.[14] Care must be taken to ensure that the correct form of tenancy agreement is being considered. In *Palmer v Sandwell MB*, [15] the tenant's attempt to enforce an obligation to repair "design defects" failed when the landlord was able to show that it had not used the correct statutory procedure for variation of the tenancy agreement and had thus not properly incorporated the new term in the agreements of existing tenants.

Various different formulations of wording, "put in repair", "keep in repair", "good and substantial repair and condition" and many others are used in express repairing obligations, and the meanings of the various permutations are examined in detail in the traditional legal textbooks.[16] Despite these grammatical differences, it is in fact not so much the wording that is important, but rather the expressed intention that the property is to be brought into repair and kept in good repair throughout the tenancy.[17]

Whatever the wording of an express term, a repairing covenant will never be construed to require the landlord to renew the whole property, ie to turn an old and decaying house into a new and sound one.[18] Accordingly, a repairing covenant is to be construed having regard to the condition of the property as it was at the date of letting.[19] The scope of the word "repair" and the standard of work it requires are considered in more detail at pp18–22.

Advisers should also be looking at tenancy agreements to find express repairing covenants dealing with "common parts" or the "overall structure" since these frequently contain obligations imposed on landlords, even in landlord-drafted letting agreements.[20]

Remedy
The remedy for a breach of an express covenant is an action in contract for damages and specific performance of the covenant: see chapter 4. The tenant will be required to show that the landlord had notice of the defect: see p28.

3 Implied terms

Because of the breadth of the landlord's exemption from liability at common law and the infrequency of express repairing obligations imposed on landlords, the legislature (and to a much lesser extent the common law) has sought to protect tenants, especially those with short or periodic tenancies, by the compulsory implication of repairing responsibilities into tenancy agreements.

(a) Fit to be lived in

Furnished/unfurnished premises
As we have seen,[21] the common law did not even require a landlord to have carried out sufficient work prior to the letting of premises to ensure that they were fit for the purpose for which they were let (ie to be lived in) at the commencement of the tenancy. This exception from liability apparently continues today for unfurnished houses[22] and land generally.[23]

But in the case of *furnished* houses and flats the common law implies a contractual term that they are fit for human habitation at the date of letting.[24] The landlord will be in breach if it is established that the premises were actually unfit, whether or not the landlord believed them to be fit for habitation.[25]

The obligation is strictly an *initial* one, ie that the premises were fit when they were let.[26] However, the term will be broken where there was initial unfitness but the defect becomes obvious only at a later stage of the tenancy.[27] Thus a landlord will be liable for letting premises which are unfit because plasterwork is damp, even though the tenant may discover the unfitness only months into the tenancy when wallpaper peels from the walls.

The courts have held that premises will be unfit for human habitation at common law if they are infested by bugs,[28] or have a defective drainage[29] and sewerage system,[30] or carry an infection,[31] or if there is a lack of safety,[32] or an insufficiency of water supply.[33] Note, however, that the obligation is confined to fitness for habitation and that the implied term does *not* require the landlord to ensure that the premises are in structural repair when let, eg cracked ceiling plaster may not be covered.[34] Today, the courts may be willing to look at the statutory definition of unfitness[35] which is somewhat broader, in considering whether premises are unfit at common law.

In its modern application, the implied term will still be of use to furnished tenants whose homes were in very poor condition when let. Examples would include premises which were affected by penetrating dampness, infested with cockroaches or fitted with dangerous electrical wiring or fitments.

Subject to the requirements of the Unfair Contract Terms Act 1977, the implied terms may be excluded from any letting by an express term to the contrary. (Of course, if the landlord expressly warrants that premises are fit for human habitation s/he may be sued for breach of warranty without regard to the implied term.[36])

The courts have been increasingly ready to impose a requirement of fitness for purpose into *licences*, so that it may now be the law that premises made available for occupation under a licence must be fit for human habitation whether they are furnished or unfurnished.[37]

The position on the letting of *unfurnished flats* is more problematic. The principle underlying the general implication of a requirement that premises be fit for habitation if furnished, is that the landlord will obviously be aware that the premises are immediately to be occupied. If this logic is followed through, it would dictate that unfurnished flats let for immediate occupation should be fit for habitation. This proposition would have been adopted by the courts had not an earlier case on commercial leases been followed. However, in *Cruse v Mount*[38] it was clearly held that unfurnished flats were without the protection of the implied term. The decision itself is questionable since an earlier authority – in which it had been assumed that the implied term applied to flats – was not cited.[39] Indeed, the Court of Appeal has expressly left open the question of whether it might apply to all unfurnished property available for immediate occupation.[40] It is accordingly well worth arguing in an appropriate case that the implied term applies to unfurnished flats. In Ireland, the Supreme Court has held that the implied term does apply to unfurnished council flats.[41]

Regrettably, the Court of Appeal has recently indicated that if a covenant of fitness is to be extended to unfurnished council flats in Britain, the initiative must come from Parliament and not from the courts.[42]

Remedy

Where the landlord has failed to observe the terms of this implied covenant the tenant may *immediately*[43] quit the premises without liability for rent[44] or may sue for breach of contract.[45] See further chapter 4 for civil remedies.

Scotland
In Scotland, the common law requires (as an implied contractual condition) that the property let must be wind and watertight and in habitable and tenantable condition.[46]

Premises let at low rent
The Landlord and Tenant Act 1985 (LTA 1985) s8 implies into lettings at a low rent (for example long-standing periodic tenancies and long leases) two separate contractual terms which are *absolute* and *non-excludable:*
(a) that the premises are *fit for human habitation* on the date of letting; and
(b) that the premises will be *kept fit* for habitation, by the landlord, throughout the duration of the tenancy.
See Appendix 4 for the full text of s8.

Both terms apply to lettings of whole houses or parts of houses (s8(6)). The apparently wide scope of s8 is, however, limited by the narrow range of lettings to which it applies. In order to have the benefit of these implied terms the annual rent[47] (irrespective of who paid the rates[48]) must be *less* than:

Date of letting	
Before 31 July 1923	£40 London £26 a borough or district with over 50,000 people £16 elsewhere
On or after 31 July 1923 and before 6 July 1957	£40 London £26 elsewhere
On or after 6 July 1957 and before 1 April 1965	£80 London £52 elsewhere
On or after 1 April 1965	£80 inner London £52 outer London £52 elsewhere

If the letting was *originally* at a rent not greater than the maximum figure shown above, the tenant has the benefit of the implied terms. The *current* rent is irrelevant. As will be apparent, very few periodic tenancies remain which can benefit from s8. The failure to uprate the rent levels to give protection to more recent tenants has attracted judicial comment in the Court of Appeal.[49] The Government has declined to increase the rent levels, as in its view the s8 provisions are "effectively out of date", having been overtaken by the more modern provisions of s11.[50] A Department of the Environment (DoE) consultation paper (*Repairing obligations under the*

Landlord and Tenant Act 1985 June 1989) has invited comment on the continuing usefulness of s8.

Section 8 is not applicable to a letting for a fixed term of three years or more where it is expressly agreed that the tenant will put the premises into a condition reasonably fit for habitation (s8(5)). If the letting contains no such term, the benefit of s8 extends to any long lease which fulfills the low rent condition, in addition to periodic tenancies.

The section gives the landlord an express power to enter and inspect premises after giving the tenant or occupier 24 hours' notice in writing of his/her intention to do so (s8(2)).

In determining whether a house is fit for human habitation, regard is to be had to its condition in respect of: repair, stability, freedom from damp, internal arrangement, natural lighting, ventilation, water supply, drainage/sanitary conveniences, facilities for the preparation and cooking of food, and facilities for the disposal of waste water (not the new "unfitness" standard described in chapter 6). The house is deemed to be unfit for human habitation if, and only if, it is so far defective in one or more of these respects that it is not reasonably suitable for occupation in that condition (LTA 1985 s10).

Breaches of the terms implied by s8 have been successfully established in a wide range of cases, for example a small house in which the sole window in a main room could not be safely opened,[51] premises where plaster had fallen from the ceiling,[52] the complete collapse of a ceiling,[53] and accommodation in which a sanitary convenience was defective and serious dampness had accrued from defective guttering.[54]

It should be noted that liability arises only in relation to the defects *within* the premises let to the tenant, so that for example defective common staircases[55] and incursions of vermin from elsewhere,[56] will be outside the scope of the terms implied by s8.

A "rule of thumb" guide to the standards required by s8 was set out by Atkin LJ in 1926:

> "If the state of repair of a house is such that by ordinary use damage may naturally be caused to the occupier, either in respect of personal injury to life or limb or injury to health, then the house is not in all respects reasonably fit for human habitation".[57]

The courts have, however, developed a serious limitation to the usefulness of s8 by confining its application to premises which can be made fit by the landlord at reasonable expense: *Buswell v Goodwin*.[58] This controversial decision rests on a concession made in argument and has no foundation within s8 itself but it has stood unchallenged for two decades.

Advisers already using s8 should note that the exemption of lettings of temporary accommodation owned by local authorities in clearance areas or as individual unfit properties, is now to be found in Housing Act (HA) 1985 s302.

Remedy

If the landlord is in breach of either of the terms implied by s8, the tenant may recover damages for breach of contract and may abandon the tenancy without liability for the rent.[59] *But*, the obligation to keep the premises fit for habitation throughout the letting does not become enforceable until the landlord is given notice of the defects rendering the premises unfit: *McCarrick v Liverpool Corporation*.[60] See p28 on the notice requirement and, generally, chapter 4 for civil remedies.

(b) Obligation to repair common parts

All tenants

Tenants often suffer much difficulty and inconvenience resulting from the disrepair of the *common parts* they share with other tenants or resident landlords. Complaints of defective stairways, lifts, hallways, paths and courtyards are commonplace. In dealing with the disrepair of these "common parts" where there are no relevant express terms in a tenancy agreement, certain *common law implied terms* are of importance:

(a) a landlord is under an obligation[61] to ensure that if s/he retains control of part of a building and lets another, s/he takes reasonable care to maintain the condition of the parts retained so as to prevent injury to the tenant or damage to the premises let: *Dunster v Hollis*.[62] Thus where a landlord lets a flat but retains control of the roof and gutters, s/he is obliged to repair them so as to prevent dampness getting into the flat: *Cockburn v Smith*.[63] There will however be no grounds for implying a term as to repair of the common parts where provision is comprehensively made for such repairs in a written tenancy agreement: *Gordon v Selico Co Ltd*;[64]

(b) if the tenant is given a contractual right to use another part of a building in addition to the part let (for example a shared lavatory), the landlord is under an obligation to maintain that part for the use of the tenant: *Miller v Emcer Products*;[65]

(c) if a landlord lets premises but retains control of facilities which are essential or necessary for the tenant the landlord is under a contractual obligation to take reasonable care to maintain those facilities reasonably so that they remain available for the use of the tenant: *Liverpool Corporation v Irwin*.[66] "Facilities" for this purpose include lifts,[67] stairways[68] and rubbish chutes serving upper-storey lettings. This implied term would, for example, impose an obligation on a landlord to maintain artificial lighting on an internal staircase shielded from natural light, since the stairway is a facility for the use of the tenant and artificial light is essential to permit safe use;[69]

(d) a landlord is to give the tenant "quiet enjoyment" of the premises for the duration of the letting. This may be breached in circumstances of disrepair, for example by a landlord failing to keep watertight the building containing the tenant's flat, thereby allowing the flat to be penetrated by rainwater or dampness,[70] or by carrying out work on other parts of the building causing noise and nuisance to the tenants;[71]

(e) a landlord shall not "derogate from his grant" of a tenancy to the tenant. This implied term may be breached in relation to disrepair if a landlord allows premises retained in his/her ownership or occupation to be in such a state as to interfere with the tenant's tenancy. However, the act or omission of the landlord must be shown to stem from the landlord's own deliberate or voluntary behaviour.[72]

Because the common parts are deemed to be within the landlord's control, the tenant is *not* required to give notice of disrepair, before the obligation to repair arises.[73]

In so far as these obligations arise as implied contractual terms, they may be excluded by express terms to the contrary.[74]

Tenancies granted on or after 15 January 1989

It is an implied term of a periodic tenancy (or a tenancy for less than seven years) granted on or after 15 January 1989 that the landlord will keep in repair the structure and exterior of any part of the building owned by the landlord of which the dwelling let to the tenant forms part (LTA 1985 s11(1A)). This is in addition to the landlord's ordinary obligation to keep in repair the structure and exterior of the individual dwelling let to the tenant (see below p18). Therefore if the tenancy is of a flat in a block of flats the landlord must keep in repair the parts of the block (both common parts and other flats) of which s/he is owner.

Tenants can enforce the repairing obligation imposed by s11(1A) only if the disrepair interferes with the enjoyment of their own dwelling or their use of the common parts (s11(1B)).

This provision will be exceptionally helpful to tenants affected by disrepair in the common parts (eg broken stairtreads and missing bannister rails on communal staircases, crumbling balcony walls, potholes in elevated walkways etc) and to tenants with repairs problems arising from disrepair to empty flats in a block (eg where the roof to an empty flat above the tenant is leaking, allowing water penetration into the tenant's home).

Even though the landlord will be presumed to know of the disrepair in the parts of the property s/he retains, it is not certain that the courts will presume that the landlord knows of the effect on the individual tenants. It may therefore be advisable to ensure that the landlord has actual knowledge (preferably by notice) of both the defect and effect before proceeding for breach of s11(1A). It is a defence for the landlord to show in such proceedings that, despite using reasonable endeavours, s/he was unable to obtain the right to carry out the works to the particular part of the building concerned (eg where the disrepair emanates from a flat of which the landlord is the freeholder but where the leaseholder is exercising the right to refuse access): s11(3A).

Advisers dealing with complaints of disrepair affecting a whole block may (in the light of the availability of s11(1A) to post-January 15 1989 tenants) find it useful to identify one of the newer tenants for the "lead case" on action concering the common parts.

Remedy

Where the obligation in relation to common parts takes effect as an implied contractual term, the remedy lies in an action on the contract. In other cases, an action lies for breach of the landlord's duty of care. See generally chapter 4 on civil remedies.

(c) Basic repairs (LTA 1985 s11)

The LTA 1985 s11 implies into tenancy agreements an obligation upon landlords to effect basic repairs which is both *absolute* and *non-excludable.* (Section 11 consolidated the Housing Act 1961 s32. For the full text of ss11-17 see Appendix 4).

The obligation is:

> "(a) to keep in repair the *structure and exterior* of the dwelling-house (including drains, gutters and external pipes),
> (b) to keep in repair and proper working order the *installations* in the dwelling-house for the supply of water, gas and electricity and for sanitation (including basins, sinks, baths and sanitary conveniences but not other fixtures, fittings and appliances for making use of the supply of water, gas or electricty), and
> (c) to keep in repair and proper working order the *installations* in the dwelling-house for space heating and heating water." [italics supplied]

The landlord cannot seek to avoid the obligation imposed by s11 by the use of express contractual terms. Any such term seeking to exclude the liability (s12(1)(a)) or transfer it to the tenant (s11(4)) is void.

The landlord or the landlord's agent is given a statutory right to enter premises for the purpose of viewing the condition and state of repair on giving the tenant 24 hours' notice in writing: s11(6).

Interpreting s11

Owing to the breadth of the implied terms contained in s11, the component parts have been subject to close scrutiny:

- *"... keep in repair ..."* The covenant to keep in repair is a continuing obligation to keep up the standard of repair in the dwelling throughout the duration of the tenancy. Moreover, it also requires the landlord to *put the premises into repair* if they were not in good repair at the outset of the tenancy.[75]

But what exactly does the word "repair" cover and how is it to be applied?

Ultimately, the question of whether a disputed item of required work is repair or renewal or maintenance or improvement will be one for the courts based on the facts of the individual case,[76] but some earlier decisions give a useful indication of the principles to be applied. For example, in *Lurcott v Wakeley*[77] it was said that repair means the restoration by renewal or replacement of subsidiary parts of the whole; whereas renewal, as distinguished from repair, means the reconstruction of the whole. So that in *Lurcott*'s case, repair was held to cover the replacement of a deteriorated wall, since the wall was only a subsidiary part of the whole.

Denning LJ has given further guidance as to the test to be applied:

> "If the work which is done is the provision of something new for the benefit of the occupier, that is, properly speaking an improvement; but if it is only the replacement of something already there which has become dilapidated or worn out, then, albeit that it is a replacement by its modern equivalent, it comes within the category of repairs not improvements."[78]

More recently still, Sachs LJ has said that the correct approach is to

> ". . . look at the particular building, look at the state which it is in at the date of the lease, look at the precise terms of the lease, and then come to a conclusion whether, on a fair interpretation of those terms in relation to that state, the requisite work can fairly be called repair."[79]

If it is necessary, to comply with the covenant, that the landlord should replace part after part until the whole is replaced, s/he will have to do so.[80] On the other hand, the landlord cannot be required to rebuild the whole dwelling at once if that is what is required.[81] It should also be noted that the requirement to "repair" carries with it an obligation upon the landlord to make good or redecorate on completion of works.[82]

• *"repair" and s11* For s11(1)(a) to apply it must be shown that there is actually some part of the structure or exterior which is in a state of disrepair and therefore requires "repair", ie "the covenant will only come into operation where there has been damage to the structure and exterior which requires to be made good".[83] Evidence of damage to decoration, clothing, bedding, curtains, etc is all to no avail unless some part of the structure or exterior can be shown to require repair, for instance window frames or wall plaster.

• *responsibility for major repair work and design defects* Advisers frequently have to consider cases of disrepair so fundamental as to be critical to the integrity of the dwelling as a whole, for example replacement of the roof, underpinning, damp-proof coursing, remedying design defects etc.

In recent years the courts have reviewed the circumstances in which such major work can be brought within the "repairing" obligation. (Such consideration has not been confined to areas of housing law.[84]) Much that has emerged from this caselaw is helpful to tenants.[85]

From the cases, the following broad propositions have been extracted for testing whether an item of major work falls within the covenant of "repair":

(a) the particular words of the covenant are to be construed and given their ordinary meaning to determine whether they would cover the works necessary;
(b) the particular works required are to be considered to see whether, as a matter of fact and degree, they fall within the covenant;
(c) in determining the issue of fact and degree the courts will have regard to:
  (i) the intention of the parties at the time of the letting as expressed by the letting agreement or otherwise;
  (ii) the cost or value of the repairs as compared to the value of the property as a whole;
  (iii) the difference (if any) between the nature of the dwelling in its state of "repair" as opposed to disrepair.

In *Ravenseft Properties Ltd v Davstone (Holdings) Ltd*[86] expansion joints had been omitted from a 16-storey tower block because at the date of construction building technology had not recognised the need for such joints. Forbes J held that the remedial work did fall within the repairing covenant having regard to the low cost of repairs compared to the value of the building as a whole, and the fact that the works would not affect the character of the property.

The Court of Appeal gave authority to this approach in *Smedley v Chumley & Hawkes Ltd.*[87] A repairing covenant was held to extend to works of underpinning a property which had begun to subside, since it was the intention of the parties that the repairing clause should operate so as to give the tenant a stable and structurally sound property. Similarly, in *Elmcroft Development v Tankersley-Sawyer*,[88] a repairing covenant was construed to require extensive remedial work. A block of modern private flats was subject to acute penetrating dampness due to the laying of the damp proof course at below ground level. The tenants succeeded in an action for breach of the covenant on the basis that the obligation to repair required the landlords to remedy the problem properly by insertion of a silicone injected damp proof course at the proper level. The "*Ravenseft* test" was adopted and applied.

In *Elite Investments Ltd v Bainbridge Silencers Ltd*,[89] the repairing covenant was held to require the complete replacement of a substantial, defective roof. However, in *Murray v Birmingham CC*,[90] the tenant was unable to prove that the roof had deteriorated to such an extent that the only proper repair would be complete replacement. The court found repeated patch repairs sufficient to satisfy s11.

In *McDougall v Easington DC*,[91] considerable work had been undertaken to a council house of system-built, concrete panel construction. In deciding that the work undertaken constituted improvement rather than repair, the Court of Appeal reviewed the modern authorities. Mustill LJ said that in any dispute as to whether major works are of repair or improvement:

> ". . . three different tests may be discerned, which may be applied separately or concurrently as the circumstances of the individual case may demand, but all to be approached in the light of the nature and age of the premises, their condition when the tenant went into occupation, and the other express terms of the tenancy:
> (i) whether the alterations went to the whole or substantially the whole of the structure or only to a subsidiary part;
> (ii) whether the effect of the alterations was to produce a building of a wholly different character than that which had been let;
> (iii) what was the cost of the works in relation to the previous value of the building and what was their effect on the value and lifespan of the building?"

In the light of these developments it will no longer be open to a landlord of relatively modern property to escape liability for repair by suggesting that the work required arises from a "design defect" or "inherent fault".[92] Indeed, where the "design defect" or fault arises in circumstances where the landlord has designed or built the dwelling, there may be an additional liability in negligence (see below pp37–39). It is important to stress, however, that the design defect complained of must be such as to have caused disrepair before the repairing covenant can be used to require remedial work.[93] If there is such disrepair or damage "caused by an unsuspected inherent defect then it may be necessary to cure the defect, and thus to some extent improve without wholly renewing the property as the only practicable way of making good the damage to the subject matter of the repairing covenant."[94]

For the particular difficulties, both in law and practice, arising from chronic condensation dampness see chapter 7 p114.

• *repairing older buildings* At the present state of the law, the covenant to "repair" will not be used to require a landlord of an older property to bring it up to modern standards.[95] However, there is no reason to believe that the test of "intention at time of letting" mentioned above is confined in its application only to new property. If the parties to a letting of an older house contemplate that it should provide sound living accommodation throughout, then the covenant to "repair" will be interpreted to require the landlord to repair, renew and replace the "subsidiary parts" of the whole so as to keep the dwelling in a fit state to provide sound living accommodation.

• *patching-up or complete repair?* A landlord may accept that a particular part of the dwelling is in disrepair but propose to deal with it by "patch" repairs. For example, if a flat roof leaks, the repair proposed may be a further application of bitumen rather than a complete overhaul, or if a floorboard is rotten that board may be replaced without tackling the source of the rot. The issue is whether such "patching" work meets the obligation to *keep in repair*. In *Elmcroft v Tankersley-Sawyer*[96] the landlords conceded that the repairing obligation would require them to hack-off and replace damp wallplaster but denied that it would oblige then to tackle the source of the dampness (rising damp). Ackner LJ said:

> "The patching work would have to go on and on, because as the plaster absorbed (as it would) the rising damp, it would have to be renewed and the cost to the [landlords] in constantly being involved in this sort of work, one would have thought, would have outweighed easily the cost in doing the job properly. I have no hestitation in rejecting the submission that the appellant's obligation was repetitively to carry out futile work instead of doing the job properly once and for all."

The notion that patch repairing was sufficient to discharge the duty was similarly rejected in *Stent v Monmouth DC.*[97] In that case there had been a problem for over 30 years of rot to a wooden front door and frame. The landlords had repeatedly cut out and repaired parts of the door and frame and from time to time replaced the rotten wooden door with another wooden door which then rotted. The Court of Appeal had no hesitation in holding that the obligation to "repair" was not discharged by these patching repairs. The council "had the obligation to make good the design defect which caused the collection of water which occasioned the rotting". This was achieved by installing a self-sealing aluminium door.

Quick v Taff Ely[98] does not fit happily with this line of authority. In that case a window sill and wallplaster required replacement because of acute condensation dampness. That in turn could be cured by double glazing, insulation etc. However, insufficient findings of fact had been made in the county court to show that the only "proper" way of tackling the limited disrepair which had been proved was the major work urged by the tenant.

In summary, the test of whether patching will suffice is whether tackling the root cause would be a "mode of repair which a sensible person would have adopted; and the same reasoning applies if for the word 'sensible' there is substituted some such word as 'practicable' or 'necessary'."[99] The burden is on the tenant to lead the evidence which shows that further patching will not suffice and that a more generalised repair or replacement is necessary.[100]

• *"... dwelling-house ..."*: the building or part of a building which is let to the tenant wholly or mainly as a private residence; LTA 1985 s16(b).[101]

• *"... keep in ... proper working order ..."* These words necessarily presuppose that at the inception of the letting the relevant installations *were* in proper working order, so that, if by reason of disrepair or technical design fault the item has *never* been in proper working order, a landlord with knowledge of the defect will be in continuing breach of the implied term.[102]

• *"structure and exterior"* Repairs which are *structural* are those which concern the fabric of the building or the integrity of the dwelling as constructed, however small the particular unit of the structure may be.

A useful definition of structural repairs has been provided by the courts:[103]

> "A house is a 'complex unity', particularly a modern house. 'Structural' implies concern with the 'constituent or material' parts of that unity. What are the 'constituent or material parts'? In my judgment in any ordinary sense they involve more than simply the load bearing elements, for example the four walls, the roof and the foundations. The constituent parts are more complex than that. [The judge then suggested a definition of 'structural' as being] . . . appertaining to the basic fabric and parts of the house as distinguished from its decorations and fittings."

The *exterior* is the outside or external part of the dwelling-house. The liability under the covenant extends to all outside parts of the demised dwelling.

The interpretation of the words "structure" and "exterior" may be illustrated as follows:

(a) a partition wall between the dwelling and another house or flat is part of the structure or exterior;[104]
(b) in relation to a house, the path and steps which are the immediate and ordinary means of access are within "exterior"[105] but the paving of the back yard is not;[106]
(c) whether underpinning of subsiding walls is within the covenant to repair the structure is a question of fact and degree;[107]
(d) the roof[108] (if any) is part of the structure of a house as is any skylight it contains (see below for roofs of *flats*);[109]
(e) the walls are part of the structure, together with any wallplaster[110] or cement rendering;[111]
(f) woodwork will usually be part of the structure, and failure to paint external woodwork so as to protect it from rot will be a failure to repair;[112]
(g) windows will be part of the structure if they are a substantial and integral part of the wall.[113] On the other hand, the ordinary windows in a house or flat are part of the exterior of the dwelling.[114]

Where the dwelling-house is a *flat*, "structure and exterior" has been held to extend to: the outside wall(s) of the flat, the outside of the inner party wall of the flat, the outer sides of the horizontal divisions between the flat and the flats above and below, ceilings and walls of the flat.[115] Where the ceiling and roof of a top-floor flat form an inseparable structural unit, the roof will be within the structure or exterior of the flat. In the case of other flats, whether a common roof is within the covenant will be a question of fact according to the particular circumstances.[116]

The "structure and exterior" with which s11(1)(a) is concerned is the "structure and exterior *of the dwelling-house*" let to the tenant, ie the tenant's own house or flat (see p22 for the definition of "dwelling-house"). Normally, therefore, the provision could not be used by the tenants of the lower of two flats to get the roof over the upper flat repaired, since on any view the roof would not be part of the structure or exterior of their own flat. The position is now different for tenancies commencing on or after 15 January 1989. In these more recent tenancies, the term implied by s11 is extended to include not only the structure and exterior of the demised premises but also the remaining parts of the building in which the landlord retains an estate or interest (s11(1A)). The effects of this extension of s11 and the circumstances in which it can be applied are discussed above at p17.

• *"... the installations in the dwelling-house ..."* The landlord is obliged to keep in repair *and* in working order the installations specifically mentioned in s11(1)(b) and (c). The provision also extends to other installations for the supply of water/gas/electricity/sanitation/heating/hot water. Thus water or gas pipes, electrical wiring, water tanks,[117] boilers, radiators and other space heating installations such as vents for underfloor heating will be within the repairing obligation.

It should be noted that the installations must normally be *in* the tenant's dwelling. However, some tenants (and particularly those in high rise flats) experience major problems as the result of the failure of installations serving blocks or estates but sited outside their homes, for example central heating boilers. The courts have declined to extend the benefit of the repairing covenant to such tenants. In the *Campden Hill Towers* case[118] Megaw LJ said:

> ". . . the installations in the physical confines of the flat must be kept in repair and capable, so far as their own structural and mechanical condition is concerned, of working properly. But no more than that."

The requirement that the defective installations must be *in* the dwelling has been lifted for more recent tenants. If the tenancy was granted on or after 15 January 1989 the obligation to repair and keep in proper working order is extended to any installation which (a) either directly or indirectly serves the dwelling and (b) is either owned by or under the control of the landlord or is part of a building owned by the landlord (s11(1A)). This provision effectively overcomes the *Campden Hill Towers* case and gives these more recent tenants rights to require repairs to, for example, the communal heating boiler, the pump in the district heating system, the water tank on the roof of the tower block etc. The extended obligation can be enforced only by a tenant whose home is actually affected by the deficiency of the installation: s11(1B).

Advisers concerned with complaints from groups of tenants with such problems should accordingly aim to identify those with the benefit of the new extensions to the implied term as the "lead" cases.

Apart from the installations specifically mentioned in the section, the repairing obligation does *not* extend to fixtures, fittings, and appliances for making use of water/gas/electricity and sanitation (s11(1)(b)).

In *Wycombe AHA v Barnet*[119] the Court of Appeal held that the obligation in s11(1)(b) and (c) to keep the installations in the premises in proper working order did not impose a duty on the landlord to lag water tanks and pipes so as to avoid damage in exceptionally severe cold weather. The Court did indicate however that a landlord would be liable if the pipes were prone to burst within the normal temperature range, and that since there was in any event no liability on the part of the tenant, any prudent landlord would insulate the pipes to avoid damage being caused to his/her reversion. Additionally, in certain circumstances a landlord may be liable in negligence to the tenant for damage caused by pipes bursting.[120]

Standards for s11 repairs

The repairing obligations implied into tenancy agreements by s11 are subject to the important qualification that in determining the standard of repair to be required, regard is to be had to the age, character, and prospective life of the dwelling-house and the locality in which it is situated (s11(3)). Some assistance as to the interpretation of this provision is given by the caselaw.

In *Proudfoot v Hart*[121] it was said that:

> "The house need not be put into the same condition as when the tenant took it, it need not be put into perfect repair, it need only be put into such state of repair as renders it fit for the occupation of a reasonably minded tenant of the class who would be likely to take it" (per Esher LJ).

However, this does not allow a landlord in an area of derelict housing to escape liability for repair, because the standard to be maintained by the requirement to repair is a full repaired standard as at the date of the letting. Thus:

> "We are bound to look at the character of the house and its ordinary uses at the time of the demise . . . An improvement of its tenants or its neighbourhood will not increase the standard of repair, *nor will their deterioration lower that standard.*"[122]

Accordingly, a dwelling which was in poor repair at the date of letting and is presently a worthless property in an area of very poor quality housing, does not fall to be comprehensively repaired under s11.

In *Patel v LB Newham*,[123] the Court of Appeal found no breach of s11 where a tenant lived for five years in premises so damp and poorly-repaired that they had been condemned as both unfit for habitation and a statutory nuisance, since the premises had been scheduled for redevelopment for 14 years and money spent on them would have been wasted. Alternatively, the Court upheld the judge's finding that the tenant was not entitled to recover damages even if a breach were established, since the rent payable had been set artificially low as a result of the condition of the property and no special damage had been proved. Similarly, in *Wainwright v Leeds CC*[124] the Court of Appeal declined to hold that s11 required the council to insert a damp proof course in a run down back-to-back terraced house built in the early 1900s even though it was subject to acute penetrating dampness.

However, *McClean v Liverpool CC* [125] demonstrates that if the dwelling has not yet reached the end of its useful life, s11 will require repairs to be carried out even though the house is otherwise unmodernised and lacks many facilities.

Advisers dealing with very dilapidated properties where local housing conditions were poor at the date of letting should accordingly consider whether other remedies are more appropriate than s11. Finally, it should be noted that the standard of repair required by s11 is no higher for local authorities than for private landlords.[126]

Time limits for s11 repairs

The obligation of the landlord under s11 is complied with if the landlord carries out a repair on being informed of the need for such repair. It follows that there can be no breach of the obligation until the landlord knows of the disrepair and "a reasonable time has elapsed in which the repair could have been carried out".[127] There is no prescribed "reasonable time" so the length of the period for completion of repairs will vary according to the circumstances in each case.

If the landlord has given some advance indication to the tenant of the times within which particular repairs will usually be completed (perhaps by showing "target periods" in a tenant's handbook) these will be strongly indicative of what a "reasonable time" would be for repairs falling within those categories. Some landlords may even have placed such time limits within the tenancy agreement (in which case they can be directly enforced without reliance on s11).

In other cases, the courts (and initially those advising tenants) will determine the reasonable period taking into account a variety of factors. Obviously the scale and severity of the disrepair will be critical factors but also relevant will be: whether the tenant is actually living in the property, the availability of replacement parts and (in the case of municipal landlords) the overall workload.[128] The burden of proving that a reasonable time has been exceeded lies on the tenant. This will require firm evidence rather than inference. For example, even where the repair required is the replacement of a missing or damaged front door and door frame, it does not necessarily follow that a landlord allowing a week to pass before effecting repairs is in breach of s11.[129]

Limitations of s11

The operation of s11 is circumscribed in a number of ways:

(a) the provision applies only to tenancies commencing on or after the passage of the Housing Act 1961, ie 24 October 1961 (s13(1));

(b) it applies only to periodic tenancies and fixed-term leases of a shorter duration than seven years. Lettings for longer periods are also covered where the landlord has an option to end the letting within seven years of commencement. But, by s13(2), lettings for less than seven years may fall outside s11 if the tenant can renew for a further term, making more than seven years in total. These provisions, together with those relating to renewed lettings, are somewhat complex and an adviser should pay close attention to the terms of ss12-15 before giving a conclusive opinion;

(c) s11 does not apply to certain agricultural tenancies within the Agricultural Holdings Act 1948;

(d) no liability can be imposed upon the landlord for breach of s11 until s/he has *notice* of the defects complained of (see below);

(e) (except in the case of post-15 January 1989 tenancies) it does not extend to *common parts* of the building containing the accommodation let to the tenant, nor to parts of the premises retained by the landlord but which the tenant is permitted to use;

(f) s11 does not extend to any item which the tenant is entitled to remove from the premises, nor does it relieve the tenant of the obligation to use the premises in a tenant-like manner, nor does it require the landlord to reinstate premises destroyed by act of God or inevitable accident etc (s11(2));

(g) s11 does not assist most business tenants (s32(2));

(h) s11 does not apply to certain properties let *to* local authorities and other public bodies (s14(4));

(i) s11 does not bind the Crown. It cannot therefore be relied on by the tenants of most government departments and agencies.[130]

Important note for pre-1961 tenancies

Tenancies which would otherwise be outside s11 because they started before 24 October 1961 may nevertheless gain the benefit of the provision. For example, where a fair rent has been registered on the basis that the tenancy is subject to s11 and the landlord has accepted rent following that registration, the landlord will be bound by the repairing obligation: *Brikom Investments v Seaford.*[131] Alternatively, a pre-1961 tenant may be able to show that s/he is covered by s11 because the earlier tenancy has been determined and replaced by one commencing after 1961. This will be the case for all local authority tenants because in the 1960s and 1970s council rent increases were achieved by a process of notice to quit and regrant.[132]

Pre-1961 tenants[132A] not covered by s11 may be able to rely on one of the implied terms described below.

Remedy

The remedy for breach of s11 will generally be an action in contract for damages and specific performance (see generally chapter 4). In such actions the tenant will be required to establish breach of the covenant on the ordinary balance of probabilities.[133] If there is a dispute as to whether s11 applies to a property at all, a declaration may be sought from the county court (s15).

(d) An implied term on general structural repair?

For those tenants who fall outside the scope of s11, there may possibly be other implied terms which may be of assistance.

There is authority for the proposition that in respect of very short term or periodic lettings a landlord will be taken to have assumed a contractual liablity to maintain the structure or exterior of the property, at least to the extent of preventing a dangerous state of disrepair from arising.[134] Of course, this assumption may be displaced by any express term to the contrary.

If a tenant is obliged under an express term of a tenancy to carry out repairs to the interior of a dwelling, the courts are prepared to impose a collateral implied term that the landlord must repair the exterior of the property.[135] The implication is justified by the need to give "business efficacy" to the tenancy agreement.

The notice requirement

The general rule at common law applicable to both express and implied repairing obligations in tenancy agreements is that a landlord is under no liability to attend to repairs until s/he has knowledge of the need for repair.[136] Although a "common law" rule, it has been consistently held to apply where the repairing obligations are imposed by statute.[137]

The strict common law rule required the landlord to have *actual knowledge* of the repair, notwithstanding any express or implied right of the landlord to enter premises and inspect for disrepair.[138] The landlord's knowledge of the defect must be proved even if the disrepair is undetectable, so that a tenant injured by the collapse of a ceiling which no one could have expected to be liable to fall, cannot recover damages from his/her landlord for breach of repairing obligations.[139]

It should be noted that it is the "knowledge" of the landlord which is important. Usually this knowledge will arise from notice of disrepair given by the tenant. However, a landlord may be imputed with knowledge if the disrepair is brought to the attention of his/her workmen,[140] rent-collector or any other person, for example a resident caretaker, employed by the landlord and having express or implicit authority to receive complaints of disrepair on behalf of the landlord.

The route by which the landlord receives knowledge of the disrepair is not significant save that it has been suggested that the informant must be a "responsible source".[141] In *Dinefwr BC v Jones*,[142] the council was held to have actual notice of the disrepair seen at the property by an environmental health officer (EHO) even though the EHO was not from the housing department and was inspecting the property after complaints relating to cleanliness rather than disrepair. The EHO however was *not* treated as having implied knowledge on behalf of the council about defects other than those obviously visible (ie not those which would have been discovered only on a thorough inspection). The *Jones* case also indicates that notice will be established where the landlord receives information about the defects in a property from an independent valuer (in that case from the valuation officer following a right-to-buy application). This was confirmed in *Hall v Howard*,[143] where the landlord received an offer for purchase from a private tenant accompanied by a surveyor's valuation report, listing (and costing) repairs needed. Receipt of the report was sufficient to fix the landlord with knowledge of the defects. Similarly, service by a local authority of some form of statutory repair notice is sufficient to establish knowledge on the part of the landlord and thus, liability.[144]

The information received by the landlord must be sufficient to put a reasonable person on enquiry as to whether works of repair are needed.[145] It will therefore be necessary for the tenant to make the landlord aware of the need for specific disrepair to be tackled, but the notice given need not particularise the degree or extent of the disrepair nor the remedial works required.[146] Where the tenant informs the landlord that s/he will be preparing a detailed list of items of disrepair and estimates for the works required, notice is not actually given until the list and estimates are served.[147] Save in the case of an inspection by an EHO or specialised tradesperson (see above), a tenant cannot necessarily rely on the proposition that because the premises were inspected by the landlord or landlord's agent, it follows that the landlord knew of the defects in the premises. It is for the tenant to show that the landlord or unqualified agent saw the defect.[148]

Where no notice or knowledge can be established, the Defective Premises Act 1972 s4 may be helpful (see p42).

Access for the landlord

For the purposes of carrying out repairs[149] or inspecting for repairs, landlords may have rights of access at either common law or under statute.

• *Common law* The landlord who is subject to an express or implied duty to keep premises "in repair" will have certain rights at common law:

> "I have construed that covenant to mean that he shall put them into good condition if necessary and it is my judgment that the covenant carries with it an implied licence

to the lessor to enter upon premises of the lessee and to occupy them for a reasonable time to do what he has covenanted to do"

per Fry J in *Saner v Bilton*.[150] The right to enter is subject to an obligation to give the tenant reasonable notice.[151]

• *Statute* Most statutory repairing obligations carry within them express rights of entry for the landlord (see particularly the discussions of the LTA 1985 ss8 and 11 at pp15 and 18 above).

In addition, the Rent Act 1977 s148 gives landlords an express right to enter for the purpose of carrying out repairs in the case of protected or statutory[152] tenancies. The Housing Act 1988 s16 gives the same right of access to the landlord of an assured tenant.

1 *Robbins v Jones* (1863) 15 CB (NS) 221 at 240.
2 See further chapter 3, especially pp35-41.
3 *Longrigg, Burrough and Trounson v Smith* (1979) 251 EG 847.
4 *Gott v Gandy* (1853) 2 E & B 845; see also *Sleafer v Lambeth BC* [1960] 1 QB 43, CA.
5 *Hart v Windsor* (1844) 12 M & W 68 (houses); *Cruse v Mount* [1933] Ch 278 (flats); and see *Edwards v Upton* (1980) 253 EG 818.
6 *Arden v Pullen* (1842) 10 M & W 321.
7 *Manchester Bonded Warehouse Co v Carr* (1880) 5 CPD 507.
8 *Middleton v Hall* (1913) 108 LT 804; *Ryall v Kidwell & Son* [1914] 3 KB 135.
9 Per O'Higgins CJ in *Siney v Dublin Corp* [1980] IR 400.
10 *The civil liability of vendors and lessors for defective premises* Law Comm Report No 40 para 45.
11 See below pp18-28.
12 See below pp14-16.
13 See Arden and Partington *Housing Law* (Sweet & Maxwell).
14 Housing Act (HA) 1985 s104(1).
15 (1988) 20 HLR 74, CA.
16 See Woodfall *Landlord and Tenant* (Sweet & Maxwell) Vol 1 para 1-1429 or Hill and Redman's *Law of Landlord and Tenant* (Butterworth, 18th edn, 1988).
17 Per Banks LJ in *Calthorpe v McOscar* [1924] 1 KB 716 at 722; and M Pawlowski "Construction of repairing covenants" (1989) 20 EG 20.
18 *Lister v Lane* [1893] 2 QB 212, CA; *Pembery v Lamdin* [1940] 2 All ER 434, CA.
19 *Walker v Hatton* (1842) 10 M & W 249; *Proudfoot v Hart* (1890) 25 QBD 42; *Calthorpe v McOscar* n17.
20 This is particularly true of fixed-term lettings and long leases. See, eg, *Minchburn v Peck* (1987) 20 HLR 392, CA.
21 See p10.
22 *Hart v Windsor* n5.
23 *Sutton v Temple* (1843) 12 M & W 52.
24 *Smith v Marrable* (1843) 11 M & W 5.
25 *Charsley v Jones* [1889] 5 TLR 412.
26 *Sarson v Roberts* [1895] 2 QB 395.
27 *Harrison v Malet* (1886) 3 TLR 58.
28 *Smith v Marrable* n24.
29 *Wilson v Finch-Hatton* (1887) 2 Ex D 336.
30 *Harrison v Malet* n27.

31 *Bird v Greville* (1884) C & E 317; *Collins v Hopkins* [1923] 2 KB 617.
32 *Edwards v Etherington* (1825) Ry & M 268.
33 *Chester v Powell* (1885) 52 LT 722.
34 *Maclean v Currie* (1884) Cab & El 361.
35 See further pp92-95.
36 *Bunn v Harrison* (1886) 3 TLR 146, CA.
37 *Smith v Nottinghamshire CC* (1981) *Times* 13 November, CA; *Wettern Electric Ltd v Welsh Development Agency* [1983] 2 All ER 629. But see *Morris-Thomas v Petticoat Lane Rentals Ltd* (1987) 53 P&CR 238, CA.
38 [1933] Ch 278.
39 *Sarson v Roberts* n26.
40 *Bunn v Harrison* n36.
41 *Siney v Dublin* Corp n9.
42 *McNerney v LB Lambeth* (1988) 21 HLR 188, CA.
43 Thus, in the case of a weekly or monthly tenancy, the tenant should take action before renewal of the tenancy; otherwise s/he will be treated as having consented to the unfitness.
44 *Wilson v Finch-Hatton* n29.
45 *Harrison v Malet* n27.
46 *Gunn v NCB* 1982 SLT 526; *Davis v Edinburgh* DC (1984) June *Scolag* 86, Edinburgh Sheriff Court. And see Brown and Gordon "Rights to a decent home - condensation, cold and mould" (1989) April *Scolag* 55 and (1989) 8 *Scottish Housing Law Notes* 1.
47 Formerly defined as "annual contractual rent", see *Whitcombe v Pollock* [1956] 106 LJ 554 (but see, contra, *Kirkpatrick v Watson* [1943] Ir Jur Rep 4).
48 *Rousou v Photi* [1940] 2 KB 379.
49 *Quick v Taff Ely BC* [1985] 3 All ER 321, CA.
50 Lord Skelmersdale. HL Debs col 370, 22 October 1986.
51 *Summers v Salford Corp* [1943] AC 283.
52 *Walker v Hobbs & Co* (1889) 23 QBD 458.
53 *Fisher v Walters* [1926] 2 KB 315.
54 *Horrex v Pidwell* [1958] CLY 1461.
55 *Dunster v Hollis* [1918] 2 KB 795.
56 *Stanton v Southwick* [1920] 2 KB 642.
57 *Morgan v Liverpool Corp* [1927] 2 KB 131, adopted and applied by House of Lords in *Summers v Salford Corp* n51.
58 [1971] 1 WLR 92.
59 *Walker v Hobbs & Co* n52.
60 [1947] AC 219.
61 It is not clear whether this obligation arises in contract or tort (*Cockburn v Smith* [1924] 2 KB 119). *Gordon v Selico Co* (1986) 18 HLR 219, CA, suggests that the better categorisation of the duty, where it arises, is an implied contractual term.
62 [1918] 2 KB 795; *Duke of Westminster v Guild* [1984] 3 WLR 630; *Gordon v Selico Co* n61.
63 [1924] 2 KB 119.
64 N61.
65 [1956] Ch 304.
66 [1977] AC 239.
67 *De Meza v Veribest Mfg* (1952) 160 EG 364.
68 *Miller v Hancock* [1893] 2 QB 177.
69 *Liverpool Corp v Irwin* n66.
70 *Booth v Thomas* [1926] Ch 397; *Gordon v Selico Co* n61.
71 *Mira v Aylmer Square Investments Ltd* [1988] EGCS 172, (1989) 21 HLR 284, QBD.
72 *Chevron Petroleum (UK) Ltd v Post Office* 1987 SLT 588.
73 *Melles & Co v Holme* [1918] 2 KB 100; *Bishop v Consolidated London Properties* (1933) 102 LJKB 257 and see *Loria v Hammer* [1989] EGCS 126, ChD.

74 *Gordon v Selico Co* n61.
75 *Proudfoot v Hart* n19; *Luxmore v Robson* (1818) B & Ald 584; *Saner v Bilton* (1878) 7 ChD 815.
76 *Manprop v O'Dell* [1969] 2 Ch 378.
77 [1911] 1 KB 905.
78 *Morcom v Campbell-Johnson* [1956] 1 QB 106.
79 *Brew Bros Ltd v Snax* [1970] 1 QB 612; and see Wilkinson "The lessons of Ravenseft" (1979) NLJ 839.
80 *Lurcott v Wakeley* [1911] 1 KB 905 at 916, 917.
81 *Collins v Flynn* [1963] 2 All ER 1068.
82 *McGreal v Wake* (1984) 13 HLR 107 followed and applied in *Bradley v Chorley BC* (1985) 275 EG 801.
83 *Quick v Taff Ely BC* n49 per Dillon LJ at 325.
84 See PF Smith "Repairs and maintenance in two contexts" (1983) Conv 231; *Commissioners of Customs and Excise v Sutton Housing Trust* [1983] STC 399 and [1984] STC 352, CA; *Commissioners of Customs and Excise v Viva Gas Appliances Ltd* [1983] 1 WLR 1445.
85 See D Williams "The meaning of 'repair'" (1982) 263 EG 963; Hughill and Kenny "Commercial leases: repairs" (1983) 267 EG 334; Wilkinson "Major structural repairs" (1982) NLJ 677; Hughes "Landlords and repairs" 39 *Housing and Planning Review* No 4 p6; D Williams "Repair or renewal?" (1987) LS Gaz 2253; Bonehill "Liability to remedy an inherent defect" (1987) LS Gaz 1400.
86 [1980] QB 12, followed and applied in *Halliard Property Co Ltd v Nicholas Clarke Investments Ltd* (1984) 269 EG 1257; *Rich Investments Ltd v Camgate Litho* [1988] EGCS 132, QBD; *Plough Investments Ltd v Manchester CC* [1989] EGCS 1, ChD. See D Williams "The 'repairing' covenant" (1984) LS Gaz 2369, "'Repair' considered" (1986) LS Gaz 350 and "Repairs update" (1989) 13 EG 22.
87 [1982] P&CR 50.
88 (1984) 270 EG 140, CA. And see *Post Office v Aquarius Properties Ltd* [1987] 1 All ER 1055, CA; *Savage and Savage v Harscott Ltd* (1987) September *Legal Action* 12.
89 (1986) 280 EG 1001; (1986) 12 CL 148.
90 (1988) 20 HLR 39, CA.
91 (1989) 21 HLR 310, CA.
92 For an alternative view see D Hughes "Housing repairs: a suitable case for reform" (1984) JSWL 137 at 145.
93 *Stent v Monmouth DC* (1987) 19 HLR 269, CA; *Post Office v Aquarius Properties Ltd* n88.
94 *Quick v Taff Ely BC* n49 at 325.
95 *Lister v Lane* (1893) 2 QB 212; *Wright v Lawson* (1903) 19 TLR 510.
96 N88.
97 N93.
98 N49.
99 Per Stocker LJ in *Stent v Monmouth DC* n93 at 284-285.
100 N90.
101 On "dwelling-house" see *Gravesham BC v Sec State for Environment* (1984) 47 P&CR 142.
102 *Liverpool Corp v Irwin* n66.
103 Per HH Judge White in *Pickering v Phillimore* (1976) 10 May (unreported), cited with approval in *Pearlman v Harrow School* [1979] 1 All ER 356.
104 *Green v Eales* (1841) 2 QB 225.
105 *Brown v Liverpool Corp* [1969] 3 All ER 1345.
106 *Hopwood v Cannock Chase DC* [1975] 1 WLR 373.
107 *Pembery v Lamdin* n18; *Smedley v Chumley and Hawkes* (1981) 261 EG 775; *ACT Construction v Customs and Excise* [1981] 1 WLR 1542.

108 *Commissioners of Customs and Excise v Sutton Housing Trust* n84.
109 *Taylor v Webb* [1937] 2 KB 283.
110 *Patel v LB Newham* [1979] JPL 303; *Palmer v Sandwell MB* (1988) 20 HLR 74, CA at 89; *Savage and Savage v Harscott Ltd* n88.
111 *Granada Theatres v Freehold Investment (Leytonstone)* [1959] 1 WLR 570.
112 *Crawford v Newton* (1886) 2 TLR 877, CA. And see *Blight on Britain's buildings: a survey of paint and maintenance practice* Paintmakers Association of Great Britain, 1984.
113 *Boswell v Crucible Steel Co of America* [1925] 1 KB 119; *Holiday Fellowship v Hereford* [1959] 1 WLR 211.
114 *Ball v Plummer* (1879) *Times* 17 June, CA; *McKay v Norwell* (1980) 30 October, unreported, Edinburgh Sheriff Court (see (1983) March *LAG Bulletin* 35); *Hastie v City of Edinburgh* 1981 SLT 61 and generally A Samuels (1973) 39 Conv 91.
115 *Campden Hill Towers v Gardner* [1977] QB 823.
116 *Douglas-Scott v Scorgie* [1984] 1 All ER 1086; *Rapid Results College v Angell* (1986) 277 EG 856, CA; *Straudley Investments v Barpress Ltd* (1987) 282 EG 1124, CA; *Hatfield v Moss* (1988) 40 EG 112.
117 *Sheldon v West Bromwich Corp* (1973) P&CR 360.
118 N115.
119 (1982) 264 EG 619.
120 *Cameron v Glasgow DC* (1984) January *Scolag* 9 and see p40 below.
121 [1890] 25 QBD 42.
122 *Calthorpe v McOscar* n17.
123 [1979] JPL 303.
124 (1984) 13 HLR 117, CA.
125 (1988) 20 HLR 25, CA.
126 N124.
127 *Calabar Properties v Stitcher* [1983] 3 All ER 759, CA at 769.
128 *Morris v Liverpool CC* (1987) 20 HLR 498, CA.
129 Ibid.
130 *Department of Transport v Egoroff* (1986) 18 HLR 326, CA.
131 [1981] 1 WLR 863.
132 *Benson v Liverpool CC* (1989) March *Legal Action* 22.
132A If the tenant was previously a pre-1961 licensee s/he will be within s11: *Davies v Brenner* [1986] CLY 1874; (1989) June *Legal Action* 24.
133 *Foster v Day* (1968) 208 EG 495.
134 *Mint v Good* [1951] 1 KB 517.
135 *Barrett v Lounova (1982) Ltd* (1988) 20 HLR 584, CA.
136 *Makin v Watkinson* (1870) LR 6 Ex 25.
137 *Morgan v Liverpool CC* n57.
138 *McCarrick v Liverpool Corp* [1947] AC 219.
139 *O'Brien v Robinson* [1973] AC 912.
140 *Sheldon v West Bromwich Corp* n117.
141 Per Bush J in *Dinefwr BC v Jones* (1987) 19 HLR 445, CA at 448.
142 N141.
143 (1988) 20 HLR 566, CA.
144 *McGreal v Wake* n82.
145 *O'Brien v Robinson* n139; *Sheldon v West Bromwich Corp* n117.
146 *Griffen v Pillet* [1926] 1 KB 117.
147 *Al Hassani v Merrigan* (1988) 20 HLR 238, CA.
148 *Hughes v Liverpool CC* (1988) *Times* 30 March, CA.
149 For the position in relation to improvements, see chapter 8 p131.
150 N75.
151 *Granada Theatres v Freehold Investment (Leytonstone)* n111.
152 Rent Act 1977 s3(2).

Chapter Three

Landlords' Liability for Disrepair

1 Introduction

Beyond the contractual rights conferred expressly or impliedly by the terms of a tenancy agreement, English law has been extremely slow to impose any further repairing obligations upon landlords, or even to give tenants remedies for injury sustained as a result of disrepair.

Indeed, landlords letting premises were given a very broad exemption from any liability to repair or prevent injury to occupiers. So that, in the absence of any express or implied contractual obligation, a landlord was not liable in negligence or otherwise either to the tenant or any other person entering the premises during the tenancy, for any defect or disrepair in the premises rendering them dangerous or unsafe, even where the landlord knew of the defect or had caused it to be there. Since the only remedy available (if any) lay in contract, those who were not parties to the letting agreement, ie the family and visitors of the tenant, had no protection at all.[1]

This rule of general immunity was preserved by the courts throughout the early part of this century, even though the common law was increasingly imposing liability on persons other than landlords in the supply of services or goods.[2] Consequently, in a series of cases the immunity continued to protect landlords of dangerous and defective housing, even though occupiers were being seriously maimed or even killed.[3]

In recent years, however, substantial progress has been made, both through the common law and statute, in piercing the landlord's "cloak of immunity from responsibility" in respect of shoddy housing. Notwithstanding that the existence of the residual immunity was confirmed in the House of Lords as recently as 1977,[4] some have suggested that developments in the last decade have gone so far as to remove altogether the special treatment of landlords by the common law,[5] although others support a more cautious approach.[6]

This author would endorse the view that ". . . the days of the landlord's immunity are numbered, and that any last vestiges of it should be abolished. Instead of a basic rule of non-liability, with exceptions grafted on it, the converse should be the case: a basic rule of liability, subject to such exceptions as may be found necessary."[7]

In this chapter consideration will first be given to the developments in common law, followed by a discussion of the relevant statutory provisions.

2 General liability for disrepair at common law

The developments made at common law have taken place in the field of "negligence". English law of tort provides that a person injured physically or materially by the negligence of another can recover recompense from that other, if a duty of care is owed and the wrongdoer failed to take reasonable care.

However, throughout its development, the common law avoided including tenants and their families among the class of persons to whom a landlord owed a duty of care. It is within only the last 20 years that caselaw has made significant changes to this approach.

The various stages in the progression towards full liability for dangerous or defective premises can best be considered by looking at the different categories of persons now subject to legal responsibility in respect of inadequate buildings.

(a) Builders[8]

Those who build property for human habitation have a duty to exercise reasonable care in the work they do, the duty being owed both towards those for whom they build under contract and to subsequent occupiers. The builder is liable, however, only for latent defects, ie those causing harm to person or property without warning.[9] Thus, tenants are able to sue builders for negligent work carried out on property prior to letting.[10] (Builders also have statutory liabilities to occupiers – see p42.)

(b) Developers

Individuals, companies and public bodies undertaking the development of land for building are liable to future occupiers, including tenants, for failure to take reasonable steps to ensure that the site acquired and developed was one on which premises fit for human habitation could be erected.[11] This obligation arises in negligence in addition to other statutory[12] or contractual rights.[13]

(c) Local authorities

In certain circumstances, an occupier of defective property (including a tenant) may properly sue a local authority where the personal injury or damage to property has arisen from the negligent failure of the authority to inspect properly the plans or the site of the works, or its failure to enforce the Building Regulations appropriate to the development.[14]

(d) Architects, engineers etc[15]

Those professionally engaged in work related to construction of dwellings owe a duty of care to future occupiers (including tenants) to exercise reasonable care in their work. A present tenant can therefore sue such experts on the basis of injury caused by defects attributable to their negligence.[16]

In many cases (particularly where it is not clear where responsibility for the defect lies) it will be reasonable to take action against more than one of those listed above. Less commonly, an occupier may successfully recover damages against all those involved in the construction of a defective building.[17]

The prime responsibility of builders, developers, etc is towards those by whom they are contracted to work. In *Murphy v Brentwood DC*[18] the House of Lords held that beyond that contractual liability there is no liability for negligence at common law unless and until harm is caused to the person or property of a third party. If a defect in the property caused by the builder, developer, etc is discovered before it causes harm then there can be no liability. The House accordingly overruled its earlier landmark decision in *Anns v Merton LBC*[19] and all cases following and applying it. If the defect is discovered before harm occurs, the cost of rectifying it is pure economic loss which cannot generally be recovered in negligence.[20] Where, however, tenants or other occupiers are personally injured by the latent defect they can recover damages in negligence.[21] Damages can also be recovered where the defect in the property let causes damage to other property and possessions of the occupier. For these purposes, however, structural damage to the property actually occupied caused by a defect in its construction does not count.[22] The courts are accordingly not willing to take general liability at common law beyond the limits prescribed by contractual or statutory[23] obligations.

It must also be shown that the architect, developer, etc failed to observe professional standards at the time of construction, modernisation etc. Later improvements in technical knowledge or professional standards cannot be used to impute liability for earlier work.[24]

It is the development of liability for defective premises established in the categories mentioned above that has indirectly led to the impending downfall of the landlord's immunity. This is best examined by looking at various potential areas of landlord responsibility.

(e) Landlords

Landlord/builder

Where the landlord is also the builder of the defective property the "cloak of immunity" no longer offers protection against an action in negligence brought by the tenant.

The extension of liability to landlords who were also builders was authoritatively made by the House of Lords in *Anns v Merton LBC.*[25] Although it did not form the point directly at issue in the case, Lords Wilberforce and Salmon were clear that the immunity of the landlord/builder was no longer good law:

> "The immunity of a landlord who sells or lets his house which is dangerous or unfit for habitation is deeply embedded in our law. I cannot, however, accept the proposition that a contractor who has negligently built a dangerous house can escape liability to pay damages for negligence . . . just because the contractor happens to have been the owner of the land upon which the house stands."

Although in the *Anns* case the builders were a private company, local authority landlords who build defective property are equally liable to be found accountable in negligence to injured tenants. In *Rimmer v Liverpool CC*[26] the council's architects designed, and the direct works department built, a block of flats each of which contained a dangerously thin glass panel. The tenant occupier having been injured in falling through the glass successfully sued the council in negligence at common law. The Court of Appeal held that:

> "The landowner who designs *or* builds a house or flat is no more immune from personal responsibility for faults of construction than a building contractor, or from personal responsibility for faults of design than an architect, simply because he has disposed of his house or flat by . . . letting it."

Quite apart from negligence, the law of contract provides that it is an implied term of any tenancy entered into while the premises are still being built, that the property will be fit to be lived in upon completion.[27]

Landlord/developer

Where the landlord does not actually build the property, but is instead responsible for the development of the site, employment of the builder and supervision of the work, the tenant will be able to recover damages for any negligence, notwithstanding the "landlord's immunity". Thus long leaseholders have been able to recover damages in both contract and tort from negligent landlord/developers.[28]

Landlord/housing authority

Where a local authority is concerned with the design, construction or development of properties subsequently let to tenants, a duty of care is owed to all those who might be affected by latent defects in the property (including the tenant) in exactly the same way as suggested for private builders and developers in the preceding paragraphs.

However, it is increasingly being argued that local housing authorities owe a higher and more particular duty of care to their tenants since they carry wider responsibilities for the quality of housing than their private counterparts. Such an argument has already received the attention of the superior courts in another jurisdiction.[29] In *Rimmer v Liverpool CC*[30] the Court of Appeal said:

> "We have not investigated the statutory powers under which the council built these flats; but the decision of the Supreme Court in Eire in *Siney v Dublin Corp* (1980) IR 400 suggests that the council's position as housing authority might provide another reason for making them liable to the plaintiff in negligence, even though they are not liable in contract."

The position was canvassed in *McNerney v LB Lambeth*,[31] where the argument was put that local authorities (as compared with private landlords) owe a general duty of care, but Dillon LJ said "I cannot see why or on what basis such a distinction is to be made or what power this court has to make it."

Landlord who does work after letting

A landlord who does work on the tenanted premises after commencement of the tenancy – be those works of repair, improvement or otherwise – is under a general duty to exercise reasonable care so as to avoid defects or the causing of damage to person or property.[32] The duty extends to using reasonable materials to ensure that the work is effective, so that for example where a landlord tries to treat an infestation of bugs with inadequate materials s/he will be liable to the tenant for subsequent damage caused.[33]

Landlord who does work before letting

The common law has not yet expressly imposed upon landlords any liability in tort to tenants or others for defective work carried out prior to the letting (but see Defective Premises Act 1972 s3. at p42 below). However, in *Hone v Benson*[34] purchasers of a property recovered damages for loss caused by defects in a central heating system which owners had negligently installed prior to the sale. An extension of this decision may possibly be to hold *landlords* liable at common law for negligent works of construction, modernisation or installation carried out prior to the letting, but so defective as to cause damage to the subsequent tenant. The Court of Appeal recently reviewed the common law authorities regarding the liability of landlords for their own defective pre-letting workmanship in *Rimmer v Liverpool CC*[35] and held that a landlord may now no longer be able to rely on a common law "immunity" but will be liable to the tenant for defects rendering the premises dangerous if they were created by the landlord. As yet, the author knows of no case in which the tenant has successfully relied on pre-letting defective work other than construction of the whole property.

Landlord who does no work

The immunity of a landlord who lets a defective, dangerous or unsafe property on which s/he has done no work, is the last aspect of the immunity remaining to be struck down by the common law and caselaw is presently developing in this area to such an extent that even this last barrier may now no longer be legally supportable. The Court of Appeal has recently expressed the view that the immunity of the bare landlord, although questionable, is still "too deeply entrenched in our law for any court below the highest to disturb or destroy it" and that to do so would possibly be "so great a change in the law as to require legislation."[36] At the time of writing, no such legislation is proposed. An attempt to show that the old immunity of the "bare landlord" had been overtaken by developments in caselaw failed in *McNerney v LB Lambeth.*[37] In that case, the landlord had not negligently constructed the building but it was unable to cope with modern usage and was prone to chronic condensation dampness. The Court of Appeal held that the fundamental immunity of the landlord in negligence had survived into the modern age and could be removed only by a change in law made by statute.

Remedy

Where it can be shown that the common law duty of care is owed, and as a result of a failure by the landlord to take reasonable care the tenant or the tenant's possessions have been damaged, proceedings may be taken in the civil courts (see chapter 4).

Landlord liable in nuisance

If the landlord retains some part of the building let to the tenant, s/he may be liable in nuisance if defects in that part cause interference with the tenant's reasonable use and enjoyment of the premises let. For example, if a landlord retains control of the roof and gutters, and, as a result of failure to keep them free of debris, rainwater gathers, pools and eventually pentrates the let property, tenants may recover compensation for the interference with their tenancy under the tort of nuisance.[38]

Landlord liable for common parts

The immunity of landlords in negligence does not extend to protect a landlord who negligently fails to repair or maintain the common parts of a property with the result that a tenant or others using the common parts are injured or their property damaged.[39] Compensation may be recovered in an action for negligence (and in an appropriate case - see above - in a combined negligence and nuisance action).

Landlord liable for actions of others

If disrepair to the dwelling occupied by the tenant is caused by a third party, the landlord will be liable to carry out repairs required by any contractual or statutory obligation even though the landlord him/herself did not cause or contribute to the disrepair. Thus, if a burglar breaks a door of the tenant's property in order to gain admission, the landlord, once given notice of the disrepair, is usually obliged to replace or repair the door.

In recent years the courts have had to consider whether a landlord might be liable in negligence for allowing a third party to get into a position to cause damage and disrepair to a tenant's property.[40] In *King v Liverpool CC*,[41] the tenant's flat was flooded when burglars broke into the vacant flat above (owned by the council landlord) and ripped out the sanitary fitments. The tenants claimed that the landlords owed a duty of care to secure the vacant flat against the known possibility (or probability) that the flat would be vandalised. It was held that no duty of care was owed, especially since there were no reasonable further measures the council could have taken to secure the vacant flat against vandals. The same conclusion was reached in *Ion v Liverpool CC*,[42] where the council had boarded the windows to the vacant flat and locked the door in the normal way. They were not liable for the actions of vandals who smashed through the door and caused damage which affected the tenant's flat below.

The result will however be different if the *landlord* creates the opportunity for damage by the third party, or, where damage is a known likelihood, the landlord stands by and does nothing about it. In *Nolan v Liverpool CC*,[43] the landlords were undertaking repairs to the tenant's window frames and in doing so smashed panes of glass. Pending the arrival of glaziers, thin sheets of plywood were placed over the windows by the council and secured by panel pins. Burglars removed the plywood sheets gaining access and causing damage to the property. The landlords were held liable in damages. In *Morris v Liverpool CC*,[44] a third party had damaged the tenant's front door. The landlord knew of the need for repair but (pending replacement of the door) simply secured the opening with plywood sheeting through which burglars gained admission. The Court of Appeal left open the question of whether the landlords might have been liable in negligence (the case having been argued on the basis of contractual liability).

Landlords have also been found liable in negligence for not acting to prevent avoidable harm to tenants. In *Stockley v Knowsley MBC*,[45] the tenant reported a loss of water supply presumed to be due to the freezing of the cold-water tanks and pipes in the communal loft area. The landlords simply told the tenant to turn off the water supply. The tenant did not know where the stopcock was (in the communal yard area) and did not have authority to shut off the stopcock and thus deprive all the tenants of water. The landlords were found liable in negligence for the damage caused to the tenant's flat when the tanks and pipes burst. Once appraised of the danger which was within their control the landlords should have at least told the tenant where the water supply control was and how to shut it off. A similar conclusion was reached in *Mattis v Islington LBC.*[46]

(f) Limitation

In those cases where liability in tort might be established, the limitation period within which legal proceedings must be commenced runs from the date on which the personal injury or damage to the tenant's property occurs – even if at that date the damage is not identified, or is incapable of discovery.[47] This initial limitation period (Limitation Act 1980 s14A) could therefore run out before the tenant or other occupier is directly affected by the defect. If that occurs, the prospective plaintiff then has a further period of three years running from the date on which significant damage is, or should reasonably be, discoverable in which to bring the claim (s14A(5)). However, no action may be based on a defect created more than 15 years before the launch of proceedings (s14B). For the purposes of these provisions, it is the date on which the defect causes damage that is important, rather than the date on which the defect itself arose.[48]

Any question of limitation should be dealt with at full trial rather than on an interlocutory basis and the burden of proving the application of a limitation rule is on a defendant who seeks to be protected by it.[49]

Where the damage which results is personal injury, the limitation period starts to run from the date of injury even though this may be many years after the defect was first constructed.[50] Where the damage suffered is damage to property, the date from which the limitation period runs may be unclear, as the legal position is generally more complex.[51]

3 General liability for disrepair under statute

Before the recent advances in the common law, Parliament had already recognised the need to give additional protection to tenants and others, and enacted legislation to impose general liability upon landlords in relation to the letting of defective premises.

(a) Occupiers' Liability Act 1957

In many common situations a landlord will retain in his or her "occupation" part of the property directly related to the part let to tenants. For example, the courtyard, entrance steps, staircases, boiler-house, lifts and roof of a block of flats may be retained in the landlord's occupation even though all the individual flats are let.[52]

Section 2 of the Act provides that in such circumstances the landlord owes a common duty of care to *all* visitors and that this is a duty "to take such care as in all the circumstances of the case is reasonable to see that the visitor will be reasonably safe in using the premises." The statute prohibits any attempt by a landlord to exclude or reduce his/her obligations to persons, not party to the contract, who are visitors, under the terms of the tenancy agreement.[53] Indeed, attempts to exclude or transfer liability in this way probably now fall within the ambit of the Unfair Contract Terms Act 1977.

Although the 1957 Act imposes a liability on the landlord for injury caused to, say, the tenant's spouse, by defects in the part of a building "occupied" by the landlord, it does not provide a mechanism by which the landlord may be forced to repair such defects in the common parts, in advance of the accident.

(b) Defective Premises Act 1972

This Act was a broader attempt by the legislature to fix builders and lessors with liability for defective premises. Although it received critical legal comment at the time of its passage,[54] the wide scope for litigation does not yet appear to have been appreciated.

Section 1 of the Act imposes a duty on those who undertake work for, or in connection with, the provision of a dwelling to:
(a) do the work in a professional or workmanlike manner; and
(b) use proper materials; and
(c) ensure that the dwelling is fit for human habitation when completed.

The duty is owed by builders as well as all others doing work in connection with the provision of the dwelling, for example architects, surveyors, specialist sub-contractors etc. It is also owed by, for example, local authorities and property development companies who engage the builder to do the work.[55] The duty is owed to the person for whom the dwelling was provided *and* to any person acquiring a subsequent legal or equitable interest. Section 1 is available in relation to property on which work commenced after 1 January 1974.[56]

Section 1's operation is limited by s2 which excludes dwellings covered by an "approved scheme" of purchaser protection, ie the National House Building Council scheme which covers nearly all private residential development. Thus, in relation to the *private* sector, s1 will operate, effectively, only in the case of conversions and alterations.

A tenant will accordingly have a statutory civil remedy against a landlord for defects in a property badly built wholly or partly by the landlord. Given prevalent problems of design defects in relatively recently constructed tower blocks and other high density dwellings, it is surprising that legal actions have not been more frequently initiated by tenants and their advisers. All the more so, given that if the builders are not available to be sued, the section gives a clear right of action against the architects and planners. (Builders may also be subject to enforceable civil liability for breach of building regulations: Health and Safety at Work etc Act 1974 s71.)

Section 3 abolishes the old immunity available to lessors, in relation to damage caused by defects in work done prior to the start of the letting. Wholly apart from contract, where a tenant or a person who might "reasonably be expected to be affected by the defects . . . created by the doing of the works" is owed a duty of care in negligence by the landlord because of any repair, maintenance, construction or other work on or in relation to premises, the duty of care is not abated by the selling or letting of those premises.[57] This means that the tenant's family and visitors are covered by s3.

The most important provision of the 1972 Act is contained in s4 (see Appendix 1 for text). This imposes on a landlord civil liability for damage caused by defects for which s/he is liable, but has failed to repair. The section, which applies to tenants, licensees, members of their households and visitors, gives rise to a remedy for personal injury or damage to their property.

Section 4(1) provides that where premises are let on a tenancy[58] under which the landlord has an obligation to repair or maintain, the landlord:

> "owes to all persons who might reasonably be expected to be affected by defects in the state of the premises a duty to take such care as is reasonable in all the circumstances to see that they are reasonably safe from personal injury or from damage to their property caused by a relevant defect."

The repairing or maintaining obligation concerned may be an express contractual term or may be implied into the contract by common law or statute: s4(5).

Section 4(4) extends "obligation" to mean that where a landlord has a right to enter in order to carry out any description of maintenance or repair, "he shall be treated for the purposes of [s4(1)-(3)] . . . as if he were under an obligation . . ." Thus the section provides great assistance to tenants and others who do not have the benefit of express or implied contractual repairing covenants, but in respect of whom the landlord has expressly reserved the right to enter and do certain repairs (possibly in default). Advisers should consider carefully how such a "useful" clause may be incorporated into new tenancy agreements, particularly those negotiated with local authorities.

In the case of a protected or assured tenant, if it can be shown that the landlord is entitled to do a particular repair, the landlord will owe a duty of care in respect of such a repair, since the statute confers a power upon the landlord to enter and do those repairs.[59] In the case of any other form of tenancy, if the landlord has the express or implied right to enter and carry out repairs, then s4 prima facie operates in relation to any defects in the property which might be corrected as a matter of repair.[60]

Two important issues arise in connection with s4 concerning (a) avoiding the usual requirement to give notice of the need for repairs and (b) the meaning of "relevant defect". These points are considered below.

No notice needed

One of the main drawbacks of contractual rights to repair is the rule that liability does not arise until the landlord has notice of the need for repair. Section 4(2) enables tenants to avoid this rule.[61] It is clear from the terms of s4(1) that the duty arises as soon as any property is let provided that the landlord is under an obligation to repair or maintain. Section 4(2) goes on to provide that the duty is owed "if the landlord knows . . . or if he ought in all the circumstances to have known of the relevant defect." Section 4(4) provides that liability for relevant defects arises "as from the time when he first is, or by notice or otherwise can put himself, in a position to exercise the right" to enter and repair.

Recent litigation turning on the use of s4 has shown the great scope it offers for those situations in which the tenant has not notified the landlord of the defect which subsequently causes injury.

In *Clarke v Taff Ely BC*,[62] injury occurred when the floor of rented council accommodation collapsed. The tenant had not notified the council of any defect but it was conceded that s4(3) and (4) applied in that the council had an obligation to carry out repairs and was entitled to exercise a right to enter and inspect. The council was held liable in substantial damages in that it ought reasonably to have known that houses of the age and type of that occupied by the tenant were susceptible to dampness and rotting floorboards, and that such defects could easily have been discovered by simple inspection.

Similarly, in *Smith v Bradford Metropolitan Council*,[63] the tenant was injured when the external patio of his council house gave way. The council had not constructed the patio, and the tenant had not reported any defect. However, the council had retained an express power in the tenancy agreement to enter and inspect and carry out repairs. Section 4(3) and (4) thus operated to impute the landlord council with knowledge of the defects and liability to take reasonable care to avoid injury to the tenant. The duty of care was held to have been breached and damages were awarded. Donaldson LJ observed that, since s4(4) applies equally where powers of entry to repair are *implied*, it must apply to almost all periodic tenancies since the court will usually imply a power to enter and inspect and carry out repairs in the absence of express provision.

The landlord in *Barrett v Lounova (1982) Ltd*[64] was held to be in breach of s4, having regard to the state of disrepair to the exterior of the premises. Again the duty to take care had been brought into play, not by any obligation to repair, but rather by an express provision allowing the landlord to enter the premises for the purposes of repair. The Court of Appeal held that in an appropriate case the s4 duty could be enforced by injunction.

Proceedings under s4 have also been taken, somewhat less successfully, on behalf of young children injured in tenanted properties. In *Ryan v LB Camden*,[65] the local authority let a flat containing pipes which protruded into the rooms and carried hot water for the estate district heating system. The tenant's child was seriously burned on falling against the pipes. The Court of Appeal was prepared to accept that a duty of care was owed by the landlord, even though negligence was not established on the particular facts of the case. Similarly, in *Issitt v LB Tower Hamlets*,[66] the tenant's child fell through a window as a result of a defective catch. The Court of Appeal was prepared to hold that the duty of care was owed, but (overruling the judge) held that there had not been breach of the duty of care on the particular facts of the case.

Finally, a local authority was held liable in negligence to a council tenant's visitor in *Marsden v LB Havering*.[67] The visitor was injured when the door-knocker came away as she was pulling the front door closed. The council was deemed to have known of the use of door-knockers in this way and was held liable for failing to carry out systematic inspection and maintenance.

It is to be hoped that those advising tenants will continue to use s4 as a more common remedy for damage caused by disrepair. For comment on its potential use in cases of condensation dampness see chapter 7 p114.

Meaning of "relevant defect"

The person suffering damage (be it the tenant or another) may rely upon the duty of care only if the damage arises by reason of a "relevant defect". Section 4(3) defines this as "a defect in the state of the premises" arising from or continuing because of:

(a) an act or omission of the landlord in failing to carry out the obligation to repair or maintain; or
(b) such an act or omission for which the landlord would have been liable had notice been given.

The relevant defect must exist at or after the "material date". In relation to pre-1974 tenancies, this is defined as being 1 January 1974. For all other tenancies the material date is the earliest of the following:

(a) the date the tenancy commenced;
(b) the date the tenancy agreement was entered into; or
(c) the date the tenant went into occupation under the tenancy.

The defect complained of must be of a type covered by the obligation to repair or maintain. Chronic condensation dampness, causing discomfort but falling short of disrepair, probably does not amount to a relevant defect for the purposes of s4.[68]

The duty owed by s4 cannot be excluded or restricted by the landlord (s6(3)).

An illustration of the usefulness of s4 would arise in the following case:

> A grants B a contractual right to occupy an unfurnished room for one year which contains no repairing obligation on the landlord's part. One clause of the licence does say that "on giving 24 hours' notice, the landlord may enter the premises and carry out structural repair, or improvement therein". If the floorboards are defective, A will owe a duty of care to B and be liable to him/her for any injury caused thereby, at any time 24 hours after the agreement is entered into.

Without the benefit of the 1972 Act, a licensee injured in the circumstances of this illustration would have no recourse arising from any injury sustained.

Remedy

The general rule is that these statutory obligations upon a landlord to "take care" cannot be enforced until there has been some damage or injury caused to the tenant or the tenant's possessions. Once damage has been suffered, the usual remedies are available (see generally chapter 4).

1 *Middleton v Hall* (1913) 108 LT 804; *Ryall v Kidwell* [1914] 3 KB 135.
2 See *Donaghue v Stevenson* [1932] AC 562 and the cases which follow and apply it.
3 *Cavalier v Pope* [1906] AC 428; *Bottomley v Bannister* [1932] 1 KB 458; *Travers v Gloucester Corp* [1947] KB 71; *Davis v Floors* [1940] 1 KB 116.
4 *Anns v Merton LBC* [1977] 2 WLR 1024.
5 Speaight and Stone *The Law of Defective Premises* (Pitmans, 1982) chapter 7.
6 Holyoak and Allen *Civil Liability for Defective Premises* (Butterworth, 1982) chapter 7.
7 J Martin "Recent developments in negligence liability" 1984 CLP 85 at 109.
8 See N Green "The scope of builders' negligence liability and related problems" (1981) NLJ 82 and T Bailey "A rejoinder" (1981) NLJ 671; and N Green "Scope of a builder's negligence liability: the third party" (1982) NLJ 284.
9 *Murphy v Brentwood DC* [1990] 3 WLR 414, HL.
10 *Gallagher v McDowell Ltd* [1961] NI 26.
11 *Batty v Metropolitan Property Realisations* [1978] QB 554.
12 See Defective Premises Act 1972 s1, p42 below.
13 *Esso Petroleum v Marden* [1976] 1 QB 801.
14 *Murphy v Brentwood DC* n9 explaining *Dutton v Bognor Regis UDC* [1972] 1 QB 373; *Anns v Merton LBC* n4; *Acrecrest v Hattrel (WS) & Partners* [1983] 1 All ER 17; *Dennis v Charnwood BC* [1982] 3 All ER 486, CA; *Lyons v Booth (FW)(Contractors) and Maidstone BC* (1982) 262 EG 981; and Holyoak and Allen "Recent developments – III: local authorities" (1987) NLJ 299.
15 See also Defective Premises Act 1972 s1, p42 below.
16 *Cedar Transport Group v First Wyvern Property Trustees Co* (1981) 258 EG 1077.
17 *Eames London Estates v North Hertfordshire DC* (1981) 259 EG 491, discussed in D Alton "Liability for defective premises" (1982) 263 EG 331.
18 N9.
19 N4.
20 *Peabody Donation Fund Governors v Sir Lindsay Parkinson & Co Ltd* [1985] AC 210, HL.
21 See, e.g, *Rimmer v Liverpool CC* [1984] 1 All ER 930, CA.

22 *D & F Estates Ltd v Church Commissioners for England* [1989] AC 177, HL; *Department of Environment v Thomas Bates & Son* [1990] 3 WLR 457, HL.
23 See p41.
24 *Wimpey Construction Co v Poole* (1984) *Times* 3 May; 128 SJ 969.
25 Overruled on other grounds in *Murphy v Brentwood DC* n9.
26 N21; and see Holyoak and Allen "Premises liability: Recent developments - IV" (1984) NLJ 425.
27 *Miller v Cannon Hill Estates* [1931] 2 KB 113; *Perry v Sharon Development Co* [1937] 4 All ER 390.
28 *Batty* n11, but as the loss was purely economic, damages would no longer be recoverable.
29 See *Siney v Dublin Corp* [1980] IR 400; and see "Council housing, implied terms and negligence" 1980 *Irish Jurist* 32.
30 N26.
31 (1988) 21 HLR 188, CA.
32 *Ball v London CC* [1949] 2 KB 159; *Billings (AC) & Sons v Riden* [1957] 3 All ER 1.
33 *Sharpe v Manchester Metropolitan DC* (1982) 5 HLR 71; and see *Hudson v RB Kensington and Chelsea* (1985) 22 October, Bloomsbury and Marylebone County Court, noted at (1985) December *Legal Action* 171.
34 (1978) 248 EG 1013, QBD.
35 N26.
36 Stephenson LJ in *Rimmer v Liverpool CC* n21; and see Williams "Landlords' liability at time of letting" (1982) LS Gaz 1567 and "Landlords' new duty of care" (1983) 266 EG 235.
37 N31.
38 See *Tennant Radiant Heat Ltd v Warrington Development Corp* (1988) 11 EG 71, CA.
39 *Taylor v Liverpool Corp* [1939] 3 All ER 329 and more generally Hill and Redman's *Law of Landlord and Tenant* (Butterworth, 18th edn, 1988).
40 Hoath "Damage caused by vandalism: responsibility as between landlord and tenant" (1986) February *Legal Action* 22.
41 [1986] 1 WLR 890, CA.
42 (1987) 10 June, unreported, QBD, Liverpool District Registry, Official Referee HHJ Stannard.
43 (1988) 14 March, unreported, Liverpool County Court, HHJ Stannard.
44 (1987) 20 HLR 498, CA.
45 (1986) 279 EG 677, CA.
46 (1987) March *Legal Action* 20.
47 *Pirelli General Cable Works Ltd v Faber (Oscar) & Partners* [1983] 1 All ER 65; *Ketteman v Hansel Properties* [1984] 1 WLR 1274; and see C Baxter "Latent damage in defective construction work" (1983) NLJ 414 and 437.
48 *London Congregational Union v Harriss* [1988] 1 All ER 15, CA.
49 *Holland v Yates Building Co Ltd* (1989) 45 LS Gaz 36.
50 *Rimmer v Liverpool CC* n21.
51 Brown "Latent damage - the remaining uncertainties" (1987) NLJ 191.
52 *Jordan v Archara* (1988) 20 HLR 607, CA.
53 S3(1).
54 North "Defective Premises Act 1972" (1973) 36 MLR 628; and Spencer "Defective Premises Act 1972" (1974) CLJ 307 and (1975) CLJ 38.
55 S1(4).
56 *Alexander v Mercouris* [1979] 3 All ER 305.
57 The section applies only to lettings made after 1 January 1974: s3(2)(a).
58 S4(6) extends "tenancy" to any right of occupation given by statute or contract.
59 Rent Act 1977 s148 (see chapter 2 p30) and Housing Act 1988 s16.
60 *Hamilton v Martell Securities* (1984) 48 P&CR 69.
61 See Ruth Holt "Notice in disrepair cases" (1978) January *LAG Bulletin* 13.

62 (1984) 10 HLR 44.
63 (1982) 44 P&CR 171, CA.
64 (1988) 20 HLR 584, CA.
65 (1982) 8 HLR 75, CA. And see generally as to liability for child visitors to defective premises Allen and Holyoak "Premises liability: Recent developments - III" (1984) NLJ 411.
66 (1983) 6 December, unreported, CA, Ub Transcript 1115.
67 (1983) 11 March, unreported, CA.
68 *McNerney v LBC Lambeth* n31.

Chapter Four

Civil Remedies for Disrepair

1 Introduction

Notwithstanding the availability to tenants of detailed legal rights under contract (see chapter 2), in tort and by statute (see chapter 3) to secure repairs from landlords, large numbers of tenanted dwellings remain in exceptionally poor repair. For some tenants, the only prospect of decent accommodation lies with use by local authorities of the procedures available under environmental protection and housing legislation (which will be dealt with in later chapters), but for many others a range of civil remedies should be considered.

For the purposes of each of the avenues of redress, discussed below, three matters have been assumed:

(a) the landlord is liable to undertake the appropriate type of repair;
(b) the tenant has given notice of the existence of disrepair and the need for remedial works;
(c) the landlord has failed to carry out the repairs within a reasonable period.

In such circumstances, the tenant has accrued a right to both financial compensation (damages) and an order requiring the landlord to discharge his/her obligations. Advisers may accordingly consider that there is little to be gained by simply encouraging the landlord to comply with repairing duties, since, even if the work is belatedly carried out, the landlord is unlikely to volunteer any payment of the compensation to which the tenant has become entitled. At this stage the tenant should certainly be directed to good legal advisers.

Preparing for legal action

Much preparatory work in disrepair cases may be undertaken using the green form scheme. This can cover initial research on the law, drafting of letters and notices, and advice to the tenant. Where necessary, extensions to the green form should be sought for preliminary reports from experts as to the cause of the disrepair and the scale of remedial works required.

An initial medical report may also assist in identifying any past ill-health or continuing health risk to the tenant caused by disrepair.

The identity of an elusive landlord should be established as early as possible, using the Landlord and Tenant Act 1985 (LTA 1985) s1,[1] which requires the person to whom rent is paid to disclose the name and address of the landlord upon request.

The appropriate venue for court proceedings should be considered. Where a lengthy period in unrepaired property is suffered by the tenant, action in the High Court may be appropriate given the county court limit of £5,000. Alternatively, the landlord may be persuaded to consent to waive the county court limit so as to keep the matter within the jurisdiction of the county court and save High Court costs.[2] It should be noted that there is no limit to the amount that can be sought as a counterclaim.

2 Direct action

(a) Using rent to pay for repairs

Where landlords are in plain breach of their contractual repairing obligations, tenants have a right at common law to undertake the necessary repairs (either personally or by engaging a contractor) and recover the costs and expenses of so doing, by deduction from future rent.

The origins of this right are to be found in precedents of considerable antiquity,[3] but its availability to tenants was reaffirmed in *Lee-Parker v Izzet*, decided in 1971.[4]

Before exercising the right to use rent to pay for repairs in default, tenants should follow carefully certain preliminary steps:

(a) inform the landlord of the intention to take this form of action if repairs are not carried out;
(b) allow a further reasonable period for the landlord to comply with the repairing obligations;
(c) obtain three estimates for the cost of carrying out the remedial works and submit copies of these to the landlord with a "final warning";
(d) engage the contractor at the lowest tender and have the work carried out;
(e) submit a copy of the contractor's invoice to the landlord and request reimbursement;
(f) if no money is forthcoming, recoup the cost by deduction from future rent.

This right, which is wholly separate from the right to "set-off against rent" (see below), will provide a tenant who is sued for unpaid rent, with a complete *defence* to the landlord's action.

This procedure will be most attractive to the tenant with sufficient funds to finance the remedial works in default. Its usefulness has also been tenuously extended. In *Asco Developments & Newman v Lowes, Lewis and Gordon*,[5] it was held that a tenant was entitled to raise a defence to an action for arrears of rent on the ground that the rent monies had been expended on remedial works following the landlord's default in carrying out repairing obligations. The benefit of this right to deduct costs has accordingly been extended to the impecunious tenant who saves up rent to pay the contractor to carry out the works.

Limitations of the right to use rent for repairs

1 The right to recoup from rent (whether from future rent or arrears) is confined to the actual costs and expenses of remedial works and does not allow for the recovery of monies for damage suffered as a result of disrepair. Also, given the length of time necessary to accumulate sufficient withheld rent to pay a contractor, the right is of only limited use to the poorer tenant suffering severe disrepair.

2 There is no clear authority as to whether a landlord may exclude the right by an express term in the tenancy agreement.[6]

3 If a tenant can effectively use this procedure to obtain repairs in default, it may be open to a landlord to argue that a tenant who neglects this remedy is guilty of failure to mitigate loss arising from breach of the landlord's repairing obligation.[7]

4 Where the tenant is receiving housing benefit, it will be advisable to inform the paying authority that this procedure is being used in order to avert the possibility of payment being withheld (Housing Benefits Regs 1987[8] reg 95). Similarly, where a council tenant receives housing benefit, it will be necessary to secure payment in cash rather than by way of rent credit in order to operate this procedure (Housing Benefits Regs 1987 reg 88(1)).

From 1 January 1986, secure tenants of local authorities and most housing associations have had access to a statutory scheme for the use of rent to pay for repairs. The scheme, which is in almost all respects more limited than the common law right, is to be found in HA 1985 s96 and is detailed in the Secure Tenancies (Right to Repair Scheme) Regulations 1985 SI No 1493. Despite an extensive literature[9] on the potential application of s96, the statutory procedure is hardly ever used in practice.[10] Its scope is limited to repair work in the range of £20-£200, it requires the service of a multiplicity of forms and counter-notices, it involves the tenant discharging what are the landlord's responsibilities and provides no compensation for the fact of disrepair or the need for the tenant to use the remedy. It is in almost all respects a less satisfactory remedy for tenants than the use of legal proceedings.

(b) Withholding rent and rent strikes

The tenant has no right in law simply to withhold rent in protest at the landlord's failure to carry out repairs. Indeed, in addition to inviting possession proceedings against themselves, tenants organising rent strikes may well be guilty of unlawful interference with the contracts (ie tenancy agreements) of other tenants.[11]

Tenants are permitted to withhold service charges and service elements in rent, but only where the landlord is seeking to impose the expenses of remedial works on the tenant which by statute are the liability of the landlord, for example where the service charge includes an amount for LTA 1985 s11 repairs.[12]

In other circumstances advisers assisting those who have withheld rent should consider:

(a) applying the accrued arrears towards the payment of a contractor to carry out works in default (see above); and/or
(b) defending possession proceedings based on arrears of rent, on the ground that it would not be reasonable,[13] given the circumstances of the tenant's action, to order possession (such a defence is clearly not available if the landlord can establish the mandatory rent arrears ground – HA 1988 Sch 2 ground 8 – against an assured tenant); and/or
(c) a defence of set-off (see below) and counterclaim to the landlord's proceedings for arrears of rent.

The dangers of advising the tenant to withhold some or all payment to the landlord, on the basis that substantial balancing sums will be recoverable by a claim or counterclaim for damages are well illustrated by *Al Hassani v Merrigan*.[14] There the counterclaim for damages was dismissed and the judge found it reasonable in the circumstances to grant a possession order for arrears of rent.

(c) Set-off against rent

In many cases the tenant will seek to recover from current rent, or set against existing arrears of rent, a sum equal to the damages and expenses to which s/he would be entitled as a result of the landlord's default (for example the costs of redecoration or for replacement of damaged furniture etc). In practice, such considerations usually arise where the landlord has commenced a rent action and/or possession proceedings based on rent arrears, and the tenant has withheld the rent or spent it on new furnishings etc. Can the tenant raise a defence to the landlord's claim on the basis that the arrears of rent can be "set-off" against the damages resulting from the landlord's failure to repair?

There has been considerable doubt about this, particularly as it seeks effectively to match a debt (rent arrears) against damages which will usually not be liquidated (ie ascertained). The older cases raise difficulties of approach between the ancient jurisdictions of common law and equity, and between "cross-actions" and counterclaims.[15]

The authorities were reviewed in *British Anzani v International Marine*,[16] where it was held that an unliquidated claim in damages for breach of a contractual repairing obligation could be set-off against accrued arrears of rent. Where the value of the unliquidated damages matches the rent arrears in full, the tenant is entitled to an equitable set-off amounting to a complete defence to the landlord's action.[17] The equitable set-off has the advantage over the common law right to recoup from rent discussed above, in that it goes beyond costs of remedial works to include ordinary damages to which the tenant is entitled by reason of the landlord's default.

The set-off should formally be raised in the defence to the landlord's claim, and will usually be accompanied by a counterclaim setting out the breach complained of and particularising the damage suffered.[18]

It must be shown that the set-off arises under the tenancy and that it would be inequitable to allow the landlord to recover the amount claimed, in the face of the tenant's counterclaim; such conditions will usually be automatically satisfied in the case of damages resulting from the landlord's breach of a contractual repairing obligation.[19]

Levels of damages (see below) awarded in disrepair cases have, until recently, been notoriously low, but nowadays the tenant should be able to establish a set-off sufficient to amount to a complete defence to the landlord's claim in most disrepair cases. Experience indicates that even the most straightforward set-off raised in a defence will serve to delay the final hearing of proceedings for arrears or possession for considerable periods (particularly where the landlord is a local authority).

(d) Reduction in rent

A tenant paying a registered fair rent may apply to the rent officer for a reduction in the registered rent at any time if there has been a change "in the condition of the dwelling" since the last assessment.[20] However, this right should be exercised only in a clear-cut case of substantial deterioration in condition, since such application allows a complete reassessment of the rent, not confined to the simple question of deterioration.[21]

In respect of council and housing association tenancies it is worth consulting the tenancy agreement to identify any available "unusable rooms allowances" and rent reductions for lift or service failures. The express terms of secure tenancies are available for inspection from the appropriate local authority or housing association on request (Housing Act 1985 s104).

(e) Reduction in rates

Where disrepair is such as to affect the value of the property itself, a tenant would be well advised to seek a reduction in the rateable value and thus the rates payable for any period before the abolition of domestic rates on 1 April 1990.[22] Cases where disrepair has rendered the property unfit will be relatively straightforward and lead to substantial reductions (but see chapter 8 as to the effect on any home loss payment).[23] The procedure involves application to the local Inland Revenue valuation officer. Several useful guides to the steps to be taken are readily available.[24]

(f) Appointing a receiver or manager

Not infrequently, the reason for extensive disrepair will be persistent landlord neglect. In the private sector, situations commonly arise in which the present landlords are not known or cannot be traced and urgent repairs await attention. In such cases the common sense solution is to have one person officially appointed to collect all the rents and then pay for the repairs from the money received. In legal terms, this process is known as the appointment of a receiver, and the High Court has power to implement the procedure in any case where it appears just and convenient to do so (Supreme Court Act 1981 s37(1)). The power has been exercised to the benefit of a group of private tenants where no repairs had been carried out and no rent collected for two or three years (see *Hart v Emelkirk Ltd*[25]). In an appropriate case, the county court may appoint a receiver to like effect.[26] The remedy of appointment of a receiver is not available to tenants of local authorities.[27] As to the remuneration of the receiver, see *Evans v Clayhope Properties*.[28] In an appropriate case, a receiver may be appointed even if the landlord is known but s/he resists the application.[29] Once the appointment has been made, the ability of the landlord to frustrate the order by selling the property can be avoided by registering the appointment as a caution or land charge.[30]

For situations where there are two or more flats in a single block, the procedure for appointment of a manager is now codified in Landlord and Tenant Act 1987 Pt II. This requires, in the usual case, that a preliminary "warning notice" be served on the landlord or agent (s22). If this does not produce the required effect, the county court (s52) may, on application, appoint a manager to take over and run the block for the purpose of making good the disrepair (s24). The appointment can be registered against the title of the property or as a land charge to prevent the landlord avoiding the consequences of the order by selling-on (s24(8)). For a review of the procedure under Pt II see (1988) November *Legal Action* 17.

3 Court proceedings

(a) Preliminaries

Most disrepair claims will start as ordinary civil actions commenced by summons in the local county court, although much the same issues are frequently raised in counterclaims to a landlord's action for rent arrears and/or possession. Several precedents of Particulars of Claim have been published and can provide useful aids to drafting.[31] Careful attention should be paid to the particulars given of damage suffered, and to the forms of relief sought, and advisers should consider use of the Official Referee's Court (1990 November *Legal Action* 12).

Gathering of evidence should start as early as possible, and include photographs of the disrepair, copies of the letters containing notice of defects, the tenancy agreement, receipts for the purchase of replacement furniture, medical expenses, experts' reports etc.

Where appropriate an application should be made for civil legal aid, although the tenant should be warned that, where s/he is successful, the statutory charge could substantially reduce the amount of money s/he will receive. It should be noted that there is still no right of audience in the courts for representatives of tenants' associations, and no capacity for unincorporated tenants' associations to take proceedings to enforce the repairs rights of their members (*Hermitage Court Owners Assoc v Clyftville Properties*[32]).

Limitation periods

The tenant contemplating use of legal action as a remedy for disrepair should ensure that proceedings are issued before the expiry of any relevant limitation period. The basic period is three years in personal injury claims and six years in other cases, running from when the cause of action accrues (Limitation Act 1980). The key date therefore is that upon which the cause of action accrues, and this may vary:

(a) *Claims in contract:* the cause of action accrues at the date of breach of the obligation to repair. Where premises are in disrepair, breach usually occurs when the landlord has had notice of the disrepair and failed to remedy it within a reasonable period. If repairs are not carried out thereafter the cause of action is a continuing one but proceedings should be commenced within six years of the initial breach in order to ensure that the tenant is compensated for the whole period. If there has been a continuing breach of obligation for more than six years, the consideration of damages will be limited to the circumstances over the six years preceding the launch of proceedings.[33]

(b) *Claims in negligence:* where the claim arises from a personal injury, the limitation period runs from the date of injury even though the landlord's negligent act (eg letting the premises in dangerous condition) may have occurred many years earlier: *Rimmer v Liverpool City Council.*[34] Where the claim is for damage to property, the initial limitation period runs from the date of damage even though it may not have been discoverable at that date.[35] Modifications of this rule, introduced by the Latent Damage Act 1986, are discussed in chapter 3 (p41).

The same principles apply whether the duty of care which has been breached arises in common law or by statute (eg Defective Premises Act 1972 s4).

(c) *Claims arising from defective building etc:* actions based on a breach of the duty imposed by Defective Premises Act 1972 s1 are subject to the normal rules as to limitation.[36] The cause of action in most cases arises at the date of completion of the works (s1(3)).

Many disrepair claims will contain elements of both personal injury (eg ill health caused by dampness) as well as damage to property (damage to personal possessions etc). In order to ensure that both forms of injury attract recompense, advisers should pay close attention to limitation periods.

(b) Interim injunctions

In cases of really severe disrepair causing serious and continuing interference with the tenant's enjoyment of the property, an application for an interim or "interlocutory" injunction should be considered. Such an application may be made even though no injunction is sought in the particulars of claim.[37] The county court even has power to grant such an injunction in the absence of a claim for damages.[38] An application for an interlocutory injunction will ensure that the matter is brought before a judge in a matter of days rather than months. (See Appendix 7 for precedent.)

The onus will be upon the tenant to secure an early date from the court office, and to serve notice of the application on the landlord, although only one clear day's notice is necessary.[39]

In an appropriate case an application should be made notwithstanding the fact that the courts are reluctant to grant mandatory injunctions on interlocutory applications and that this form of relief has been described as "very exceptional"[40] and as one to be approached with "caution" and utilised only in a "clear case".[41]

In order to ensure a successful application, a tenant should:

(a) proceed on notice;
(b) file a detailed affidavit;
(c) have available the report of a surveyor or other expert; and
(d) prepare a detailed draft order containing a realistic schedule of works for basic repair and a time-scale.

If appropriate, an application should be made for emergency legal aid.

The tenant will be required to satisfy the normal rerequisites to the grant of interlocutory injunctive relief, namely:

(a) that there is a serious question to be tried (ie a more than frivolous assertion that the landlord is in breach of a repairing obligation); and
(b) that damages alone would not be adequate compensation (for example because of a serious risk to health) or that the landlord would not be in a financial position to meet the damages to which the tenant would be entitled; and
(c) that the tenant will be in a position to meet the costs incurred by the landlord in performing works required by the injunction, if it is later found that the order should not have been made; and
(d) that, if there is doubt as to these last two factors, the balance of convenience (ie comparative hardship) favours the tenant.[42]

In a clear example of breach of an explicit repairing obligation, the courts are likely to grant an injunction where the case is plain and uncontroversial notwithstanding the applicant's inability to fulfill all the normal pre-conditions.[43]

However, in addition to the hurdles prescribed for interlocutory relief, the tenant will have to go on to justify the making of a *mandatory* order ie an order that the landlord actually carry out works. The tenant must show:

(a) the imminent danger of further serious harm to person or property;[44] and
(b) unless the landlord has acted unreasonably or with wanton disregard to the law, that the cost of remedial works is outweighed by the harm the tenant will suffer; and
(c) the order sought is sufficiently precise in terms as to tell the landlord exactly what remedial works have to be undertaken and by what date.[45]

In a straightforward case of severe disrepair the tenant should easily satisfy these criteria, onerous as they are. In *Allport v Securities Corp*[46] a mandatory interlocutory injunction was granted where a landlord had begun to dismantle a staircase in breach of the tenant's rights. The order required the landlord to reinstate the stairway. Similarly, in *Peninsular Maritime v Padseal*[47] an interlocutory mandatory injunction was issued to secure the proper working of a lift. The availability of such orders is not confined to "restorative work" alone. The Court of Appeal held clearly in *Astro Exito Navegacion SA v Southland Enterprise Co Ltd and Others*,[48] that an interim mandatory injunction for the performance of a contractual obligation may be granted, even though it amounts to forcing the defendant to comply positively with contractual obligations. This has now been applied in the disrepair context to enable tenants to achieve interim orders for specific performance of repairing obligations.[49] Although still rare, mandatory interlocutory injunctions are thus becoming more readily available.[50]

The Court of Appeal has now sanctioned the use of interlocutory interim injunctions in appropriate cases of breach of landlord covenants. An appropriate case would be ". . . an undoubted breach of covenant giving rise to actual and immediate major discomfort and inconvenience and to a real risk of damage to health flowing from the admitted breach."[51]

If the application fails, the evidence put before the court suggesting risk to health or safety should at least found a direction for an early trial.[52]

Limitations of interlocutory injunctions

Despite the attractions of this method of securing immediate remedial works, it should be remembered that the injunction is granted purely to avoid the risk of further danger or damage, and that for these purposes the landlord may successfully convince the court that basic "patch" repairs will suffice.

Further, the grant of an injunction, being an equitable remedy, may well be refused to applicants who are themselves in breach of contract (for example tenants in arrears of rent).[53]

(c) Landlord's undertakings

The commencement of legal proceedings may prompt a landlord to seek to negotiate a settlement of the matter by performance of some works (notice of application for an interim injunction is particularly salutary in this regard[54]). Such negotiations should be approached with care, since landlords rarely make concessions equivalent to the full extent of tenants' rights.

However, a landlord may be willing to offer both compensation and undertakings to perform remedial works which are realistic and will ensure repair earlier than a court hearing.

A tenant willing to accept the compromise offered by the landlord should ensure that the form of agreed court order (for example, that the matter be adjourned) incorporates the landlord's assurances as "undertakings to the court". Breach of an undertaking given to the court may be enforced by committal, and additionally, the tenant is entitled to seek a direction that the works be done and that the landlord pays the contractors' costs.[55] In one disrepair case, a county court judge fined a local authority landlord £10,000 for breach of an undertaking (reduced to £1,000 by the Court of Appeal).[56]

(d) Specific performance

If the matter proceeds to trial, a tenant should first seek an order that the landlord comply with the contractual repairing obligation. The order will be for "specific performance" of the express or implied terms of the tenancy agreement. For non-contractual repairing obligations the equivalent remedy will be a mandatory injunction. The duty imposed by Defective Premises Act 1972 s4 (see p42) can also be enforced by injunction.[57]

Specific performance is a remedy available at common law[58] and by statute. The LTA 1985 s17 (see Appendix 4 for text) provides:

> "(1) In proceedings in which a tenant of a dwelling alleges a breach on the part of his landlord of a repairing covenant relating to any part of the premises in which the dwelling is comprised, the court may order specific performance of the covenant, whether or not the breach relates to a part of the premises let to the tenant and notwithstanding any equitable rule restricting the scope of the remedy, whether on the basis of a lack of mutuality or otherwise."

Several points arise:

(a) for the purposes of s17, "tenant" includes sub-tenants and statutory tenants (s17(2));

(b) specific performance of obligations to maintain common parts can be ordered on the application of a single tenant;

(c) the old equitable rules that "the applicant must have clean hands" (ie not also be in breach of obligations, such as for payment of rent) and that "an order must be capable of supervision by the court" may be abrogated by the proviso to s17 but the grant of specific performance remains entirely at the discretion of the court.

It will be no defence for the landlord on an application for specific performance to raise the prospect of severe financial hardship as a result of the terms of the order. Indeed in *Francis v Cowliffe Ltd*[59] an order for the provision and maintenance of lifts was made notwithstanding the very real prospect of bankruptcy of the landlord as a result of compliance.

(e) Remedies for breach of orders

Failure to perform works directed in an order of specific performance or by injunction is punishable by committal for contempt. To deal with circumstances in which the landlord is a local authority or company, the initial injunction should be addressed personally to an officer who can be committed for breach.[60] Although proceedings to commit the landlord for contempt of court may provide an incentive for the landlord to do the repairs ordered, neither a fine nor the imprisonment of the landlord actually helps the tenant get the work done. As an alternative to the use of committal, RSC Ord 45 r8 allows a court faced with breach of a mandatory order to direct that the necessary action be taken by or on behalf of the plaintiff at the expense of the landlord defendant. The court may select and direct the individual or company which is to carry out the action required. The availability of Ord 45 r8 (which is also applicable in the county court: County Courts Act 1984 s76) for repairs cases was confirmed in *Parker v LB Camden*.[61] For a discussion of the procedure and subsequent cases in which it has been applied, see (1989) November *Legal Action* 19.

The court may enforce the financial element of the Ord 45 r8 procedure, either by directing a payment into court (as in *Barrett v Lounava (1982) Ltd*[62]) or by an order of sequestration on the landlord's assets (as in *Rose v Laskington Ltd*[63]).

If there is reasonable cause to believe that the landlord will sell a property to avoid the effect of judgment in a repairs case, or will dispose of assets to avoid an award of damages, advisers should apply for a Mareva injunction, whether proceedings are in the county court or High Court. (For a draft order and the procedure, see (1989) October *Legal Action* 16.) This is necessary because a pending action for breach of a repairing covenant is not registerable as a pending land action.[64]

(f) Declarations

The county court has power to grant a declaration relating to rights over real property, even if it is the only relief sought.[65] Where a mandatory order is unlikely to be effective (either because it cannot be served or will not be complied with) and the tenant would prefer to carry out the works and recoup the costs from future rent, or simply where an injunction is refused, the grant of a declaration may be a useful alternative remedy. In a disrepair case the court should be invited to make a declaration providing:

(a) that the landlord is in breach of a specified repairing obligation; and
(b) that the tenant is entitled to do the necessary works of repair in default; and
(c) that the works may be financed by deduction from future rent; and
(d) that the tenant's compliance with stages (b) and (c) will not constitute breach by the tenant of any express terms of the tenancy agreement which prima facie prohibit such action.[66]

Armed with such a declaration the tenant may in fact secure the performance of the works earlier than the date on which they would have been carried out by the landlord under a mandatory order.

(g) Damages

Where a tenant has succeeded in establishing breach of the landlord's repairing obligation or has shown that the landlord's negligence (or breach of statutory duty) has caused personal injury or damage to property, the appropriate remedy in most cases will be an award of substantial damages ie financial recompense. If the case has not yet come to trial but the claim for damages is clear, application may usefully be made for an award of interim damages under RSC Ord 29.[67]

The purpose of damages

The fundamental principle in the award of damages in disrepair cases is that the amount allowed should as far as possible place the tenant in the position s/he would have occupied if s/he "had not suffered the wrong complained of, be that wrong a tort or breach of contract".[68]

It should be noted that the purpose of awarding damages will go no further than that. The object is not "to punish the landlords but, so far as money can, to restore the tenant to the position he would have been in had there been no breach."[69]

The approach to assessment

Bearing in mind the principle to be applied, the courts have offered only broad guidance on the assessment of damages, although the usual rule—that both general and special damages will be available—is applied in disrepair cases.[70] An assessment cannot be achieved by applying one set of rules to all cases regardless of the circumstances of the particular case. The facts of each case must be looked at to see what damage the tenant has suffered and how they may be fairly compensated by a monetary award.[71] "So, the true measure of damages for persons . . . occupying land, whether in tort or contract, depends on the position of the plaintiffs and all the circumstances in which they have suffered loss and damage".[72]

General damages

In disrepair cases the award of general damages is assessed as the loss of value of the tenancy to the tenant.[73] The calculation of this "loss of value" will vary according to the circumstances of the case as follows:

(a) If the tenant remains in residence during a period of disrepair, the general damages will be a substantial award for all the inconvenience, disappointment, discomfort, ill health and mental distress[74] as well as loss of enjoyment suffered by the tenant and his or her family.[75] The period attracting compensation runs from the date of landlord's knowledge of the disrepair up to the date of assessment or the carrying out of the repairs.

As the court must also make an award for loss of value to the tenant of the tenancy and as this is a rather difficult sense of "loss of value" to measure in the abstract there has been a tendency in the past to use as a guideline a method of "discounting" from the rental value.[76] By this method, the court looks at the rent due under the letting and then awards as damages a "discount" representing the extent of loss of use and enjoyment suffered by the tenant. For example, if the rent were £30 per week and the disrepair affected one third of the property, a weekly figure of £10 might provide a starting point. This rather artificial approach tends to underestimate compensation, particularly where the rent is relatively low in comparison to the hardship suffered.[77] However, nowadays the courts are concerned to ensure that tenants affected by disrepair are awarded "substantial sums" as opposed to "nominal or cosmetic amounts".[78]

A global approach to the assessment of general damages under this head, however, can be properly adopted and will produce more generous awards for tenants. For example, the Court of Appeal did not interfere with the approach of a county court judge who first applied the "discounting" method to assess the degree of loss of value to the tenant of the tenancy itself and then went on to add to it a substantial award for inconvenience, discomfort and injury to health.[79] The fact that the rent had been registered as a fair rent and therefore in a sense had been fixed with regard to the state of repair did not affect the assessment.[80] As a guide to the current "going rate" for the assessment of general damages for disrepair, see Appendix 6.

It appears that the court is not obliged to "take account of the rent as a prima facie indication of the level of any proper award" and may instead just make a single global assessment of the general damages for inconvenience and distress.[81] Thus the Court of Appeal would not interfere with the assessment of damages under that head at £30 per week where the contractual rent for the entire premises was only £8 per week.[82]

(b) If the tenant is required to move out (either temporarily while works are undertaken or, if conditions are sufficiently serious, before remedial work starts) any specific costs of removal or alternative accommodation can be recovered as special damages. However, a separate element of general damages will be awarded for the inconvenience of having to move and live for a time in temporary accommodation. Such award will be increased if undertakings as to the length of the stay in temporary housing are broken by the landlord.[83]

(c) If the tenant has rented the property for the purpose of sub-letting it (or is going away temporarily and wishes to sub-let) and as a result of disrepair is unable to sub-let it or can only sub-let for a reduced rent, the damages awarded will be measured by the loss of rental income from the sub-letting.[84]

(d) If a long lessee is driven out of occupation by the disrepair and forced to sell the lease (or bought the lease intending to offer it for re-sale), then the damages awarded can be measured as the difference between the selling price and the price s/he would have obtained if the landlord had carried out the repairs.[85] Indeed, if it can be established that the landlord deliberately prepared the leasehold premises for sale in such a way as to disguise a serious repairing problem, the lessee may recover damages in deceit as well as for breach of contractual obligation.[86]

It will be obvious that certain of these heads represent compensation for quite specific loss. Accordingly, the courts will expect the tenant to give notice in the pleadings as to the loss suffered; it will not be sufficient just to claim "damages".[87] The claim may also embrace the effects of the disrepair on other members of the tenant's family.[88]

Special damages

The tenant is entitled to recover damages representing the loss in value of items of furniture and other personal belongings destroyed or damaged as a result of the landlord's failure to repair. The most common examples are carpets, furniture, curtains and clothing corrupted by dampness. Additionally, special damages may be sought for other specific loss capable of calculation in monetary terms, for example:

— cleaning costs
— loss of earnings
— extra heating costs (eg for "drying-out" dampness)
— costs of alternative accommodation (see below)
— expenses of repairs, cleaning up and redecoration (see below)
— travelling and medical costs (eg arising from personal injury)
— cost of eating out (eg if food storage or cooking facilities have been damaged).

If the tenant actually has to carry out works of repair, clearing-up or redecoration, damages will be awarded to compensate for any such expenses reasonably incurred.[89] Even if the works actually improve the property no reduction is made from the damages on account of this element of betterment, if the tenant was unable to make good the damage without betterment.[90] These specific costs may be pleaded as special damages. If VAT is payable on the repair work, the VAT may also be recoverable by the tenant.[91]

If the disrepair renders the premises uninhabitable, the tenant may recover as damages any expenses reasonably incurred in taking alternative accommodation from the date that the premises could no longer be occupied up to the date of assessment or repair.[92] Such damages will include the costs of any removals, storage of furniture etc. Such costs should be specifically pleaded as special damages. (As to general circumstances surrounding the displacement of tenants see chapter 8.)

Each specific item for which special damages are claimed must be identified in the pleadings and at trial it will be necessary to prove the loss in respect of each item. It is therefore vital that the tenant collects and retains where possible all receipts, accounts and invoices relating to items replaced or repaired. Where there is likely to be a dispute over the damages claimed the tenant would be well advised to retain (or at least photograph) any damaged item pending the trial.

Tenants' duty to mitigate loss
In an action for damages for breach of a contractual repairing obligation, it is important for tenants to show that they took whatever reasonable steps were available to mitigate or prevent loss or damage — for example, that a bucket was placed under a leak, rather than simply allowing dampness to rot the floorboards and carpets. Thus, if a tenant delayed giving notice of disrepair to the landlord so that the eventual damage was greater than it would otherwise have been, that tenant may see a reduction in damages on account of the failure to mitigate the loss.[93]

However, in cases where landlords have patently neglected to repair property, the duty to mitigate does not impose an obligation on tenants to do the work themselves.[94] Nor are tenants to be penalised for any refusal (other than a capricious one) to move to alternative accommodation.[95] But tenants are expected to take reasonable measures, such as blocking up the source of draughts or temporarily covering broken window glazing.[96]

Interest
As it is not unknown for disrepair cases to take months or years before the stage is reached for assessment of damages, advisers should ensure than any award for a retrospective period carries with it interest assessed under County Courts Act 1984 s69.

4 Using the ombudsman

Council tenants aggrieved by their landlords' failure to carry out repairs, and private tenants concerned at the failure of local authorities to intervene to improve their housing conditions, may seek redress against the council concerned from the Local Commissioners for Administration or "ombudsmen". Ombudsmen have the power to investigate complaints of maladministration, delay or injustice made against local authorities by tenants and their associations.[97] If there is a genuine dispute over the cause of disrepair or the appropriate remedy, the ombudsman may even appoint an independent surveyor to help in the investigation of a complaint (Investigation 315/L/85). Past investigations of repairs complaints have led to recommendations for compensation and public apologies equivalent to those which might have been obtained by seeking redress in the courts.[98]

Even though the full investigation of a complaint can take over a year, the formal process of instituting a complaint is often sufficient to propel a recalcitrant local authority into action. The local ombudsmen have made it clear that they do not expect council tenants to take court action in order to get repairs done. Accordingly, they are prepared to investigate complaints even in cases where the tenant could clearly sue in damages.[99] Indeed, the ombudsmen are ensuring that their recommendations for compensation awards reflect the amounts that are being awarded in comparable civil litigation.[100]

CAUTIONARY NOTE

Despite the possible superficial attractions of these civil remedies for disrepair, such proceedings can be a slow, costly, and ineffective means of securing repairs and financial recompense except in the most straightforward cases.[101] Advisers should consider whether other remedies (used instead of or as well as civil proceedings) such as tenants' collective action, involvement of a local authority councillor (in the case of a council tenancy) or use of Environmental Protection Act and other HA powers, might achieve a speedier or otherwise more effective result for the individual tenant.

1 Perri 6, A Jessup and S Burrage "Landlord and Tenant Act 1987" (1988) *Legal Action* 14.

2 County Courts Act 1984 s18 applied in *Kinch v LB Lambeth* (1988) June *Legal Action* 20.

3 *Taylor v Beal* (1591) Cro Eliz (1) 222; *Waters v Weigall* (1795) 2 Anstr 757; *Weigall v Waters* (1796) 6 Term Rep 488.

4 [1971] 1 WLR 1688. For a step-by-step guide to the procedure, including draft letters, see *The new small repairs kit* (Brixton Law Centre), *Dear Landlord...* (Manchester Law Centre), *How to get your repairs done* (Tottenham Law Centre), *Housing repairs and how to get them done* (Tower Hamlets Law Centre) or *Housing repairs: tenants' rights and landlords' responsibilities* (Manchester Law Centre). For the procedure in Scotland see *The right to withhold rent* (Shelter (Scotland) Housing Action Notes No 1, 1983).

5 (1978) 248 EG 683.

6 See Yates and Hawkins *Landlord and tenant law* (Sweet & Maxwell, 2nd edn, 1986) pp254-255.

7 See Sedley (1973) August *LAG Bulletin* 173 and Rank (1976) 40 Conv 196. Advisers should strongly resist any such argument – and rely on *Porter v Jones* [1942] 2 All ER 570 and *Perry v Phillips (Sidney) & Son* [1982] 3 All ER 705, CA.

8 SI No 1971.

9 Young "Complexities of the right to repair" (1985) *Local Government Chronicle* 96. Maughan-Pawsey "Landlord's disrepair: a new statutory remedy?" (1986) NLJ 829. "The right to repair scheme: a new charter for secure tenants" (1986) SJ 380. Rank "Landlords' repairs: self-help for tenants" (1986) LS Gaz 1376.

10 Only 75 applications were approved between 1986 and 1989: HC Written Answers col 535, 31 October 1990.

11 *Camden Nominees v Forcey* [1940] Ch 352.

12 See *Campden Hill Towers v Gardner* [1977] 1 All ER 739 where recovery of part of the service charges was prohibited by [Landlord and Tenant Act 1985 ss11-16].

13 Rent Act (RA) 1977 s98(1) and HA 1985 s84(2)(a). See *Cophil v Blair* (1978) January *LAG Bulletin* 14 and *Lal v Nakum* (1982) 1 HLR 50, CA.

14 (1988) 20 HLR 238, CA.

15 See Sedley "Setting-off damages against rent" (1974) July *LAG Bulletin* 161.

16 [1979] 2 All ER 1063. See further Waite "*British Anzani* and set-off against rent: a new departure?" (1982) NLJ 815; "Disrepair and set-off against rent" (1983) Conv 373 and "Set-off and distress for rent" (1984) June *Legal Action* 66.

17 See *Melville v Grapelodge Developments* (1978) 39 P&CR 179.

18 See White "When to withhold payment – 2" (1981) August *LAG Bulletin* 182 (including precedent).

19 See Arden "Set-off against rent" (1979) September *LAG Bulletin* 210.
20 RA 1977 s67(3)(a).
21 *London Housing and Commercial Properties v Cowan* [1977] QB 148, DC.
22 *Saunders v Maltby* (1976) 19 Rydes Rating Cases 33; (1976) 239 EG 205.
23 *Black v Oliver* [1978] 1 QB 870; *Udechuko v Lambeth LB* (1982) Rating Appeals 291; (1982) 262 EG 1309; [1983] JPL 124 and *Kind v Cox (Valuation Officer)* LVC/265/1984 noted at (1986) LS Gaz 2914.
24 N Martyn "Bringing down the rates" Jan/Feb 1984 *Roof* 15 or "Rates: how to pay less" 1984 *Which?* 103 or "Getting a rate reduction" 54 *Community Action* 30 or D Forbes "Revaluation" (1987) January *Legal Action* 22. See also chapter 8 n76 below.
25 [1983] 3 All ER 15; *Daiches v Bluelake Investments Ltd* (1985) 17 HLR 543 and *Clayhope Properties v Evans* (1986) 18 HLR 361, CA.
26 *Yorston v Crewfield Ltd and Ors* (1985) 11 July, unreported, Clerkenwell County Court; and see generally Madge "Appointing receivers to repair and manage flats" (1985) NLJ 1215.
27 *Parker v LB Camden* [1985] 2 All ER 141.
28 *Evans v Clayhope Properties* (1988) 20 HLR 176, CA.
29 *Blawdziewicz v Diodon Establishment* (1988) 35 EG 83.
30 *Clayhope Properties v Evans* n25.
31 For an example see Appendix 7 below, (1976) January *LAG Bulletin* 16 and 1977 *Roof* 159. A typical pleading is also reproduced in *The emergency procedures handbook* (LAG, 2nd edn, 1989) p240.
32 (1979) 18 May, unreported, CA, CAT 79/304.
33 As in *Sturolson & Co v Mauroux* (1988) 20 HLR 332, CA at 334.
34 [1984] 1 All ER 93.
35 *Pirelli General Cable Works v Faber (Oscar) & Partners* [1983] 1 All ER 65; *Ketteman v Hansel Properties* [1984] 1 WLR 1274.
36 See Baxter "Latent damage in defective construction work" (1983) NLJ 414 and 437.
37 CCR Ord 13 r8. A useful draft application and supporting papers are contained in *The emergency procedures handbook* n31 pp243-247.
38 County Courts Act 1959 s51(A) as substituted.
39 CCR Ord 13 r1.
40 *Canadian Pacific Rly v Gaud* [1949] 2 KB 239 at 249.
41 *Locabail International Finance Ltd v Agroexport* [1986] 1 All ER 901.
42 These principles are extracted from the judgment of Lord Diplock in *American Cyanamid v Ethicon* [1975] AC 396, HL.
43 See *Office Overload v Gunn* [1977] Fleet Street Reports 39, CA.
44 As defined in *Hooper v Rogers* [1974] 3 All ER 417.
45 These principles are extracted from the judgment of Lord Upjohn in *Redland Bricks Ltd v Morris* [1970] AC 652, HL.
46 (1895) 64 LJ Ch 491; (1895) 39 SJ 362.
47 (1981) 259 EG 860, CA.
48 [1982] QB 1248 following *Smith v Peters* (1875) 20 LR Eq 511.
49 *Clarridge and Meerschwam v Swallow Securities* (1986) January *Legal Action* 14, QBD.
50 *Worldwide Dryers Ltd v Warner Howard Ltd* (1982) *Times* 9 December and for a review of current practice see D Watkinson "Interlocutory injunctions in repairs cases" (1986) January *Legal Action* 13.
51 *Parker v LB Camden* n27 at 149.
52 As in *Whittington v Liverpool CC* (1985) 18 February, unreported, Liverpool County Court.
53 See *Consolidated Agricultural Suppliers v Rushmere* (1976) SJ 523.
54 See, eg, *Kotecha v Manchester CC* noted at (1983) March *LAG Bulletin* 35.
55 *Mortimer v Wilson* (1883) 33 WR 927; and see *Gandolfo v Gandolfo (Standard Chartered Bank, Garnishee)* [1980] 1 All ER 833, CA.

56 *Connell v Hackney LBC* (1985) unreported, CA, CAT 85/316.
57 *Barrett v Lounova (1982) Ltd* (1988) 20 HLR 584, CA.
58 *Jeune v Queens Cross Properties* [1974] Ch 97.
59 (1976) 239 EG 977; (1976) 33 P&CR 368.
60 *Rainbow v Lambeth LBC* (1986) January *Legal Action* 14.
61 [1986] Ch 162, CA.
62 N57; see (1989) November *Legal Action* 20.
63 (1989) 139 NLJ 973, DC.
64 *Regan & Blackburn Ltd v Rogers* [1985] 2 All ER 180.
65 CCR Ord 13 r1.
66 *Ideal Film Renting Co v Nielsen* [1921] 1 Ch 575.
67 *Castle v Northampton CC* (1989) September *Legal Action* 24.
68 Per Donaldson LJ in *Dodd Properties (Kent) Ltd v Canterbury CC* [1980] 1 All ER 928, CA at 938.
69 *Calabar Properties Ltd v Stitcher* [1983] 3 All ER 759, CA at 768.
70 See generally HW Wilkinson "Breach of landlords' covenant to repair" (1984) NLJ 379; Madge and Watkinson "Damages for disrepair" (1984) May *Legal Action* 51; D Williams "Tenants' remedies for disrepair" (1984) LS Gaz 1269; Luba "Disrepair: important new cases" (1984) NLJ 357; and Madge "Damages for breach of repairing obligations" (1988) LS Gaz 20 July p17 and "Further cases on breaches of repairing obligations" (1989) LS Gaz 31 May p15.
71 *Calabar v Stitcher* n69.
72 Ibid at 767.
73 *Hewitt v Rowlands* (1924) 93 LJKB 729, 1080.
74 *Jarvis v Swans Tours* [1973] 1 All ER 71, CA.
75 *Calabar v Stitcher* n69 at 766.
76 As in *McCoy v Clarke* (1982) 13 HLR 89.
77 See, eg, *Seal v LB Greenwich* (1981) October *LAG Bulletin* 237; *Daejan Properties Ltd v Elliott* (1977) September *LAG Bulletin* 208; *Horrex v Pidwell* [1958] CLY 1461; *Ahmed v GLC, Mitchell v LB Brent* and *May v Pooles Park Neighbourhood Co-op* all noted at (1984) May *Legal Action* 53-54 and *De Rosario v Dewing* (1982) August *LAG Bulletin* 91.
78 *Davies v Peterson* (1988) 21 HLR 63, CA applying *Saunders v Edwards* [1987] 1 WLR 1116.
79 *Sturolson & Co v Mauroux* n33.
80 Ibid.
81 *PRs of Chiodi v De Marney* (1988) 21 HLR 6, CA.
82 Ibid.
83 *Lubren v LB Lambeth* (1988) 20 HLR 165, CA.
84 *Calabar v Stitcher* n69 at 770; and see *Mira v Aylmer Square Investments Ltd* (1989) 21 HLR 284, QBD.
85 *Calabar v Stitcher* n69; and see *City and Metropolitan Properties v Greycroft* [1987] 3 All ER 839 at 842-843.
86 *Gordon v Selico Co* (1986) 18 HLR 219, CA.
87 *Perestrello e Companhia Limitada v United Paint Co* [1969] 3 All ER 479, CA at 485.
88 *Jackson v Horizon Holidays Ltd* [1975] 3 All ER 92, CA.
89 *Calabar v Stitcher* n69; and *Little v Glasgow DC* 1988 SCLR 482.
90 *McGreal v Wake* (1984) 13 HLR 107 at 112-113.
91 *Elite Investments Ltd v TI Bainbridge Silencers Ltd (No 2)* (1987) 283 EG 747 discussed at (1987) NLJ 869.
92 *Calabar v Stitcher* n69.
93 *Minchburn v Peck* (1987) 20 HLR 392, CA.
94 *Sturolson v Mauroux* n33.
95 *Lubren v LB Lambeth* n83.

96 *Kearns v Liverpool CC* (1985) 22 February, unreported, Liverpool County Court.
97 See "How to use your local ombudsman" 1980 *Roof* 154.
98 See, eg, Investigation No 2/Y/83; F Pedley "Ombudsman reports" 1984 *Municipal Journal* 990; and the investigation on the subject of condensation dampness noted at (1985) September *Legal Action* 123. Summaries of relevant investigations are published regularly in *Inside Housing*.
99 J Bash "Can the local ombudsman help?" (1990) January *Legal Action* 16.
100 Luba "Compensation for disrepair" (1988) September *Legal Action* 15.
101 For a comparison between the merits of civil and criminal proceedings see Fassnidge and Robson "Housing repairs in context" (1977) July *LAG Bulletin* 156.

Chapter Five

Using the Public Health and Environmental Protection Acts

1 Introduction

Since the mid-19th century, Parliament has sought to protect the general public from the worst effects of slum housing (ie disease, overcrowding and dangerous buildings) through public health legislation. These laws were largely consolidated into the Public Health Act 1936 (PHA 1936), have been amended subsequently and are now recast in the Environmental Protection Act 1990 (EPA) Pt III.[1] See Appendix 3 below for the text of EPA ss79–82. These provisions replace those found in PHA 1936 ss91–100 and came into force on 1 January 1991: EPA s164(2).

Much of this legislation can be used by tenants and others to force landlords of bad housing to effect necessary repairs, and improve the condition of property they own. The Acts are concerned with attacking the *effects* of bad housing, that is, the poor conditions in which occupiers and others are placed as a result of deterioration in the structure of dwellings and other housing defects.

The key to the use of public health legislation by tenants against bad housing is the concept of the "statutory nuisance."

2 Statutory nuisance

(a) Generally

Statutory nuisances are defined as arising in the specific circumstances set out in the EPA and related legislation. The following, contained in the EPA and PHA 1936, are the most immediately relevant to housing conditions. Statutory references are to the EPA unless otherwise stated.

- "any premises in such a state as to be prejudicial to health or a nuisance" (s79(1)(a));

- "any accumulation or deposit which is prejudicial to health or a nuisance" (s79(1)(e));
- "any tent, van, shed or similar structure used for human habitation
  - (i) which is in such a state or so overcrowded as to be prejudicial to health; or
  - (ii) the use of which, by reason of the absence of proper sanitary accommodation or otherwise, gives rise, whether on the site or on other land, to a nuisance or to conditions prejudicial to health" (PHA 1936 s268 as amended by EPA Sch 15 para 4);
- "any well, tank, cistern or water-butt used for the supply of water for domestic purposes which is so placed, constructed or kept as to render the water therein liable to contamination prejudicial to health" (PHA 1936 s141 as amended by EPA Sch 15 para 4);
- "any pond, pool, ditch, gutter or watercourse which is so foul or in such a state as to be prejudicial to health or a nuisance" (PHA 1936 s259 as amended by EPA Sch 15 para 4).

Each "species" of statutory nuisance contains two distinct limbs, which are to be read disjunctively and treated quite separately ie "prejudicial to health" *or* a "nuisance".

Several of the listed statutory nuisances deal with matters likely to be common in dwellings out of repair (blocked gutters, polluted water tanks, defective cisterns etc) but that of most relevance to general disrepair is contained in s79(1)(a). Each element of s79(1)(a) requires close attention.

(b) "Any premises in such a state as to be prejudicial to health or a nuisance"

"Any premises"

Premises are defined by the EPA to include all land.[2] Thus both private and public sector housing are covered. The courts have held that the Act directs attention to the condition of the premises, rather than to the way in which they are used.[3] Indeed, the premises need not even be occupied.[4]

In the case of a block of flats, the "premises" for the purposes of s79 may be an individual flat or flats. It is possible to allege a statutory nuisance in relation to an entire block only if either the tenants are complaining of the condition of the common parts or there is a problem "not confined to any one constituent unit in the block and which can only be related to the entire block".[5]

An open site without any permanent buildings (eg a travellers' site) may also be "premises" for the purpose of s79. Thus the EPA powers may be used to eliminate statutory nuisances on caravan sites and other areas of land used for residential purposes.[6]

"... in such a state ..."

A statutory nuisance arises if the state of the premises as a *whole* is such as to be prejudicial to health or a nuisance. This may arise either from a single major item of disrepair (for example a collapsing ceiling) or from the accumulation of a number of minor items. It should be noted that it is the *effect* of the defects which gives rise to the nuisance rather than the simple fact of disrepair. An ill-fitting window frame may contribute to premises being a statutory nuisance, not because it constitutes an item in need of repair, but rather because it allows wind and rain penetration causing damp and draughts which may render premises prejudicial to health or a nuisance.

It has been said that s79(1)(a) is directed to the type of case in which,

> ". . . the premises themselves are decayed, dilapidated, dirty or out of order, as for instance . . . where foul matter has been allowed to soak into walls or floors, or where they are so dilapidated as to be a source of danger to life and limb".[7]

However, premises may be "in such a state" as to amount to a statutory nuisance even if the origins of the nuisance are outside the premises – eg, where, because of poor insulation, the noise of local traffic and trains permeates the premises,[8] or where dampness enters from outside.[9]

"... prejudicial to health ..."

A statutory nuisance will arise where a dwelling is in such a state, through disrepair or otherwise, as to be "prejudicial to health" – defined by the EPA s79(7) to mean "injurious or likely to cause injury, to health". Thus, both actual and potential ill-health are covered.

The courts have held that the requirement of prejudice to health will be satisfied simply where it can be shown that the state of the premises is such as would cause a well person to become ill or the health of a sick person to deteriorate further.[10] Accordingly, a statutory nuisance exists where *any* premises are so defective as to cause potential or actual detriment to the health of the tenant or other occupiers, even if they are particularly prone to illness (for example the very young or very old).

"Health", although not defined by the Act, should be interpreted broadly to include physical and mental health, particularly to incorporate the medically recognised stress associated with living in bad housing.[11] Mere interference with comfort will not bring a case within the "health" limb[12] nor will defects which are merely decorative (such as stained wallpaper[13]) or simply constitute an "eyesore".[14] The tenant's general practitioner or hospital consultant should be able to identify premises which are prejudicial to health and most environmental health officers (EHOs) are trained to recognise them.[15]

Examples of premises which are "prejudicial to health" include those suffering from dampness, condensation or mould growth (see below chapter 7), falling plaster, broken glass, defective gas and electric fitments,[16] dangerous staircases etc.

"... or a nuisance ..."

The EPA does not define "nuisance". Initially, it was given the common sense interpretation of "anything which caused interference with the personal comfort of the occupier of premises".[17] A definition of this breadth extended the concept of statutory nuisance to all but the most trifling cases of disrepair, and greatly expanded the usefulness of the provision.

However, in 1975 the House of Lords threw doubt on that approach[18] and subsequently in *National Coal Board v Neath BC*,[19] the Divisional Court held that to fall within s79(1)(a), the "nuisance" must be either:

(a) a public nuisance at common law; or
(b) a private nuisance at common law.

At common law a *public* nuisance arises where an act or omission affects adversely the comfort or quality of life of the public generally, or a class of citizens.

At common law a *private* nuisance is a substantial interference by the owner or occupier of property with the use and enjoyment of neighbouring property.

Given this restrictive interpretation of "nuisance" in s79, it follows that a statutory nuisance based on this limb ". . . cannot arise if what has taken place affects only the person or persons occupying the premises."[20] Thus, if the conditions in the premises are a nuisance only to the tenant or other occupier, a "statutory nuisance" will not arise unless the prejudice to health "limb" can be satisfied as an alternative.

Moreover, only certain types of nuisance may be within the section. To constitute a nuisance at common law, it will generally be enough "that the matter complained of renders the enjoyment of property and life uncomfortable"[21] for the occupiers of adjoining property. Consequently, the nuisance can arise in circumstances short of prejudice to health, so that offensive smells, noise and dirt may be within the definition. However, the courts have required, in addition, that the nuisance be of such a nature as to relate to matters of public health, although this limitation has not been confirmed expressly in modern times.[22]

It will be apparent that the *National Coal Board* decision (above) represented a considerable setback for tenants. It has restricted the use of the nuisance limb to those tenants affected by the disrepair of neighbouring or adjacent property and those who occupy premises in such a state as to cause a nuisance to passers-by. Thus, the position at present is that tenants may take action under the "*nuisance*" limb if personal comfort is interfered with as a result of disrepair where that disrepair is in an adjacent property; action may be taken under the "*health*" limb in respect of disrepair inside the premises, as well as on neighbouring property but this does not include disrepair causing mere interference with personal comfort.

Attempts were made during the passage of the Local Government (Miscellaneous Provisions) Act 1976 to reverse this judicial narrowing of the definition of nuisance, but the relevant amendments were withdrawn as the Government gave assurances to review the position. The subsequent Department of Environment consultation document[23] recommended that a suitable amendment to "plug the gap" should be incorporated into future legislation. This was achieved to a modest degree by the HA 1985 s190(1)(b) which gave local authorities a discretionary power to tackle disrepair causing discomfort to tenants (see chapter 6 p105). However, research has indicated a continuing need for amendment of the EPA to tackle conditions which are inconvenient or of discomfort to tenants.[24]

Even within the narrow definition of a "nuisance", action can be taken against "statutory nuisance" arising from disrepair in immediately adjacent property (including common parts retained by the landlord). Examples include: leaking lavatory overflows, unhygienic rubbish chutes, backsurges of sewage, blocked pipes and gutters, falling slates and external cladding, and noisy central heating boilers.[25]

Where premises are in such a state as to cause potential or actual injury to health, or constitute a nuisance, the consequent statutory nuisance may be tackled, either by action by the local authority, or direct action by the occupier.

3 Action by local authorities

(a) Abatement notices

The existence of statutory nuisances may be brought to the attention of local authorities either by their own systematic inspections[26] of districts (for example in renewal areas) or, more commonly, by complaints from tenants and others. The investigation of statutory nuisances and enforcement of environmental protection legislation are usually delegated to individual EHOs.[27] For these purposes, EHOs have a right to enter and inspect premises which may be in such a state as to be a statutory nuisance.[28]

Once satisfied of the existence of a statutory nuisance (or the likelihood of a statutory nuisance arising or recurring), a local authority is legally bound to take action,[29] using the powers available to it under the EPA. (Remedial action may also be taken under Housing Acts and the potential overlap with these powers is dealt with below at p86.) Although obliged to follow the statutory procedures to tackle statutory nuisances, some authorities will first give the landlord an "informal notice" that EPA sanctions are being considered.

The first formal step is service by the local authority of an abatement notice on the person responsible for the nuisance.[30] The notice requires the person served (in practice, usually the landlord) to abate the nuisance (or prevent it arising or recurring) and execute "such works, and the taking of such other steps as may be necessary" for that purpose. The notice need not spell out precisely what works are required, but if precise specification is given, the works detailed must be capable of remedying the nuisance.[31] The notice also gives a time limit for completion of remedial works.[32] In cases of structural defects (for example statutory nuisances arising from disrepair), the abatement notice must be served on the "owner",[33] ie the person who does (or would) receive the rent.[34] The authority will be able to identify the owner from the tenant's rent book, or by use of its statutory powers to obtain information about the ownership of property.[35]

If the person causing the nuisance cannot be found (as is frequently the case with property in very gross disrepair), the authority can serve notice on the owner or occupier.[36]

Where more than one person is responsible for a statutory nuisance, notice may be served on each person whether or not his/her conduct alone would amount to a nuisance.[37]

The person served with an abatement notice has a right of appeal to a magistrates' court (to be exercised within 21 days of the date notice is served[38]) by way of complaint.[39] No grounds of appeal are specified in the EPA and the statute is silent as to the effect of the lodging of an appeal on the notice itself. This issue is to be tackled by regulations to be made by the Secretary of State which may also include provision for the outcome of an appeal to be more adverse to the landlord than the initial abatement notice.[40]

If the abatement notice is neither appealed nor complied with, the person served is guilty of an offence if the failure to comply is without reasonable excuse.[41] Under the former PHA 1936 provisions, local authorities were under a statutory duty to prosecute for non-compliance with abatement notices. The EPA imposes no such obligation and is silent as to whether prosecutions may be brought by the Crown Prosecution Service or occupiers directly in place of local authorities unwilling to take action.

If the offence of failure to comply is proven, the landlord or other person served is liable to a fine (up to level 5 on the standard scale) and a further fine of one-tenth the level 5 scale for each further day of non-compliance following conviction.[42] Under the old PHA 1936 procedure, the magistrates were required to issue a nuisance order directing the offender to carry out specified works. In the EPA process, the original abatement notice continues to bind the person served and the incentive for compliance with it is the prospect of incurring daily fines. There is accordingly no need for a nuisance order.

Whether or not it prosecutes for non-compliance, the authority can itself abate the nuisance "and do whatever may be necessary" for execution of the original abatement notice.[43] It can then recover its costs from the person served or from the present owner of the property.[44]

(b) High Court actions

If the local authority is satisfied that it would be inappropriate to deal with a statutory nuisance by using the magistrates' court procedure outlined above, it may take any necessary legal proceedings against the owner in the High Court.[45] Such proceedings have the advantage of giving access to broader equitable remedies, eg injunctions, and wide-ranging means of enforcement and are useful where the owner persistently defaults or repeatedly delays the summary process before the magistrates' court. For the procedure on a High Court action, see *Warwick RDC v Miller-Mead*.[46]

(c) Emergency procedure

Frequently the delays inherent in the enforcement procedures described above render them inappropriate in tackling situations of "prejudice to health" etc. A streamlined procedure for these urgent cases is to be found in the Building Act 1984.

Thus, where an authority is satisfied (usually as a result of an urgent tenant complaint) that a statutory nuisance exists and that unreasonable delay[47] would be caused by following the summary procedure, it may serve the landlord with a notice stating its intention to do the remedial works and specifying the defects it intends to remedy.[48]

Nine days after service, the local authority may carry out all the necessary work identified in the notice and may recover its costs and expenses from the person on whom the notice is served.[49] Landlords can prevent this procedure taking effect only if, within seven days of service of the notice, they serve a counter-notice upon the authority that they intend to remedy the defects. The authority cannot act thereafter unless:

(a) the landlord fails to start remedial works within a reasonable time, or
(b) having been started, remedial works proceed unreasonably slowly or make no progress at all.[50]

In either of these circumstances, the local authority can proceed directly and carry out the works, and recover the full cost from the landlord.

Advisers assisting tenants in situations where disrepair is sufficiently gross to constitute a statutory nuisance by reason of prejudice to health, should always consider pressing the Environmental Health Department to use this "nine-day notice" procedure.

(d) Recurring nuisances

Under the former PHA 1936 provisions, difficulties arose in serving abatement notices in respect of premises which were intermittently in a condition amounting to a nuisance but not constantly so. The Public Health (Recurring Nuisances) Act 1969 sought to plug this gap by introducing a prohibition notice procedure to prevent nuisances recurring.

However, the provisions are wholly recast by the EPA and the 1969 Act has been repealed in its entirety. Under the EPA a local authority can serve an abatement notice requiring works, not only when it is satisfied that a nuisance exists, but also where it is satisfied that:

(a) a nuisance is likely to occur; or
(b) a nuisance is likely to recur.

The notice can either prohibit or restrict the nuisance arising or recurring and require the necessary works for those purposes.[51]

4 Action by tenants and other occupiers

(a) Private sector

Private sector or housing association tenants will usually look to the EHOs employed by local authorities to take the necessary administrative and legal proceedings to eradicate statutory nuisances arising at their premises, using their powers described above.

Accordingly, advisers consulted by private tenants suffering prejudice to health or nuisance should immediately involve the local authority's EHO by requesting a visit and inspection of the tenant's property. Thereafter, the adviser should liaise closely with the EHO and ensure that the abatement procedures are fully used, including the nine-day notice procedure for urgent cases. In any subsequent prosecution of the landlord, the tenant may well be a witness for the local authority.

There are five situations, however, which may give rise to difficulty:

1 The EHO fails to carry out an inspection, or there is an unreasonable delay before a visit is made A local authority is required to investigate individual complaints (s79(1)). In the event of a clear default, a complaint may be made to the Secretary of State[52] who may direct the authority to inspect; alternatively a complaint may be made to the local ombudsman. In the interim, an inspection should be arranged with an independent EHO.

2 The EHO carries out an inspection but does not agree that a statutory nuisance has arisen In such circumstances, advisers should ask for the matter to be reconsidered, ensuring that the EHO is supplied with all the available medical information about the prejudice to the health of the tenant, or complaints from other tenants about the nuisance. An EHO may be persuaded to revisit if presented with a convincing report from an independent expert engaged by the tenant.

3 The EHO is not prepared to find that premises constitute a statutory nuisance, even after reconsideration In this eventuality, the tenant will need to establish the existence of the nuisance by other means (eg an inspection and report by an independent EHO, a medical report as to prejudice to health etc), and if satisfied that a statutory nuisance can be proved, take proceedings directly against the landlord using the s82 procedure (see below).

4 The EHO agrees that there is a statutory nuisance, but fails to take remedial action within a reasonable time using the EPA procedures The duties of the local authority to tackle statutory nuisances are mandatory statutory duties.[53] The tenant can challenge the failure to take action, if aggrieved by the breach of statutory duty, and move in the High Court for judicial review and prerogative orders directing the local authority to use the powers available to it.[54] Alternatively, complaint may be made to the local government ombudsman. This may, however, be secondary to the urgent need to remedy the statutory nuisance, in which case the tenant should initiate summary proceedings directly against the landlord in the magistrates' court, using the s82 procedure and secure the attendance of the EHO as a witness (see below).

5 The EHO behaves improperly or unprofessionally If the difficulty for the tenant arises from the improper or unprofessional behaviour of the EHO (eg, where the tenant is subject to racist remarks or has some evidence of corruption), complaint should be made to the chief EHO of the authority concerned. If this produces no satisfaction, the matter should be raised with the professional association of EHOs – the Institution of Environmental Health Officers.[55]

(b) Public sector

In practice, council tenants are largely outside the protection of the public health legislation—simply because EHOs, as local government officers, are usually reluctant to take enforcement procedures and serve legal notices upon their own authorities.[56] Although some EHOs will serve informal administrative notices on their housing departments, the majority take the view that public health notices cannot properly be served upon their own local authorities, and indeed there is some judicial support for that view.[57] The council tenant must therefore use the enforcement procedure contained in s82 (formerly PHA 1936 s99).

5 Section 82 proceedings

The procedure for direct action by tenants against their local authority or private landlord is contained in EPA s82 (formerly PHA 1936 s99).[58]

Under this section, action may be taken against a local authority by a council tenant for the abatement of a statutory nuisance, even though the authority is providing the accommodation in exercise of its powers as a housing authority.[59] Similarly, s82 can be used by a private sector or housing association tenant where the local authority is not itself taking proceedings to compel the landlord to repair the property.

Proceedings may be initiated by any person aggrieved by the statutory nuisance. Although this will usually be the tenant or licensee, the provision extends to all other occupiers of the premises such as the tenant's family or lodgers and "it may very well be concerned with people who come on the land".[60] Thus in *Gould v Times Square Estates Ltd*[61] justices were prepared to hold that squatters might be within the definition.

Under s82, proceedings brought by individual tenants are criminal proceedings from the outset[62] even though the Act itself refers to an action started by way of complaint.[63] The reference to "complaint" remains in s82 even though the proceedings are still criminal in nature throughout. The main change has been the introduction of a new requirement of formal written notice of intention to prosecute (see below). Provided that notice has been given, the occupier can prosecute the landlord responsible for the statutory nuisance. If successful, those proceedings produce a nuisance order – breach of which constitutes a further criminal offence: s82(8).

The first stage of s82 proceedings is commenced by the laying of an information in the magistrates' court by a person aggrieved by the existence of a statutory nuisance (ie in order to have jurisdiction the court must be satisfied that at the date of information there is a statutory nuisance rather than the prospect of a nuisance arising or recurring).[64] See Appendix 7 for a precedent of such an information. The proceedings are brought against the person responsible for the nuisance or, if s/he cannot be found, against the owner (usually the landlord) or occupier.[65] If on the hearing of the complaint the court is satisfied that a nuisance exists it makes an order requiring the defendant to abate the nuisance within a specified time and to carry out the works necessary for that purpose.[66] If at the hearing date the nuisance has abated (whether naturally or as a result of remedial measures) but the court is satisfied that recurrence is likely, it makes an order prohibiting recurrence and requiring works to prevent recurrence.[67] It will be apparent that the court's powers at this stage mirror those of the authority itself to serve an abatement notice (save that the magistrates have no jurisdiction to prevent first occurrence of a nuisance). In order to secure the most appropriate orders, tenants and their advisers should have drafts available for the court to consider. A conviction will be entered and costs will be awarded to the complainant if an order is made and the court is satisfied that proceedings have been properly brought.

Proceedings under s82 cannot be started until the landlord has been given formal written notice of the intention to prosecute: s82(6).

In order to ensure that s82 proceedings are effective, tenants should take certain preliminary steps, of which (a) and (b) are optional:[68]

(a) write to the chief EHO of the local authority specifying the defects complained of and the general condition of the property, asking for an EHO to inspect the premises. In addition to copies retained, a copy should be sent to the housing department/landlord;

(b) if no action results (for example the EHO fails to inspect or, having inspected, fails to take further steps) write again to the chief EHO and housing department/landlord, asking what remedial action is intended;

(c) if this produces no reaction, write again to the landlord, giving at least 21 days' warning of the intention to commence legal proceedings;

(d) in the absence of a start upon remedial works, lay an information before justices who issue a summons if satisfied that there is a prima facie case of statutory nuisance (see above for an outline of the procedure).

The time-lapse between each of these stages will largely be governed by the urgency and seriousness of the prevailing disrepair. Only very short periods will be needed in cases relying on "prejudice to health".

(a) Preparatory work

Legal aid is *not* available for either the private prosecution of criminal cases, nor the enforcement of orders made under s82. Accordingly, preparatory work will mainly be undertaken using the green form scheme and it may be necessary to apply for an extension at an early stage. Preparation will usually include:

(a) the engagement of an independent EHO to inspect the premises and prepare a report;[69]

(b) gathering of medical evidence, and preparation of a medical report, if the case is to proceed on the "prejudice to health" limb;

(c) the photographing of the premises, including the particular items said to contribute to the nuisance or prejudice to health;

(d) the copying and collation of correspondence passing between the tenant, EHO and the local authority/landlord concerning the disrepair. If an EHO is unwilling to disclose documents, a witness summons should be issued requiring attendance at court with all documents relevant and available;

(e) preparation of statements of the tenant and other members of the household relating to conditions at the premises, including statements which may be submitted under the Criminal Justice Act 1967 s9; and

(f) preparation of a schedule of items destroyed or damaged by disrepair, including other financial loss, to be submitted for consideration of a compensation order.

It is important that the tenant has sufficient evidence to show that the statutory nuisance exists at the date on which the information is laid, and that the tenant was "aggrieved" by the statutory nuisance *at that date*.[70] Thus, it may be necessary to be selective about the stage at which it is decided to launch the proceedings. However, at least one magistrates' court has been prepared to accept that a statutory nuisance arises from the state of premises which are structurally prone to be prejudicial to health, even though not actually prejudicial to health at the date the information was laid.[71]

For a summary of the use of s82 proceedings in relation to problems of condensation dampness see chapter 7 pp115–116 below.

(b) Procedure (see Appendix 7 for precedents)

The first step is the laying of the information in the local magistrates' court. This is largely an administrative process involving completion of a standard form or a simple written application. The information laid should disclose:

(a) an indication of the capacity in which the defendant is to be served (ie as "owner" if the nuisance arises from a structural defect, or otherwise as the person responsible for the nuisance); and

(b) the nature of the alleged nuisance.[72]

It would be usual for the tenant to be in occupation of the premises at the date the information is laid, but the absence of the tenant (perhaps driven to live elsewhere temporarily by the poor conditions) is not fatal to an application.[73]

Although many metropolitan magistrates' courts were familiar with applications made under PHA 1936 s99, advisers should be careful not to take the issue of a summons under EPA s82 for granted in other areas. It is good practice to ensure that the complaint is accompanied by a statement from the tenant, a copy of EPA s82 and a request for an early hearing date. Strictly, all that is required is that the magistrate be satisfied (whether sitting in private or in open court) as to the existence of a nuisance. Photographs of the property and an inspection report should be at hand, together with a copy of the warning of intention to prosecute (s82(6)). Once the magistrate is satisfied, the court will issue a summons to the defendant to appear on a specified hearing date and, with it, will send a copy of the information and any supporting statement from the tenant.

In cases relying on "prejudice to health", advisers should always press for an early hearing date, but in negotiating this with the court, it is essential to be realistic about the likely duration of the hearing, so that inconvenience to the tenant caused by repeated adjournments is avoided. Although the procedure up to the hearing date is comparatively straightforward, it can be intimidating to the litigant in person[74] and may prove frustrating in a busy magistrates' court with a recalcitrant defendant.[75]

As well as taking all necessary preparatory steps prior to the hearing, advisers should endeavour to discover in advance whether the landlord or local authority will be pleading guilty and is agreeable to an order being made. Even if the remedial works are commenced after the laying of the information, the tenant and adviser should attend on the hearing date to secure an order for costs (see below). The case should also proceed to hearing even if the tenants have been rehoused, since removing the tenant does not remedy the statutory nuisance.[76]

Advisers may well find that on the hearing date notified in the summons, the case appears in a list of many other actions, on the basis that it will be effective only if there is a guilty plea and agreement as to matters such as the works to be covered by an order. If this is not the case, a fresh trial date will be set.

At the substantive hearing, the proceedings before the magistrates will turn mainly on factual and expert information about "prejudice to health" or "nuisance". The use of expert EHOs, architects and others as witnesses to give specialist evidence is growing. Indeed, the whole case may turn on "scientific" evidence.[77] Recently, convictions have been overturned on appeal where tenants were unable to produce independent expert evidence of conditions relied upon before the justices.[78] On the other hand, the magistrates are not entitled to reject the evidence of expert witnesses called on behalf of the tenant unless that evidence is challenged or contradicted by witnesses for the respondent: ". . . when it comes to deciding whether the condition of premises is or is not liable or likely to be injurious to health one is moving outside the field where a tribunal is entitled to draw on its own experience. That is a matter upon which the tribunal needs informed expert evidence."[79] At the very least, cogent evidence given on behalf of the tenant by an independent EHO and/or building surveyor will establish that there is a case for the landlord to answer.[80]

Legal advisers attending the hearing with tenants whom they have been assisting under the green form scheme, can no longer invite the court to grant an extension to cover the costs of representation. Reimbursement for representation under the green form is available only to a lawyer within the precincts of the court on other business who is asked by the justices to assist the tenant.[81] It is worth checking that not only are none of the sitting justices members of the local authority,[82] but also that none of them are in any obvious way likely to be associated with the interests of the defendant.[83]

(c) Nuisance orders

At the close of the evidence, the justices are required to make certain findings, including:

(a) the actual condition of the premises: (i) at the date of the tenant's information and (ii) at the date of hearing;

(b) whether the condition at the date of the laying of the information constitutes a statutory nuisance, and whether the statutory nuisance still exists;

(c) whether the statutory nuisance is found by reason of "prejudice to health" *or* "nuisance" or both;

(d) identifying the person responsible for the statutory nuisance.

The existence of a statutory nuisance and the cause of that nuisance have to be proved to the criminal standard of proof, ie beyond reasonable doubt.[84] The fact that the matter complained of does not arise from any breach of the landlord's statutory obligation to repair may be persuasive in showing that it was not caused by any act or default of the landlord, but is not conclusive.[85] However, where the nuisance arises from any defect of a structural nature (eg, dampness resulting from a hole in the roof), the landlord is liable in the capacity of "owner" irrespective of repairing obligations[86] (s82(4)(b)) once a statutory nuisance is proved.

If matters are found in favour of the tenant,[87] the court must make an order against the defendant local authority or landlord requiring:[88]

(a) such work as the court considers necessary to abate the nuisance, within a stipulated time limit, or

(b) sufficient works to prevent a recurrence of the nuisance.

The justices must be specific as to the work required in the nuisance order.[89] Thus, advisers should ensure that the court is supplied with a full and detailed draft order. Where there has been agreement as to the facts, advisers should arrange that the fullest possible order is agreed in advance with the landlord and put before the justices. Much may be achieved through hard bargaining on the terms of orders "at the door of the court".[90] Whether or not the order is agreed, evidence in support of it must be given, since the decision as to the extent of the works necessary to abate the nuisance should be made by the court itself.[91] The order may properly require works to be done which go beyond the terms of any other repairing obligation on the landlord. The order can for instance, require improvement work or the installation of fixtures, fittings and facilities not present at the commencement of the tenancy.[92]

The court has a wide discretion as to the form and content of the order, and, in considering the remedial works to be specified, can properly have regard to the future life of the property. The justices must "look at the whole circumstances of the case and try and make an order which is in its terms sensible and just, having regard to the entire prevailing situation",[93] and this may include consideration of the overlapping provisions of the Housing Act (see below chapter 6). If the order is being made against a local authority, the court is also entitled to have regard to the general obligations that the council owes to its tenants and to the extent of its resources.[94]

Although in many cases, there will be an attempt to convince the court that simple "patch" repairs will cure the statutory nuisance, advisers should be bold in pressing for substantial orders for work sufficient to prevent recurrence of the nuisance. With the assistance of expert witnesses, tenants have been able to persuade courts to make formidable orders for remedial works. Examples include:

(a) provision of new roof covering, installation of full gas central heating, insulation of walls, ceiling and floors, and complete electrical rewiring and renovation of electrical fitments – *Christou v Islington LBC*;[95]
(b) re-pointing of external brickwork, replacement of defective sink and draining board (further works of installation of central heating and internal dry-lining having been agreed by the respondent) – *Tusting v RB Kensington and Chelsea*;[96]
(c) the provision of thermal insulation, installation of mechanical ventilation, and the overhaul of an inefficient heating system – *Brunyee v Lambeth LBC*;[97]
(d) insulation of walls, floors and ceilings, renewal of defective windows, installation of ventilators and provision of night storage heaters – *Ali v LB Hackney*;[98]
(e) installation of gas fired central heating, secondary double glazing, roof insulation, filling of cavity walls and electrical re-wiring – *Birmingham DC v Kelly and Others*.[99]

Where the only effective way to abate the statutory nuisance is to have the whole property demolished, a nuisance order requiring demolition may be made.[100] Where the property is unfit the court can prohibit occupation (see below).

Alternatively, if the only means of abating the nuisance is the provision of facilities or installations, the nuisance order may direct that such provision be made.[101]

Usually the terms of the nuisance order will be complied with before expiry of the time stated in the order. If there is a failure without reasonable excuse to comply with "any requirement" of an order made in s82 proceedings, the person subject to the order (usually the landlord) commits a further criminal offence: EPA s82(8). The tenant may then bring a prosecution for that non-compliance in the same magistrates' court where the order was made. Indeed, if the order in the earlier part of s82 proceedings was made against a private or housing association landlord, the local authority could bring the further prosecution even though it was the tenant who first obtained the order in default of the authority acting. The prosecution is launched by the laying of an information. If prima facie satisfied that an offence has occurred, the magistrates' court (or its clerk) will issue a summons requiring the attendance of the landlord for trial. Tenants should press for early hearing dates as the daily fine, which is the real pressure on the landlord to comply with the order, bites only from the date of conviction not from when the order is breached or the information laid.

Tenants should endeavour to establish in advance whether the landlord will be pleading guilty or not guilty. In particular tenants should be alive to the prospect of the defendant relying on the "reasonable excuse" defence for non-compliance. This is undefined and potentially very wide ranging.

If the magistrates are satisfied as to non-compliance or there is a guilty plea, a further conviction will be entered. Penalties are described below.

The court may direct the local authority for the area (if not itself the defendant) to carry out the works (or any part of them) specified in the original notice. Before making such an order the justices must give the authority an opportunity to be heard: s13. In order to undertake the works the authority can call in aid considerable powers to enter private property: Sch 3 paras 2–3.

(d) Penalties

Where the initial prosecution under s82(1) results in a nuisance order, the court enters a conviction and may impose a fine of up to level 5 on the standard scale: s82(2). The penalty for failure to comply with a nuisance order made by the court is a fine of up to level 5 on the standard scale plus one tenth of that scale for each subsequent day on which compliance remains outstanding (s82(8)).[102] In assessing the fine, the court will be assisted by any information about the respondent's earlier convictions relating to other properties owned.

(e) Compensation

In addition to any penalty, a compensation order[103] may be made in favour of the tenant for damage suffered to person and property. In a "prejudice to health" case, actual ill-health will usually have been proved and recompense should follow. A compensation order provides a "speedy, summary and cheap" method of obtaining financial compensation without the need to bring separate civil proceedings.[104] Full details of any personal injury should be provided[105] although in the absence of such evidence an award for anxiety and distress can be made.[106] Up to £2,000 may be awarded by magistrates (there is no limit in the Crown Court), but the court should be assisted to make a proper assessment of loss.[107] It is not necessary to show that the landlord would have been liable in civil proceedings to pay compensation,[108] but some evidence of the actual loss suffered must be available: mere representations are insufficient.[109]

It is not unusual for a magistrates' court both to impose a substantial fine and to award the maximum amount of compensation.[110] Magistrates are required to give reasons if refusing to award compensation, whether or not an application has been made.[111]

Care should be taken in identifying the actual loss in respect of which compensation is sought because, in any subsequent civil action for damages, credit will have to be given for the amount of the compensation order where the award is for the same "injury, loss or damage".[112] The magistrates should therefore be asked to award compensation for those items which will not attract civil damages.

(f) Appeals

An appeal against conviction may be made to the Crown Court.[113] Indeed, any "person aggrieved" by the outcome of the proceedings before the magistrates may appeal and therefore a tenant, unsuccessful with a prosecution, may appeal to the Crown Court.[114] The appeal takes the form of a rehearing but the Court concerns itself only with the matters as at the date of the hearing before the justices.[115] Appeal also lies to the Divisional Court of the Queen's Bench Division by way of case stated. Alternatively, the procedure for judicial review by the High Court is available. Judicial review may be necessary, eg, to compel the magistrates in EPA proceedings to prepare a case stated for the purposes of an appeal.[116] Any order made by the magistrates' court to take effect before an appeal can be heard, must be complied with.[117]

(g) Costs and legal aid

Under the old-style PHA 1936 s99 proceedings no specific provision was made for costs orders. Although it had long been thought that s94(3) operated to ensure automatic entitlement to costs if a statutory nuisance were proven, the award of costs was actually a matter for the discretion of the court.[118] The EPA now makes specific provision for costs awards in s82 proceedings. Where the court is satisfied that the statutory nuisance alleged existed at the date the information was laid then, irrespective of whether the nuisance still exists or is likely to recur, the court must order the defendant to pay the costs. The sum ordered to be paid to the occupier is "such amount as the court considers reasonably sufficient to compensate him for any expenses properly incurred by him in the proceedings".[119]

These should be sufficient to cover experts' fees, legal costs, tenant's loss of earnings etc. £1,200 costs awarded in *Ali v LB Hackney*[120] included fees of an independent environmental health officer, a heating engineer, medical reports, attendance by a GP and three sets of photographs. In one case, heard over four days, the tenant was awarded costs "limited to £4,000".[121] Costs are not usually taxed, but simply assessed from rates of costs and charges put to the court by the tenant's representative.

Although legal aid is not available to tenants in the magistrates' court (notwithstanding that the court may allow assistance by way of representation in very limited circumstances), it is available to the tenant to resist any appeal to the Crown Court,[122] or to the Divisional Court.

Even if the tenant loses a case, if it can be shown that proceedings had been reasonably commenced, an order may exceptionally be made for the payment of costs out of central funds.[123]

6 Environmental Protection Act and the Housing Act

As has been seen, local authorities have a statutory duty to take action where premises are in such a state as to be a statutory nuisance, under the EPA. However, if any premises are in such severe disrepair as to be unfit for human habitation, the local authority has a statutory duty to take action under the Housing Act.[124] Where premises are sufficiently out of repair to constitute a statutory nuisance *and* are unfit for human habitation, the courts have made it clear that local authorities should not use the statutory nuisance procedure to force full-scale repairs upon landlords of unfit housing,[125] but must instead use the Housing Act procedure.[126]

On the other hand, the fact that *council* property is unfit (even to the extent of simply awaiting demolition) is no bar to the tenant taking proceedings under s82, although in such cases justices are invited to take into account, in drawing up orders, the prospective life of the property.[127] Indeed, the HA 1985 s203(3) makes it clear that the use of Housing Act powers does not prejudice use by tenants or local authorities of other procedures including those under the EPA.

NOTE OF WARNING

Despite the attractions of the EPA procedures in providing a swift and straightforward remedy for bad housing and in imposing salutary penalties on landlords, including local authorities, several problems are relevant to tenants considering such action.

(a) EPA s82 proceedings are criminal proceedings and carry a higher burden of proof. Advisers should be certain of their evidence before laying informations. If the proceedings finally result in the acquittal of the respondent, the tenant may be landed with a heavy bill for costs.[128]

(b) The court may be persuaded that "patch" repairs will suffice to abate the nuisance, or will allow such a long period for the completion of works that the tenant receives little immediate benefit.

(c) The prosecution may result in a finding of unfitness and an order from the court prohibiting occupation of the property: s82(3). This would prevent the tenant returning to the property until it was made fit.

Note

This chapter is concerned only with the relationship between public health and environmental protection legislation and housing disrepair. The Public Health Acts and related regulations have a wide ranging application to a large number of matters touching upon housing standards, and should not be overlooked. Reference may usefully be made to "Housing Conditions" in *Social Welfare Law* (ed Pollard, Longman) and Arden and Partington *Housing Law* (Sweet & Maxwell).

1 The statutes are to be found annotated in *Encyclopedia of environmental health law and practice* (Sweet & Maxwell) (regularly updated).
2 S79(7).
3 *Metropolitan Asylum District Managers v Hill* (1881) 6 App Cas 193; *Fulham Vestry v London CC* [1897] 2 QB 76.
4 See *Lambeth LBC v Stubbs* (1980) 255 EG 789; (1980) 78 LGR 650.
5 *Birmingham DC v McMahon and Ors* (1987) 19 HLR 452 at 457.
6 *R v Sec State Environment ex p Ward* [1984] 2 All ER 556 at 560; *Day v Sheffield CC* (1988) August *Legal Action* 19. See n101 below.
7 *R v Parlby* (1889) 22 QBD 520 at 525.
8 *LB Southwark v Ince* (1989) 21 HLR 504, QBD.
9 *Pollway Nominees Ltd v LB Havering* (1989) 21 HLR 462, QBD.
10 *Malton Urban Sanitary Authority v Malton Farmers Manure Co* (1879) 4 Ex D 302.
11 See Ros Franey "Housing stress" March/April 1982 *Roof* 19.
12 Per Wilberforce LJ in *Salford CC v McNally* [1975] 3 WLR 87, HL.
13 *Springett v Harold* [1954] 1 All ER 568.
14 *Coventry CC v Cartwright* [1975] 1 WLR 845; [1975] 2 All ER 99, DC.
15 See Ormandy and Burridge *Environmental health standards in housing* (Sweet & Maxwell, 1988); Ormandy "Public health quarterly notes" (1977) September *LAG Bulletin* 206; and "The law of statutory nuisance as it relates to premises" *Environmental Health Professional Practice Series* IEHO 1985 vol 1 chapter 1.
16 *Bennett v Preston BC* (1982) 22 October, unreported, Preston Crown Court, noted at March/April 1984 *Roof* 18.
17 *Betts v Penge UDC* [1942] 2 KB 154.
18 *Salford CC v McNally* n12.
19 [1976] 2 All ER 478; [1976] 1 WLR 543, DC.
20 Per Watkins J in *National Coal Board v Thorne* [1976] 1 WLR 543 at 546.
21 Per Mansfield LJ in *R v White and Ward* (1757) 1 Burr 333; and see *R v Neill* (1826) 2 Car & P 485.
22 *Great Western Railway v Bishop* (1872) LR 7 QB 550; and *Bishop Auckland Local Board v British Auckland Iron and Steel Co Ltd* (1883) 10 QBD 138 considered in *Coventry CC v Cartwright* n14.
23 DoE 1979 *Consultation paper on review of the law of statutory nuisance and offensive trades*; see M Davey "Bridging the nuisance gap" September 1979 *Roof* 163.
24 Hawke and Taylor "The compulsory repair of individual substandard housing: the law in practice" (1984) JSWL 129.
25 *Joyce v LB Hackney* (1976) 24 June, unreported, Highbury Corner Magistrates' Court, noted at (1976) September *LAG Bulletin* 211.

26 Local authorities are under a duty to inspect regularly their districts to identify statutory nuisance (EPA s79).
27 Under Local Government Act 1972 s101.
28 EPA Sch 3 para 2.
29 *Cocker v Cardwell* (1869) LR 5 QB 15.
30 EPA s80(1).
31 *Millard v Wastall* [1898] 1 QB 342; *Whatling v Rees* (1914) 84 LJKB 1122; *R v Wheatley* (1885) 16 QBD 34.
32 See EPA s80(1) and *Bristol Corp v Sinnot* [1918] 1 Ch 62.
33 EPA s80(2)(b).
34 PHA 1936 s343(1) and see *Pollway Nominees Ltd v LB Havering* n9.
35 Local Government (Miscellaneous Provisions) Act 1976 s16; and, for the EHO's power to inspect rent books, see HA 1985 s336 and Ormandy "Housing repairs: what local authorities should be doing" (1978) July *LAG Bulletin* 164.
36 EPA s80(2)(c).
37 Ibid s81(1).
38 Ibid s80(3).
39 Ibid Sch 3 para 1(2).
40 Ibid Sch 3 para 1(4).
41 Ibid s80(4).
42 Ibid s80(5).
43 Ibid s81(3).
44 Ibid s81(4).
45 Ibid s81(5).
46 [1962] 2 WLR 284, CA.
47 *Celcrest Properties Ltd v Hastings BC* (1979) 29 October, unreported, ChD, noted in Arden *Manual of housing law* (Sweet & Maxwell, 4th edn, 1989) p266.
48 Building Act 1984 s76(1) as amended by EPA Sch 15 para 24.
49 Building Act 1984 s76(2).
50 Ibid s76(3).
51 EPA s80(1).
52 The power to make formal complaint to the Secretary of State under EPA Sch 3 para 4 should be exercised by addressing written representations to the Secretary of State for the Environment, Department of the Environment, 2 Marsham Street, London SW1.
53 *Cocker v Cardwell* n29; *McPhail v Islington LBC* [1970] 2 WLR 583, CA at 586.
54 EPA s80(1) and see generally De Smith *Judicial review of administrative action* (Sweet & Maxwell, 4th edn, 1980).
55 The Institution of Environmental Health Officers, Chadwick House, Rushworth Street, London SE1 0QT (tel 071-928 6006).
56 For a review of local practice see J Burdett "Fair weather friends" September/October 1981 *Roof* 12 and subsequent correspondence.
57 See *Cardiff CC v Cross* (1982) 6 HLR 1, CA.
58 For a review of the development of s99 as a repairing tool, see Hodge "Tenants and s99" (1974) NLJ 1161; Hughes "Public health legislation and improvement of housing conditions" 27 NILQ 1; Hughes "What is a nuisance?" 27 NILQ 131; Haddon "Public health and housing legislation" 27 NILQ 245; and Hughes "Housing and public health" 28 NILQ 233.
59 *R v Epping (Waltham Abbey) JJ ex p Burlinson* [1947] 2 All ER 537; [1948] 1 KB 79.
60 Per Widgery LCJ in *Coventry CC v Cartwright* n14.
61 (1975) 1 April, unreported, Camberwell Magistrates' Court, noted at (1975) September *LAG Bulletin* 247.
62 *Northern Ireland Trailers v Preston County Borough* [1972] 1 All ER 260.
63 *R v Newham East JJ ex p Hunt* [1976] 1 All ER 839; [1976] 1 WLR 420; and Magistrates' Courts Act 1980 s50.

64 EPA s82(1).
65 Ibid s82(4) and (5).
66 Ibid s82(2).
67 Ibid s82(2)(b).
68 For a fuller guide see *Statutory nuisance and s99* Shelter Practice Note 1 (January 1983) or *S99 repairs kit* Brixton Law Centre or Ormandy "Fixing it" May/June 1986 *Roof* 15. However, there is as yet no guide to the new EPA procedure.
69 Law centres, solicitors and legal advice agencies have access to the Health and Housing Group's panel of independent EHOs (Health and Housing Group, 120 Wilton Road, London SW1 1JZ. Tel: 071-233 7780).
70 *Hilton v Hopwood* (1899) 44 SJ 96.
71 *Brunyee v Lambeth LBC* (1981) 13 November, unreported, Camberwell Green Magistrates' Court, noted at January/February 1982 *Roof* 25. (An appeal to the Divisional Court on this point was withdrawn.)
72 *Warner v LB Lambeth* (1984) 15 HLR 42, DC.
73 *Jones v Public Trustee* (1988) September *Legal Action* 21.
74 C Blood "One woman's fight for a damp-free home" September 1979 *Roof* 162.
75 "Using s99" letter from Brixton Law Centre (1982) November *LAG Bulletin* 82.
76 *Lambeth LBC v Stubbs* n4, followed and applied in *Coventry CC v Doyle* [1981] 2 All ER 184.
77 See eg *R v Fenny Stratford JJ ex p Watney Mann* [1976] 2 All ER 888.
78 *GLC v Feroushos* (1982) March, unreported, Inner London Crown Court, noted in *South London Press* 9 March 1982.
79 *Patel v Mehtab* (1982) 5 HLR 78 per Donaldson LJ at 82.
80 *McCorley v Birmingham DC* (1984) 12 January, unreported, DC, noted at D Pollard *Social Welfare Law* (Longman) para C.6063.
81 Legal Advice and Assistance (Scope) Regs 1989 SI No 550 regs 7 and 8; and see the statement issued by the Legal Aid Board at (1989) 46 LS Gaz 11.
82 Justices of the Peace Act 1979 s64.
83 *R v Smethwick JJ ex p Hands* (1980) *Times* 4 December, DC.
84 PHA 1936 s99 procedures were also criminal throughout.
85 *Birmingham DC v Kelly and Ors* (1985) 17 HLR 572 at 579.
86 *Coventry CC v Doyle* n76.
87 Or other informant.
88 *R v Camberwell Green Magistrates' Court ex p Healey* (1984) 10 October, unreported, QBD, noted at (1985) December *Legal Action* 171.
89 *R v Horrocks ex p Boustead* (1900) 69 LJQB 688.
90 For good examples of success in bargaining see cases taken against LB Southwark (48 *Community Action* 6); proceedings against LB Greenwich (49 *Community Action* 3); and *Ali v LB Hackney* (1985) 9 September, unreported, Highbury Magistrates' Court, noted at (1985) December *Legal Action* 171.
91 *Birmingham DC v Kelly and Ors* n85.
92 Ibid at 582.
93 Per Widgery LCJ in *Nottingham Corp v Newton* [1974] 2 All ER 760 at 766.
94 *Salford CC v McNally* n12; *Birmingham DC v Kelly and Ors* n85; and *LB Southwark v Ince* n8.
95 (1980) unreported, Inner London Crown Court, noted at 51 *Community Action* 10.
96 (1975) 3 January, unreported, Inner London Crown Court, noted at 27 NILQ 16 and *Municipal Journal* 17 January 1975.
97 N71.
98 See n90.
99 N85.
100 *Brown v Biggleswade Union* (1879) 43 JP 554.
101 *Whittaker v Derby Urban SA* (1885) 55 (ns) LJ MC 8; *LB Hammersmith and Fulham*

and RB Kensington and Chelsea v Ward (1983) 7 November, unreported, Knightsbridge Crown Court, noted at May/June 1984 *Roof* 18.
102 "Nuisance fines" March 1977 *Roof* 60; and see *emPHASis* No 67, 28 January 1977 and *Savizon v Lambeth LBC* (1985) unreported, Camberwell Green Magistrates' Court, noted at (1986) June *Legal Action* 81.
103 See generally S Singh "Compensation orders and Public Health Act 1936" (1987) December *Legal Action* 11.
104 *R v Dorton* [1988] Crim LR 254, CA.
105 *R v Cooper* [1982] Crim LR 308, CA.
106 *Bond v Chief Constable of Kent* [1983] 1 All ER 456.
107 Powers of Criminal Courts Act 1973 s35 (see *R v Vivian* [1975] 1 All ER 48, CA).
108 *R v Chappell* [1984] Crim LR 574, CA.
109 *R v Horsham Justices ex p Richards* [1985] 2 All ER 1114; *R v Amey* [1983] 1 All ER 865, CA and Criminal Justice Act 1982 s67.
110 *Oliver v Islington LBC* (1987) 24 July, unreported, Highbury Corner Magistrates' Court, noted at (1987) September *Legal Action* 12; and similar cases noted in *Legal Action* in September 1988 (p15), December 1988 (p21) and March 1989 (p23).
111 Criminal Justice Act 1988 s104.
112 Ibid s105.
113 PHA 1936 s301.
114 *Cook v Southend BC* (1989) 11 CL 323, CA; *Josiah v Thames Housing Association* (1989) 7 July, unreported, Knightsbridge Crown Court, noted at (1989) December *Legal Action* 16.
115 *Northern Ireland Trailers* n62.
116 *R v Wells Street Magistrates' Court ex p Morrissey* (1988) 18 July, unreported, QBD.
117 *Hammersmith LBC v Magnum Automated Forecourts* [1977] 1 All ER 401, CA.
118 *Sandwell MBC v Bujok* (1989) 22 HLR 87, DC.
119 EPA s82(12).
120 See n90.
121 *Day v Sheffield CC* n6.
122 Legal Aid Act 1988 ss8 and 21; and *R v Inner London Crown Court ex p Bentham* (1988) 21 HLR 171, QBD.
123 Costs in Criminal Cases Act 1973; and see *Dover DC v Farrar* (1982) 2 HLR 32, DC.
124 See chapter 6.
125 *Salisbury Corp v Roles* [1948] WN 412; (1948) 92 SJ 618, DC.
126 *R v Kerrier DC ex p Guppys (Bridport)* (1976) 32 P&CR 411, CA.
127 *Salford CC v McNally* n12.
128 *Williamson v Kirklees DC* (1975) 25 June, unreported, Huddersfield Crown Court, noted at 44 *Community Action* 10.

Chapter Six

Bad Housing and the Housing Act 1985

1 Introduction

The 1986 national House Condition Survey[1] confirms that hundreds of thousands of homes remain "unfit for human habitation", with the escalating number of otherwise "unsatisfactory" houses running into millions. A similarly depressing picture of unfitness is presented by the statistics for Northern Ireland.[2] Notwithstanding the continuing decline in the country's housing stock, for many years there has been a welter of law applicable to housing standards and conditions, most of it unused. This legislation covers the whole housing spectrum from compulsory improvement to slum clearance programmes and redevelopment.[3]

In this chapter, those aspects of the housing legislation of most assistance to the individual tenant and adviser will be considered. The Housing Act will be discussed in its application to three standards of accommodation: unfit housing, housing in substantial disrepair, and housing in sufficient disrepair to cause discomfort to tenants.

Before turning, however, to the detail of the provisions, it is important to note that the judiciary have sanctioned policies of bold use of the Housing Act legislation in attempts to eradicate bad housing. Lord Denning MR has said:[4]

> "It seems to me that the policy of Parliament was to make the owners of houses keep them in proper repair. Not only so as to keep up the stock of houses, but also to see that protected tenants should be able to have their houses properly kept up. It would be deplorable if there were no means of compelling owners of old houses to keep them in proper repair; or if the owners could let them fall into disrepair – as a means of evicting tenants. Of course, if the state of the house is so bad that it should be condemned – whoever was occupying it – then let it be demolished or closed or purchased. But if it is worth repairing, then it should be repaired, no matter whether it is occupied by a protected tenant or an unprotected tenant."

Readers should note that the provisions of the consolidating Housing Act 1985 have in turn been extensively re-cast by the Housing Act 1988 and the Local Government and Housing Act 1989. What amounts to an almost wholly new regime is introduced from 1 April 1990 and it is with the operation of these new arrangements that this chapter is concerned. The hallmark of the new scheme is intended to be the greater degree of flexibility given to local authorities in deciding how to tackle bad housing and poor conditions. However, those authorities are required, in considering what action to take, to have regard to guidance issued by the Secretary of State for the Environment (in the form of circulars incorporating a code of guidance). Advisers will accordingly find it essential to be equipped not only with the new legislation but also with copies of the relevant DoE materials.

Advisers assisting tenants in cases where the local authority initiated action on or before 31 March 1990 are referred to the first edition of this work for a description of the old statutory provisions. Additionally, in such cases regard should be had to the transitional provisions contained in the commencement orders bringing the relevant parts of the new legislation into force (in particular 1990 SI No 431).

2 Housing unfit for human habitation

Part VI of the Housing Act 1985 (HA 1985) as amended, sets out a code for tackling individual properties which are unfit for human habitation. The code, which is enforced by local authorities under the guidance of the Secretary of State for the Environment, requires that whenever an unfit property is identified some form of action *must* be taken.

(a) Identifying unfit property

All local authorities are under a statutory duty to consider annually what action should be taken concerning housing conditions in their area and particularly with regard to, inter alia, properties that are unfit.[5] More commonly, individual properties are brought to the attention of authorities by complaints from tenants and their advisers. Once identified, an inspection must be carried out by an EHO in order to determine the condition of the property. (See also "Mobilising the authority" below p100.) If the EHO is satisfied that the property is "unfit" (see below), s/he must report that fact in writing to the committee or officer of the council with the delegated power to decide what action should be taken (HA 1985 s606(1)).

(b) The meaning of "unfit"

The HA 1985 s604(1),[6] sets out a definition of unfitness for these purposes:

> "(1) Subject to subsection (2) below, a dwelling-house is fit for human habitation for the purposes of this Act unless, in the opinion of the local housing authority, it fails to meet one or more of the requirements in paragraphs (a) to (i) below and, by reason of that failure, is not reasonably suitable for occupation,–

(a) it is structurally stable;
(b) it is free from serious disrepair;
(c) it is free from dampness prejudicial to the health of the occupants (if any);
(d) it has adequate provision for lighting, heating and ventilation;
(e) it has an adequate piped supply of wholesome water;
(f) there are satisfactory facilities in the dwelling-house for the preparation and cooking of food, including a sink with a satisfactory supply of hot and cold water;
(g) it has a suitably located water-closet for the exclusive use of the occupants (if any);
(h) it has, for the exclusive use of the occupants (if any), a suitably located fixed bath or shower and wash-hand basin each of which is provided with a satisfactory supply of hot and cold water; and
(i) it has an effective system for the drainage of foul, waste and surface water;

and any reference to a dwelling-house being unfit for human habitation shall be construed accordingly.

(2) Whether or not a dwelling-house which is a flat satisfies the requirements in subsection (1), it is unfit for human habitation for the purposes of this Act if, in the opinion of the local housing authority, the building or a part of the building outside the flat fails to meet one or more of the requirements in paragraphs (a) to (e) below and, by reason of that failure, the flat is not reasonably suitable for occupation,–

(a) the building or part is structurally stable;
(b) it is free from serious disrepair;
(c) it is free from dampness;
(d) it has adequate provision for ventilation; and
(e) it has an effective system for the draining of foul, waste and surface water."

As can be seen, the provisions start from the presumption that premises are fit. Houses[7] and flats which are "unfit" are those failing to meet one or more of the nine requirements or standards in (1)(a)—(i) and which *by reason of that failure* are not reasonably suitable for occupation.

The factors relevant for dwelling-houses are set out in subsection (1). This is an exhaustive list and other factors or housing conditions which might, in colloquial terms, render a home unfit are not relevant to the statutory definition. If the property is a flat however, it may be unfit either for failing the standard in subsection (1) or the alternative standard in subsection (2) or both. In the case of flats it is important to note that any defects in the common parts relied upon must be rendering the *flat* unsuitable for continued occupation as distinct from making the other parts of the block or building unsafe. (For means of addressing unsafe common parts, see chapter 2 p16.) The same factors or requirements apply for the purpose of determining fitness of houses in multiple occupation (s604(3)) or flats in multiple occupation (s604(4)). It should be noted that although premises may be deemed "unfit for human habitation" at common law (eg by reason of infestation by bugs), this is irrelevant to statutory unfitness. Nor are premises "unfit" by reason of failure to be supplied with gas or electricity or otherwise to conform to building regulations or modern standards for new housing.[8] Nor is this definition of unfitness the same as that used in Landlord and Tenant Act 1985 for the purposes of the landlord's obligation to let and keep premises in fit condition (see chapter 2 pp14–16).

The notion of a "nine-point standard" dates back to 1911,[9] but the new formulation is substantially different from that used up to 1990. In order to contribute to unfitness, disrepair must now be "serious", artificial lighting is to be considered in addition to natural lighting and, very significantly, heating is now a factor to be considered. Further changes have included the requirement that a sink be served by *hot* water,[10] that a WC be available for the occupants' exclusive use and that there must be a suitably located fixed bath or shower with both hot and cold water supply. The "internal arrangement" factor has been dropped. Although the Secretary of State has the power to amend the statutory definition by order, no changes are immediately proposed.[11]

In many cases, premises will be unfit by reference to more than one of the nine points; the section is so drafted that the dwelling must fail at least one of the specified requirements, rather than being close to failing several of the requirements. Thereafter it is the totality of defectiveness resulting from the specified factors which gives rise to unfitness.[12] It is worth noting that the cause of the unfitness need not arise from within the premises themselves, for example, premises may become unfit where the supply of water or natural light is obstructed externally.

The House of Lords has, in the past, determined that the application of the unfitness standard gives rise to questions of fact to be resolved in a quasi-judicial manner and that the test to be applied is that of the ordinary reasonable man.[13] Thus, when considering the application of unfitness legislation, advisers should ask, "would the reasonable man hold these premises to be not reasonably suitable for occupation, by reason of a defect or combination of defects covered by the nine listed factors?" – which is not necessarily a clear criterion to apply to premises in disrepair. Such difficulties of applying objectivity to the assessment of unfitness are largely relieved by the new phrase in s604 "in the opinion of the local authority", allowing it to make its own assessment, subject only to appeal.

Some assistance on the application of the unfitness standard is to be found in ministerial guidance, and judicial precedent.[14] The Standards of Fitness Sub-Committee of the Central Housing Advisory Committee's interpretation[15] of each of the nine factors in the earlier version of s604 received ministerial approval, and was recommended to local authorities in an Appendix to a 1967 Circular.[16] This has, in turn, been replaced by very detailed guidance on the interpretation of the new s604, aimed at improving uniformity in its application (DoE Circular 6/90 Annex A). The guidance is not mandatory and therefore not binding, but it is frequently used by EHOs as a guide. Accordingly, advisers should have a copy of the circular when negotiating with local authority officers.

The new s604 definition was in preparation for some considerable time[17] and aspects of it are criticised as being unduly restrictive or representing little progress over the standards it replaced.[18]

The courts have also considered the nine factors now found in s604. In *Morgan v Liverpool Corporation*,[19] which would now have relevance to the interpretation of "serious disrepair", Atkin LJ said that:

> ". . . if the state of repair of a house is such that by ordinary user damage may naturally be caused to the occupier, either in respect of personal injury to life or limb or injury to health, then the house is not in all respects fit for human habitation".

This test was approved expressly by the House of Lords in *Summers v Salford Corporation*,[20] a case in which consideration was given to another of the nine factors, "ventilation". Their Lordships approved a statement by Luxmore LJ that:

> "The usual method of providing ventilation for a room in a dwelling is by a window or windows, which is or are constructed so as to open and shut without danger to the person opening or shutting it or them. If a room, especially a bedroom, has only one window and that window cannot be opened or shut without danger to the person seeking to perform that operation, that room may in my opinion be said not to be fit for human habitation."

The court held that presence in one room of defects covered by s604 may be sufficient to render the whole of the dwelling unfit. *Summers* also demonstrates that in order to qualify as "unfit", premises need not be dirty, dilapidated and generally in appalling disrepair – unfitness was found on the basis of a single broken sashcord. The fact that the defects could quickly, easily and cheaply be remedied is irrelevant to the question of whether they render the premises unfit:

> "It must not be measured by the magnitude of the repairs required. A burst or leaking pipe, a displaced slate or tile, a stopped drain, a rotten stairtread, may each of them make a house unfit to live in, though each of them may quickly and easily be repaired."[21]

The question of whether or not premises are unfit is initially determined by the local authority. If it holds premises to be statutorily unfit as a result of defects other than those in s604, the finding would be quashed.[22] The authority will, however, be justified in having regard to factors which are present in *addition* to the statutorily relevant defects.[23] Once the local authority is satisfied that premises are unfit, it is under a mandatory duty to use its powers in the HA 1985 Pt VI to require remedial action. Advisers should be alert to the possibility of delays arising from the authority giving "informal" warnings or notices to the owner, and should ensure that the authority uses its statutory powers at the earliest opportunity.

(c) Selecting the appropriate action

Once the local authority has accepted that a property is unfit, it is bound by the statutory code to tackle that unfitness. Under the pre-1990 arrangements this was simply a question of either serving notices for the repair of the premises or preventing their further occupation. A test of whether the work could be carried out at reasonable expense[24] determined which alternative was to be pursued. Not surprisingly a considerable body of caselaw[25] developed around this criterion of reasonable expense.[26]

With effect from 1 April 1990 the arrangements have completely changed. There is no longer an issue as to reasonable expense. The local authority faced with premises which are unfit may select from a range of remedial measures prescribed by s604A. These are:

— repair notice
— closing order
— demolition order
— area clearance.

If the repairs procedure seems most attractive, the authority has available a further option of including the building in a group repair scheme (s190A) as an alternative to serving mandatory repair notices.

In determining which route to pursue, the authority is required to have regard to a statutory code of guidance issued by the Secretary of State for the Environment. This allows the authority to take into account a far wider range of factors than hitherto. Overall plans for the area may warrant pursuit of the repairs option, even at great expense to the owner, where other local housing is in good condition. Authorities should take into account the wishes of the owners and occupiers of the property, any sense of local community and the degree and type of housing need in the area. The owner is no longer in a position to divert authorities from particular forms of action by offering what were known in the old regime as statutory "undertakings". It is for the authority itself to select the "most satisfactory course of action" (see generally DoE Circular 6/90).

A landlord disappointed by the authority's selection will have a right of appeal and the possibility of persuading the court to prefer a different option (see below). The implications for the tenants and other occupiers arising from the choice made by the authority are considerable (see (h) below). While such tenants have no statutory right of appeal, they would have sufficient interest in such a decision to seek to challenge it by way of judicial review on the usual adminstrative law principles (eg failure to take into account some relevant consideration).[27]

(d) The repairs procedure (see Fig A)

If it decides that the most satisfactory course of action is the restoration of the property to a state of fitness, the local authority must[28] serve[29] a repair notice on the person having control of the premises – usually the owner or managing agent[30] (HA 1985 s189). If the property is a house occupied by more than one household, the notice may be served on the person managing the house instead of on the person having control (s189(1B)). If the property is a flat or a flat in multiple occupation and the reason for its unfitness is the defective condition of some other part of the building, the notice should be served on the person having control of that part (s189(1A)). The notice requires the execution of stated works considered by the authority sufficient to render the premises fit. The notice is not confined to specifying "repair work". It may also require work or improvement, eg the installation of a heating system or provision of a hot water supply (s189(2)(a)). The works are usually spelt out in a schedule to the notice and must be sufficiently detailed to enable the owner to see exactly what is required. (Advisers should identify the officer within the authority responsible for drafting these schedules, and stress the need for the widest possible range of improvement and remedial works.) The authority must supply copies of the notices to freeholders, mortgagees, leaseholders, and, most importantly, tenants (s189(3)). Advisers acting for licensees and

Fig A: The repair notice procedure

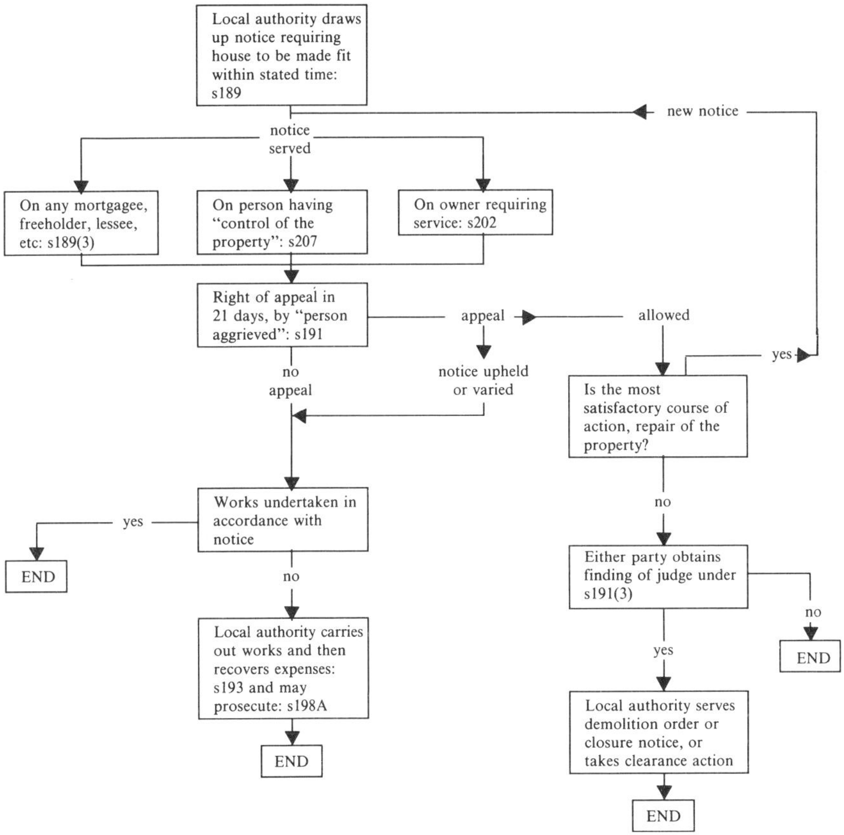

other occupiers should always request one, and if refused should check for any notices recorded in the land charges register or district land registry.[31]

The notice will specify, not only the works required, but also the date by which works must start and be completed.[32] The commencement date cannot be earlier than 28 days from the date of service of the notice (s189(2)(a)). This should give the landlord sufficient opportunity to engage contractors (and, where relevant, apply for a local authority grant). Alternatively, the landlord may invite the authority serving the notice to agree to undertake the work at the landlord's expense (s191A).

If the works are not carried out as required the local authority may undertake work in default (HA 1985 s193). This is, however, a discretionary power, rather than a mandatory duty.[33] It is exercisable where (a) work has not been started by the commencement date specified, (b) the work has not been completed by the specified completion date or (c) work is under way but "reasonable progress is not being made" towards compliance with the notice (s193(2) and (2A)). Of course advisers should ensure that authorities are given maximum possible impetus for undertaking works in default.

If the authority decides to exercise its default powers, it may enter the premises for these purposes, if it has given notice of its intention to do so, and any obstruction by the owner or their agents will be a criminal offence (s194). The cost of carrying out the necessary remedial works[34] can thereafter be recouped from the owner as a debt, or by collection from rent that would otherwise be paid by tenants or as a charge upon the property (Sch 10 paras 1, 2, 4 and 6A). Interest is also recoverable if the sum is not paid on demand.

Any person aggrieved[35] by service of a repair notice or a demand for recovery of expenses may appeal to the county court (s191). (If no appeal is entered, the notice becomes final and effective 21 days after service and may not thereafter be impugned in proceedings[36].) On an appeal, the appellant may challenge the decisions of the authority on unfitness or on the terms of the notice. New grounds of appeal allow the landlord to argue that either (a) a different owner of the property or building should more properly be served with the notice (s191A) or (b) a more satisfactory way of dealing with the unfitness would have been the making of a demolition or closing order (s191(1B)). In the former case, the landlord is obliged to join other owners in the proceedings (s191(3A)-(3C)) and in the latter case the court must have regard to the DoE code of guidance on dealing with unfit housing (s191(1B)). The judge has power to confirm, quash or vary the notice or demand challenged (s191(2)). The notice may be quashed even if in some respects it is agreeable to the owner.[37] On the appeal, the judge deals with all matters and questions with which the local authority itself could have dealt.[38] If the appeal is allowed (in whole or in part) because demolition or closure is a more satisfactory course of action than repair, the court may be invited to make a finding to that effect (s191(3)). For the authority, this finding has the advantage that it may then, with confidence, make a demolition or closing order. The local authority can no longer ask for a finding which authorises compulsory purchase (s192 has been repealed).

In the past, repair notices have proved virtually ineffective when served on recalcitrant landlords. They were often either simply ignored or, worse still (from the tenant's point of view), work was half-heartedly started and abandoned part way through. Now, however, the intentional failure to comply with such a notice is a criminal offence (s198A). "Failure to comply" can arise either from not starting work by the commencement date or not finishing it by the completion date. The landlord may be prosecuted irrespective of whether the local authority is carrying out, or intends to carry out, works in default. In addition to a conviction and fine (not exceeding level 4 on the standard scale), the landlord may be ordered to pay compensation to a tenant or other occupier affected by the offence (Powers of Criminal Courts Act 1973 s35).

(e) The closure/demolition procedure

Where the local authority is satisfied that premises would most reasonably be dealt with by being closed (either as a result of its own determination or that of the county court on an appeal), it must make a closing order (s264) for the house or house in multiple occupation (HMO). If one or more flats in a block are unfit, the closing notice may require closure of the whole or of parts of the block (s264(2)).

If the authority decides that the most satisfactory course of action is demolition, it must serve a demolition order (s265). Where the unfit properties are some or all of the flats in a block, the notice can require the demolition of the entire block (s265(2)). Tenants are not generally given a copy of the notice, but the owner or mortgagee of the property is served with notice (s268(1)). If the order relates to whole or part of a block of flats, the building owner *and* the flat owners must be served (s268(2)).

Under the pre-1990 regime, an authority considering making a closing or demolition order, was required to go through an elaborate procedure of consultation with the landlord and, in certain circumstances, an order could be avoided by an undertaking to carry out works. These statutory consultation requirements are now replaced by the DoE's code of guidance on dealing with unfit properties (s604A). Having declared a property "unfit", the authority may prefer closure or demolition to the other alternatives of repair or area clearance (see generally DoE Circular 6/90).

A demolition order requires the owner to demolish the premises after they have been vacated and clear the site, and gives rise to powers to demolish in default and recover expenses. A closing order prohibits the use of the premises for any purpose other than one approved by the local authority (s267(2)).

If the local authority considers that it could use the premises for temporary accommodation it may purchase the property instead of making a demolition or closing order (s300(1)). Notwithstanding that the premises are, a priori, unfit for human habitation and that it has earlier resolved that they are best dealt with by being closed or demolished, the authority is entitled to carry out patch repairs to the purchased property and let it to tenants,[39] who are necessarily deprived of the protection of the implied covenant of fitness (s302(a) and (c)).

Premises retained under s300(1) are notoriously used as "short life" accommodation or as "transit" lettings to homeless families, and advisers should guard against this outcome. Any attempt by the authority to retain such purchased property as a permanent part of the housing stock will be struck down by the courts.[40]

If the premises are not capable of providing temporary accommodation and are therefore not purchased, the authority must take further steps including service of notices, leading to either the demolition of the property or its closure.[41] Closure and demolition both give rise to rehousing and compensatory obligations on the part of the authority towards displaced tenants (see chapter 8 below). Furthermore, the authority may board up any premises which have become dangerous, pending demolition or closure.[42]

Closing and demolition orders may be challenged by a "person aggrieved" by appeal to the county court (s269). Tenants whose leases have less than three years to run have no right of appeal (s269(2)). It is a ground of appeal that service of the closing or demolition order was not the most satisfactory course of action (s269(2A)(a)). On the hearing of the appeal, the judge may confirm, quash or vary the notice challenged, but may not vary it in such a way as would frustrate the purposes of the legislation for example by postponing the date of demolition for several years.[43] If the appeal is allowed, the court may, on the application of either party, issue a finding that one of the alternative notices would be more appropriate (s269(3A)). This enables the local authority to serve such alternative notice with some assurance.

It should be noted that, although most tenants do not have a right of appeal, if the local authority decision is unreasonable under administrative law principles, tenants may challenge such a decision by way of judicial review.[44]

(f) Mobilising the local authority

> ". . . a majority of the authorities investigated maintained that it was the presence of a local voluntary housing advice centre or law centre which encouraged strictest compliance with statutory powers."[45]

Although authorities have substantial powers to eradicate unfit housing, as can be seen above, a frequent difficulty for advisers is mobilising an authority into taking action. Accordingly, advisers must be prepared to argue forcefully the need for action with the authority. Initially, this may take the form of letters and telephone calls to the Housing and Environmental Health Departments, and approaches to local councillors. If such pressure produces no response within a reasonable period, advisers should consider obtaining a magistrate's complaint. Under the HA 1985 s606(2), reproduced at Appendix 2, a justice of the peace for the area may complain to the local authority that certain premises are unfit. On receipt of such complaint, the authority is bound to:

(a) inspect the premises;
(b) obtain a report from the officers; and
(c) consider the question of "unfitness".

A similar complaint may be made by a parish or community council, with like effect (s606(2)(b)). See Appendix 7 for a draft complaint.

It is not procedurally difficult to arrange for such a complaint to be made. Advisers can draft all necessary documents themselves,[46] and need only satisfy a JP on the basis of either a personal inspection or written report, that certain premises are unfit.[47] Practice varies considerably in arrangements made by courts for dealing with these cases, but most justices' clerks will simply make an ad hoc arrangement for a magistrate to be available. The speediest method is to set up an inspection on an informal basis with a JP known to the adviser or tenant.

Complaints received by local authorities under s606 usually prompt an immediate inspection and officer's report, and find their way onto Housing Committee agendas.[48]

If a local authority is satisfied that premises are unfit but is dilatory in taking action, the remedy of judicial review and mandamus should be considered by advisers, since the HA 1985 code compels the authority to act.[49]

Tenants pressing for the repair of their homes (who will accordingly want to see the service of a mandatory s189 notice) should note that the authority has the alternative of including the building in a "group repair scheme" (s190A). Such schemes enable councils to work with owners to secure improvements to the external appearance of buildings. Advisers should guard against authorities "stalling" on the service of mandatory notices by saying that a group repair scheme is under consideration. It is expressly provided that a s189 notice can still be served to require the repairs (eg to the interior and rear of the property) which would not be covered by the group repair scheme.

In certain cases, complaint to the local ombudsman may be worthwhile. Failure to act when it is known that a property is unfit is maladministration, notwithstanding the resource implications for local authorities.[50]

(g) Tenants' rights to rehousing

Persons who are displaced as the result of a closing or demolition order are, generally, entitled to monetary compensation and to be rehoused.[51] For tenants' rights to compensation, see chapter 8.

Where a person is displaced from residential accommodation as a result of a demolition or closing order and suitable alternative accommodation is not available, the local authority is under a duty to provide accommodation (Land Compensation Act 1973 s39). However, the duty is for the local authority to "do its best", and it can offer temporary accommodation until permanent accommodation is available – and the permanent accommodation need not be offered on the same terms as those on which the previous accommodation was held.[52] Nevertheless, use of the HA procedures may prove attractive to a would-be council tenant not otherwise in a priority group for the allocation of council housing.

(h) Implications for tenants

Before taking any action in respect of individual unfit properties, advisers should be careful to clarify precisely the instructions given by the tenant/client. If the tenant wishes to have the premises put in *repair*, the adviser should press for use of the repair notice procedure (HA 1985 s189) and, if necessary, prosecution for non-compliance and works in default. If the process is upset by the owner establishing on appeal that the premises are more satisfactorily dealt with by closure or demolition, the adviser could ensure that the court makes a formal finding, and thereafter serves the appropriate notice in respect of the property (s191). Alternatively, the tenants of a landlord successful in a repair notice appeal may prefer to seek other means of redress (see chapters 4 and 5) rather than lose their homes under closure or demolition procedures.

If, on the other hand, the tenant wishes to be *rehoused* – usually into local authority accommodation – the approach will differ. The adviser will be pressing for a finding that the premises are most satisfactorily dealt with by closure, demolition or clearance. Thereafter, the making of a closing or demolition order will entitle the tenant to alternative housing and certain compensatory payments (see above). However, note that the accommodation need not necessarily be permanent housing of the type sought by the tenant.[53] Advisers should also be alert to the possibility of the authority acquiring the property for temporary accommodation and carrying out patch repairs (s300(1)).

Advisers should note that, although once served with a copy of the demolition or closing order the tenant is required to give up occupation (s270 – demolition orders, s277 – closing orders), that does not usually cause the tenancy to end. Special provision is made under s317 for either landlord or tenant to apply to the county court for an order terminating or varying the lease. This gives the court the opportunity, inter alia, to award compensation and damages if the tenancy should be terminated as a result of the local authority notice.[54] Statutory Rent Act tenants, however, do not enjoy the benefit of this procedure as the Rent Acts cannot prevent the recovery of possession under a demolition or closing order (HA 1988 ss270 and 276), other than by showing either that they have not received notice of the order or that it has not become operative.[55]

Whichever course is adopted, advisers should ensure that they are familiar with the way in which their own authority has delegated the exercise of Housing Act powers and duties, and at what level the principal decisions such as "unfitness" and most satisfactory course of action are determined. In at least one London borough, the powers to make these decisions and serve notices have been delegated to individual EHOs.[56]

Exercise of HA powers does not interfere with the tenant's rights to take alternative action as a result of default by landlords (s203(3)). But the tenant has no right to withhold rent[57] unless recouping the cost of repairs or exercising a set-off.[58] Application may be made to reduce any current registered rent, but the rent officer need not register a nil or nominal rent in respect of unfit property[59] although a lower registered rent may be anticipated.[60]

(i) Council tenants

The position of private sector and housing association tenants is as described above. Similarly, if a council tenant rents from one authority but lives within the area of another, there is no bar to the exercise of HA powers by the latter against the landlord authority.

However, where the council tenant's landlord is the local authority itself, it has been held that as a local authority cannot properly serve HA notices upon itself, it cannot apply the HA 1985 Pt VI in respect of its own properties.[61] Nevertheless, the authority is obliged to consider complaints of unfitness from both tenants and magistrates (see above p101). In the latter case an inspection and report must be made (s606(2)).

Modern government guidance[62] has encouraged local authorities to make local arrangements to deal with unfit council housing. It urges them to introduce and publish arrangements whereby, if a council tenant seeks the help of an EHO about the condition of a property which, in the EHO's opinion is such that, if it were private property, action under the HA would be necessary, the EHO will give notice to the Director of Housing who should ensure that necessary works are carried out within a reasonable period. Advisers should accordingly obtain copies of the relevant authorities' published arrangements and have regard to the guidance issued to EHOs as to implementation.[63]

Where council property is transferred to a housing action trust (HA

1988 Pt III), the Secretary of State may, by order, give the trust powers to deal with unfit property in substitution for, or concurrent with, those of the authority (HA 1988 s65). If no such order is made, the property conveyed to the trust is vulnerable to the unfitness procedures of local authorities in just the same way as property owned by private landlords.

3 Housing in need of substantial repair

Not all disrepair will be sufficiently serious to make a property statutorily unfit. Yet tenants may experience severe hardship as a result of that disrepair. Since 1969[64] local authorities have had the power to act in such circumstances. The HA 1985 s190(1)(a) provides that where a local authority is satisfied that:

> ". . . a dwelling-house or house in multiple occupation is in such a state of disrepair that although it is not unfit for human habitation, substantial repairs are required to bring it up to a reasonable standard . . .",

it may serve a notice on the person having control of the house (usually the landlord/owner rather than the tenant[65]) requiring the performance of specified remedial works. If the building is an HMO, notice can be served on the manager (s190(1C)). Copies of the notice must be served on any freeholder, mortgagee and, most importantly, tenants (s190(3)), although there is no requirement to serve copies on other occupiers. Although this constitutes a compulsory repair notice, the authority is not bound to inform the owner in advance of the intention to serve. The only express limitations on what may be included in the notice are that it cannot compel works of internal decorative repairs (s190(2)). The prohibition of internal decorative repair should cause no difficulty for the tenant since the landlord's performance of the other works of repair specified in the notice will in any event carry with it an obligation to make good any decoration disturbed or destroyed.[66] The authority is required to draft the notice in sufficient detail for the owner to see exactly what remedial works are required.[67]

If the tenant occupies a flat in a block, and it is disrepair in the other parts of the building which is causing problems, the authority may serve the s190 notice on the person having control of that part of the building concerned (s190(1A)). Thus, in securing the comprehensive repair of a building containing flats, the council will serve notices on leaseholders of the individual flats as well as on the freeholder (in respect of the common parts).[68]

For s190 to apply, the property concerned must either be situated in a renewal area (see p112) or have an "occupying tenant" (s190(1B)). An "occupying tenant" is either a contractual or statutory tenant or a licensee with a restricted contract or a protected or assured agricultural occupier (s207).

If the owner subsequently appeals, the county court judge, in considering whether to uphold the appeal, may take into account all relevant matters including the cost of the work, the value of the property, the circumstances of the owner etc.[69] It is also a ground of appeal that some other individual is more properly served than the appellant (s191(1A)). If such appeal is allowed, the court may vary the notice so as to require the works to be carried out by some other owner of the property (s191(3A)).

If the owner fails to commence the work or complete it by the commencement or completion dates specified in the notice, or starts work but does not make reasonable progress, the authority may enter the premises and carry out the works in default, with the same rights as to recovery of expenses as in relation to s189 repair notices. The owner retains a right of appeal under s191. The ministerial guidance given to authorities on the application of these powers is somewhat limited,[70] although the statute requires the authority to have regard to the "age, character and locality" of the property. The courts have supported the use by local authorities of the s190 provision to stop bad housing from slipping into unfitness.[71] In particular, the Court of Appeal has allowed county court judges, in dealing with appeals against s190 notices, to have regard to the policy considerations behind the legislation and weigh them against the burdens falling upon landlords who allow their properties to fall into substantial disrepair.[72]

Advisers should encourage their local authority into positive use of s190 and in particular to prosecute (see below) and carry out works in default. Landlords can no longer frustrate or avoid enforcement action by selling-on properties subject to notice, as notices must be registered as local land charges when they become operative (s190(5)). A broad illustration of the relationship between s189 and s190 is given in Fig B.

Intentional failure to comply with a s190 notice constitutes a summary criminal offence. Authorities should be encouraged to prosecute defaulting landlords and, in appropriate cases, tenants should apply for criminal compensation orders against landlords – who will also be convicted and fined (s198A).

4 Fit houses in disrepair

Local authorities have further powers to take action in respect of premises which are neither unfit for human habitation nor in severe disrepair. The HA 1985 s190(1)(b) provides that where a local authority is satisfied that:

> ". . . a dwelling-house or house in multiple occupation is in such state of disrepair that, although it is not unfit for human habitation, the condition is such as to interfere

> materially with the personal comfort of occupying tenants or in the case of a house in multiple occupation, the persons occupying it (whether as tenants or licensees). . .",

it may serve a notice on the owner requiring the execution of specified remedial works. If the tenant occupies a flat and it is part of the building outside the flat which is interfering with the personal comfort of the tenant, notice may be served on the owner of those (common) parts (s190(1A)(b)).

Exercise of this power is *discretionary* and the authority may act either on its own initiative or, for example, in response to a complaint from a tenant occupying the whole or part of the property. The existence of these alternatives means that it is no longer necessary for the authority to identify the tenant as complainant.[73] For these purposes, "tenant" includes statutory tenants and those with restricted contracts (s207).

The provision represents a half-hearted attempt to replace the mandatory duty formerly imposed on local authorities to deal with this form of disrepair under public health legislation – a duty undermined by the courts in 1976.[74]

Experience indicates that the s190 provision is under-employed as a weapon to tackle bad housing, even though it can be used to compel landlords to undertake repairs. In default, the authority has the same power to enter the property, do the work, recover its expenses and/or prosecute the landlord as it does for other repair notices (see above). The Act does not require the authority to have regard to the age, character and locality of the dwelling. However, the discomfort must arise from the condition of the property itself and external factors are probably thereby excluded unless they arise from common parts.

Almost all forms of disrepair will cause some interference with the personal comfort of occupiers, and if this discomfort is sufficiently "material" advisers should encourage authorities to use their powers under this provision.

5 "Houses"

Throughout Pt VI of the HA 1985, the term "house" has been replaced by the term "dwelling-house" or "premises" to describe the type of property subject to the unfitness and repairs procedure. For these purposes, "dwelling-house" is defined to include "any yard, garden, outhouse and appurtenances belonging to it or usually enjoyed with it".[75] Thus, if a backyard is in such a state of disrepair as to constitute a danger to the tenant, the property as a whole may be deemed unfit and subject to the Housing Act code. Furthermore, for the purposes of Pts VI and IX, the statutory powers extend to flats which are dwelling-houses (s207) and, as seen above, notices may be served in respect of buildings containing flats. The post-1990 scheme also includes both HMOs and flats in multiple occupation (s345). The revision of these technical references was made necessary by continued difficulty with the use of the word "house" in the previous statute and caselaw.[76] However, because of the improved fitness standard, the possibility of using HA 1988 notices on temporary[77] and movable structures has been withdrawn (s205 has been repealed).

Fig B: Pt VI Housing Act 1985

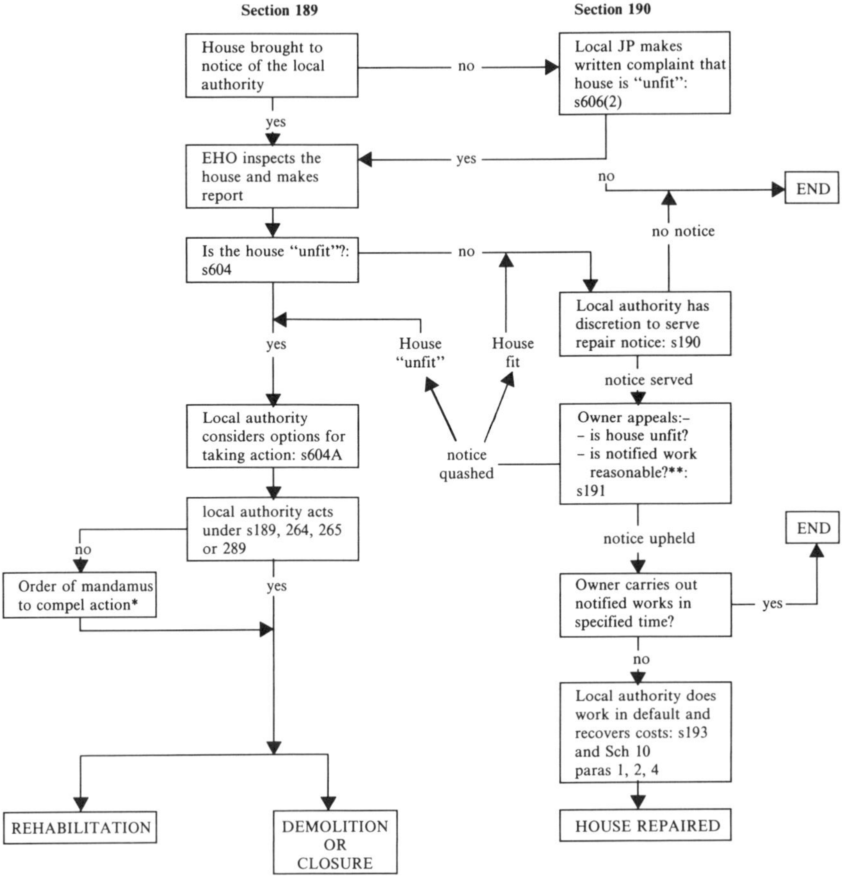

* *R v Kerrier DC, ex parte Guppys (Bridport)* (1976) 32 P&CR 411

** *Hillbank Properties v Hackney LBC* [1978] 3 WLR 260

6 Conclusion

The procedures for dealing with statutorily unfit properties constitute a double-edged sword. They may just as easily leave an owner with vacant possession or a cleared site, as provide the tenant with a repaired home. Even those tenants who would qualify for rehousing by the local authority may languish in unfit property for substantial periods awaiting an offer of accommodation, notwithstanding the statutory priorities.[78] It is for these reasons that advisers should be pressing authorities to use powers under s190 to tackle bad housing before it sinks into unfitness. It is worth remembering that the courts are not necessarily anxious to prevent slum landlords from making a profit out of their own failure to carry out repairing obligations.[79]

1 *English Housing Condition Survey 1986* (1988 HMSO).
2 "Dwelling unfitness in Northern Ireland" (1982) 31 *English Housing Review* 82.
3 The standard reference work, *Encyclopedia of Housing Law* ed A Arden (Sweet & Maxwell), now runs to four substantial volumes.
4 *Hillbank Properties v LB Hackney* (1982) 3 HLR 73 at 82.
5 HA 1985 s605 as substituted by Local Government and Housing Act 1989 Sch 9 para 85.
6 As substituted by Local Government and Housing Act 1989 Sch 9 para 83.
7 Defined by HA 1985 s623.
8 *Birchall v Wirral UDC* (1953) 117 JP 384.
9 Ministry of Health "Manual of unfit houses and unhealthy areas" Vol 1, p10, 1919, and see (1977) September *LAG Bulletin* 206.
10 *Daly v Elstree RDC* [1948] 2 All ER 13 is thereby overturned.
11 HA 1985 s604(5).
12 *Wyse (EA) v Sec State for Environment and Borough of Newcastle-under-Lyme* [1984] JPL 256.
13 *Hall v Manchester Corp* (1915) 84 LJ Ch 732.
14 See also Garner "Unfit for human habitation" (1954) JPL 833 and (1958) JPL 699.
15 The Dennington Report "Our old homes: a call for action" Cmnd 3602.
16 MoHLG Circ 69/67 (see also Circ 68/69 Appendix para 25).
17 Cmnd Paper 9513 paras 61–65 and Annex II.
18 See Ormandy 1985 *Housing Aid* 33 p11 and Parkinson "Still not a fit standard" (1985) 34 *Housing Review* 190.
19 [1927] 2 KB 131.
20 [1943] AC 283.
21 Per Lord Atkin.
22 *Estate & Trust Co v Singapore Improvement Trust* [1937] 3 All ER 324, PC.
23 *Steele v Minister of Housing and Local Government and West Ham County BC* (1956) 168 EG 37, CA.
24 See further D Morgan "Unfit housing: the issue of reasonable cost" (1979) Conv 414; Hadden "Compulsory repairs and improvements" SSRC 1978 App F; and Arden "Reasonable expense under the Housing Acts" (1982) 3 HLR (introduction).
25 Starting with *Cohen v West Ham Corp* [1933] Ch 814 and *Bacon v Grimsby Corp* [1950] 1 KB 272, and cases up to and including *Cole v Swansea CC* (1988) 21 HLR 468, CA.
26 The reported cases are usefully gathered in Housing Law Reports, Vol 3.
27 *R v LB Ealing ex p Richardson* (1982) 4 HLR 125, CA; *R v Leominster DC ex p Legg*

(1985) unreported, CA, noted at (1986) 9 *IEHO Housing Law Newsletter* 2; *R v Maldon DC ex p Fisher* (1986) 18 HLR 197, QBD; and *R v Forest of Dean DC ex p Trigg* (1989) 12 CL 254, (1989) *Times* 9 November, QBD.

28 *R v Kerrier DC ex p Guppys (Bridport) Ltd* (1976) 32 P&CR 411, CA.

29 As to service of HA notices see (1978) July *LAG Bulletin* 164.

30 See, as to "person in control", HA 1985 s207 and *Pollway Nominees Ltd v LB Croydon* (1986) 18 HLR 443, HL.

31 HA 1985 s189(5).

32 As to what is reasonable in terms of time, see *Ryall v Cubitt Heath* [1922] 1 KB 275.

33 *Elliott v Brighton BC* (1981) 79 LGR 506.

34 As to what is "necessary" see *Adams v Tuer* (1923) 22 LGR 88; and *Hodgson v Sunderland Corp* (1937) LJNCCR 187.

35 This may include the tenant.

36 HA 1985 s189(4); but see *Re Falmouth Clearance Order* [1937] 3 All ER 308; *Graddage v Haringey* LBC [1975] 1 All ER 224; and *Pollway Nominees Ltd v LB Croydon* n30.

37 *Cochrane v Chanctonbury RDC* [1950] 2 All ER 1134.

38 *Fletcher v Ilkeston Corp* (1931) 96 JPLGR 7.

39 Who will not usually be secure: HA 1985 Sch 1 para 3.

40 *Victoria Square Property Co v LB Southwark* [1978] 2 All ER 281; and see *R v Birmingham CDC ex p Sale* (1983) 9 HLR 33.

41 *R v Epsom and Ewell Corp ex p RB Property Investments (Eastern)* [1964] 2 All ER 832.

42 Local Government (Miscellaneous Provisions) Act 1976 s8.

43 *Pocklington v Melksham UDC* [1964] 2 All ER 862.

44 *R v LB Ealing ex p Richardson* n27.

45 Hawke and Taylor "Compulsory repair of individual physically substandard housing" (1984) JSWL 129 at 132.

46 See Appendix 7 and "Unfitness" Shelter Practice Note No 2 for standard forms.

47 See case discussed at (1973) June *LAG Bulletin* 117.

48 See "Action Notes on s157" in 48 *Community Action* 26-28; and for the use of s606 (formerly HA 1957 s157) in Manchester see 53 *Community Action* 4, and in Newham see *Municipal Engineering* 11 February 1977, and March 1977 *Roof*.

49 *R v Kerrier DC ex p Guppys (Bridport) Ltd* n28.

50 Investigation No 171/C/84.

51 Land Compensation Act 1973 ss29-39.

52 *R v Bristol Corp ex p Hendy* [1974] 1 All ER 1047, CA.

53 Ibid.

54 HA 1985 s317(2) and *Malik v Politi* [1964] CLY 1703.

55 *Beaney v Branchett* (1987) 19 HLR 471, CA.

56 Under Local Government Act 1972 s101.

57 *Stevenson (Westminster) v Mock* [1954] JPL 275.

58 See chapter 4 p52.

59 *Williams v Khan* (1981) 258 EG 554, CA.

60 See D Ormandy "Conditions and rent" (1978) April *LAG Bulletin* 91.

61 *R v Cardiff CC ex p Cross* (1983) 6 HLR 1, CA.

62 DoE Circ 21/84 para 117; WO Circ 42/84.

63 See Ormandy *Housing Aid* 30 p6 and 32 p18.

64 HA 1969 s72.

65 S207 and see *White v LB Barnet* (1989) 21 HLR 346, CA.

66 *McGreal v Wake* (1984) 13 HLR 107, CA; and *Bradley v Chorley BC* (1985) 17 HLR 305, CA.

67 *Church of Our Lady of Hal v LB Camden* (1980) 255 EG 991, CA.

68 DoE Circ 1/89 para 9.

69 S191 and *Hillbank Properties v LB Hackney* n4; and see H Wilkinson "Capable of being rendered fit" 1985 NLJ 831.

70 DoE Circ 64/69 para 17.
71 N69.
72 *Kenny v Kingston upon Thames LBC* (1985) 274 EG 395, (1985) 17 HLR 344.
73 DoE Circ 1/89 para 11.
74 See chapter 5 p72.
75 HA 1985 s207 and see *R v Camden LBC ex p Rowton (Camden Town)* [1984] LGR 614.
76 In *Pollway Nominees Ltd v LB Croydon* n30, it was accepted, for the purposes of the appeal, that s189 might be applied to a "house" consisting of a purpose-built block of flats.
77 See the "henhouse" declared unfit by Caradon DC *Times* 15 October 1980.
78 HA 1985 s22.
79 *Buswell v Goodwin* [1971] 1 WLR 92.

Chapter Seven

Housing Conditions

Introduction

This chapter notes other housing conditions related to disrepair: its purpose is to draw readers' attention to problems which are likely to be encountered when advising tenants. There is no attempt here to go into detail; the intention is solely to give pointers to more appropriate sources where specialised and comprehensive information can be obtained.

1 Area action

In addition to dealing with unsatisfactory individual houses and flats through the Housing Act (chapter 6) and Environmental Protection Act (chapter 5), local authorities may resolve to tackle *areas* of unsatisfactory housing. Where the most appropriate action is the clearance of the unsatisfactory housing, the authority may declare a clearance area. On the other hand, if housing can be renovated and rehabilitated, the appropriate action is declaration of a renewal area. Under the arrangements applicable before April 1990, rehabilitation on an area basis was achieved by the declaration of housing action areas and general improvement areas. Housing action areas declared on or before 31 March 1987 will continue until their natural expiry; those declared after that date will terminate on or before 1 April 1991. All general improvement areas must expire on or before 1 April 1991. No housing action areas or general improvement areas can be declared after 31 March 1990. Former housing action areas or general improvement areas can be redeclared as renewal areas if they meet the conditions for such declaration (see below).

(a) Clearance areas (HA 1985 ss289-306)
Local authorities have extensive powers to deal with areas of unfit housing. Where there is an area of mainly unfit housing, declaration by the authority of a clearance area leads to a process of the acquisition by compulsory purchase of the properties in that area and their subsequent demolition.

The cleared site is then available to the authority for its own purposes – usually the provision of new housing. This form of area action may be extensive and lead to the displacement of local communities. It has therefore, until recently, been seen as a last resort with increased emphasis being placed on improvement and rehabilitation of individual properties. However, in 1990, central government resolved that it was no longer appropriate to give preference to renovation (DoE Circ 6/90). Accordingly, it can be expected that area clearance programmes will be more common than in the past. With effect from 1 April 1990, new processes are introduced to:

- ensure that owners and occupiers are informed at an early stage (s289(2A) and (2B));
- require the authority to take account of a wide range of factors before declaring a clearance area (s604A and the code of guidance issued thereunder); and
- increase compensation paid to displaced owners (Pt XVII as extensively amended).

There has been no improvement in the rights of displaced tenants (see chapter 8), indeed, "well-maintained" payments, formerly available to some displaced tenants have been abolished (Schs 23 and 24 have been repealed).

(b) Renewal areas

From April 1990, local authorities have new powers to take area action in respect of unsatisfactory housing through the declaration of renewal areas. Areas which might benefit from such treatment are identified from the annual review of housing conditions in the district which the council must undertake (HA 1985 s605). In selecting areas for declaration, the authority must have regard to directions and guidance issued by the Secretary of State (DoE Circ 6/90). Declaration requires either that conditions specified in the circular are met, or that the Secretary of State gives individual consent. Renewal areas will usually comprise between 500 and 3,000 dwellings, at least 75 per cent of which are privately owned or privately rented and 75 per cent of which are in serious disrepair or are unfit. A programme of public consultation is required prior to declaration. Once declared, the renewal area will usually last for 10 years. Declaration vests the local authority with considerable additional powers over housing in the area (including the right compulsorily to acquire and repair property), and may attract additional central government and privately funded financial help to the area.

References

Arden and Partington *Housing Law* (Sweet & Maxwell), "Clearance areas".

Dawn Oliver "Clearance areas" (1975) December *LAG Bulletin* 314; (1976) January 12; February 37.
Social Welfare Law (ed Pollard, Longman) Section C chapter 3, "Area action: Pt III - Clearance areas".
DoE Circular "Area renewal, unfitness, slum clearance and enforcement action" 6/90, March 1990.

2 Asbestos

Asbestos, and building materials containing asbestos, have been used in the construction and modernisation of housing for more than a generation. Asbestos and its derivatives may be found, for example, in insulation boards used for panels or in the form of sprayed-on insulation coverings as well as in some older types of textured paint. It was heavily used in system-built blocks of flats where industrialised building techniques were employed and has been extensively applied in pipe-lining.

It is now widely recognised that asbestos fibres released in air may prove prejudicial to human health. Tenants with homes containing asbestos or suspected asbestos will be best advised initially to contact their local EHO.

According to the circumstances it may be possible to take such action as will cause the removal of the asbestos by the landlord. (Technical support and assistance may be available from either Services to Community Action and Trades Unions (SCAT) or the London Hazards Centre - addresses on p160.) Asbestos fibres loose in air as a result of disrepair are probably prejudicial to health and accordingly action may be taken either under the Environmental Protection Act (chapter 5) or directly under other repairing obligations (chapters 2 and 3).

References

Fighting asbestos at home and work Labour Research Department.
R Widdison "Asbestos in the home" (1982) October *LAG Bulletin* 114.
Asbestos materials in buildings Department of Environment HMSO.
Dalton and Summers "Asbestos: killer dust" Jan/Feb 1981 *Roof* 10.
"Danger asbestos" 46 and 47 *Community Action*.
Asbestos on housing estates Hackney Tenants' Federation.
Asbestos in dwellings and buildings LB of Hackney, Environmental Health Division.
Asbestos and you Health and Safety Executive.
Asbestos in housing Department of Environment and COI (1985).
Asbestos: Part 1 Policy and practice in local authorities AMA (1985).
Asbestos in the community GMBATU.
Asbestos in the home Asbestos Information Centre.
Raising the dust SCAT.

Church v Ministry of Defence (1984) NLJ 623.
C Hughes "£2 billion needed to make asbestos safe" *Times* 10 September 1985.
"Fighting the invisible enemy" May/June 1984 *Roof* 20.

3 Condensation

Approximately 2 million homes in England, Scotland and Wales are officially classified as "seriously damp". Of those some two-thirds are damp by reason of severe condensation. The presence of acute condensation dampness brings with it conditions of mould growth, excessive humidity and, often, insect infestation. The grave effects of these conditions on the health and well-being of tenants have now been extensively documented.

In very basic terms, condensation dampness arises when a dwelling is incapable of dealing with normal levels of water vapour due to: lack of insulation, lack of ventilation, inadequate heat input, or a combination of such factors. Its presence is observed as condensed water on cooled surfaces, mould spores, damp wall coverings and plaster, infestation by house mites and destruction of soft furnishings in severe cases.

For some time tenants and their advisers have been using legal remedies amongst others to seek redress in such circumstances. The following short summary deals with various legal remedies and the condensation dampness problem.

(a) LTA 1985 s11 or DPA 1972 s4

The more traditional contractual and common law remedies against landlords (see chapters 2 and 3) are difficult to apply in condensation cases due to the need to show specific disrepair to the structure or fabric of a building rather than a design problem or planning defect. County court actions using s11 or s4 (sometimes in conjunction) produced varying results in the 1980s.[1] The Court of Appeal has, however, recently and authoritatively settled that s11 cannot provide a remedy for a tenant suffering the effects of condensation dampness unless there is actual disrepair to the structure or exterior of the dwelling.[2] Where such disrepair can be shown (for example because the condensation has corrupted woodwork or caused plaster to crumble) it will become actionable.[3]

Because s4 in turn springs from an obligation to repair or maintain the property, it too is of limited usefulness in the absence of actual damage to the structure or "fabric" of the property.[4] If work to rectify condensation fails to eradicate it, a possible action may lie for breach of DPA 1972 s1 in relation to that work (see p42). If the dwelling was negligently designed or constructed so as to generate condensation, an action may lie in negligence against the landlord or designer or builder (see chapter 3 pp35-37).

(b) EPA s82 (formerly PHA 1936 s99)

In recent years public health and environmental protection legislation has increasingly been recognised as the more satisfactory means of securing redress, since acute condensation dampness invariably gives rise to conditions which are "prejudicial to health" and thus a statutory nuisance (see chapter 5). The period between 1975 and 1980 saw extensive use of PHA 1936 s99 (and now EPA s82) proceedings in condensation cases in the magistrates' courts.[5] Indeed, by 1980/81 it had become well recognised that dampness was prejudicial to health and that condensation dampness itself was capable of potential or actual injury to health.[6]

However, in order to establish a succesful prosecution the tenant must be able to show that (unless the problem arises from structural defects) the conditions are the responsibility of the landlord. Thus in *Dover DC v Farrar*[7] a conviction was quashed on appeal where the local authority landlord successfully established that the dwellings concerned had been constructed by it in accordance with prevailing standards and that with sufficient use of the supplied heating system, the provision made for ventilation and insulation was adequate to avoid condensation. The fact that fuel price increases subsequent to construction meant that the tenants were unable to use the heating system was held not to be the responsibility of the landlord authority.

Regrettably, the *Dover* case has been used by local authorities and other landlords to persuade tenants, their advisers and magistrates that s82 proceedings could not successfully be founded on condensation dampness. In fact the contrary is the case. The *Dover* decision is clear authority for the proposition that landlords can be prosecuted in relation to condensation dampness. Later cases have shown that with the careful use of specialist written evidence and expert witnesses (especially independent EHOs) it is possible to prove in the majority of condensation cases that the dampness does arise from the landlord's failure to get the condensation equation (heat/moisture/ventilation/insulation) right.[8]

In *Tower Hamlets LBC v GLC*[9] the Divisional Court dismissed an appeal against a conviction in relation to condensation dampness. The tenants and prosecuting authority claimed that the dwellings were insufficiently ventilated and insulated and that the inability of the flats to cope with normal moisture led to condensation for which the landlord was responsible. Considering the *Dover* case, Griffiths LJ said he did not read it as authority for the proposition that tenants should be required to use abnormal quantities of fuel to avert condensation. The Court held that "a landlord is required to apply his mind to the necessity of ventilation and, if need be, to insulation and heating. The landlord must provide a combination of these factors to make a house habitable for the tenant."

Applying these authorities, the Divisional Court in *Birmingham DC v Kelly and Others*[10] was able to uphold convictions even though the landlord was not in breach of any contractual or other obligation to repair. Liability for the condensation dampness was established from the evidence that there was some default by the council in relation to the design of the premises which caused the condensation difficulties and thus the mould.

(c) Ombudsmen

The local ombudsmen have regularly accepted that failures to investigate properly or to resolve complaints of condensation dampness amount to maladministration. Their reports frequently contain not only strong recommendations for compensatory payments but also useful guidance on the proper approach to be adopted by councils in condensation cases. See, for example, the report on Investigation 746/1/84 noted at (1986) March *Legal Action* 33.

The authorities on liability for condensation dampness are extensively reviewed by David Watkinson at (1985) November *Legal Action* 153 and (1986) April *Legal Action* 49. Related developments (in particular decisions of the ombudsmen) are reported regularly in *Legal Action* in a quarterly series "Recent developments in housing law" (September, December, March and June, each year from September 1985).

1 Contrast *Griffiths v Swansea CC* (1984) unreported, noted at March/April 1984 *Roof* 18; *Mitchell v Brent LBC* (1984) unreported, noted at (1984) May *Legal Action* 53; and *Steel v Newham LBC* (1985) unreported, noted at 34 *Housing Aid* 11, (1985) December *Legal Action* 171, and (1986) April *Legal Action* 49.
2 *Quick v Taff Ely BC* [1985] 3 All ER 321.
3 *Abdullah and Ors v South Tyneside BC* (1987) September *Legal Action* 12.
4 *McNerney v Lambeth LBC* (1988) 21 HLR 188, CA.
5 *Portsmouth v Treleavan* (1975) unreported, noted at January 1976 *Roof* 21; *Fitzpatrick v Dawnray* (1976) unreported, noted at May 1976 *Roof* 92; *Piper v GLC* (1977) unreported, noted at July 1977 *Roof* 122 and the cases mentioned above at chapter 5 p83.
6 *Patel v Mehtab* (1982) 5 HLR 78; *Dover DC v Farrar* (1982) 2 HLR 32 and now DoE Circular 6/90 annex A5.
7 N6.
8 See *Lawton v East Devon DC* (1982) unreported, noted at July/August 1982 *Roof* 28; and *McGourlick v Renfew DC* (1982) unreported, noted at 1982 *Scolag* 182 and 1986 *Scolag* 83 (Lord McCluskey).
9 (1983) 15 HLR 54, QBD, applied in *Law v Hillingdon LBC* (1989) December *Legal Action* 16.
10 (1985) 17 HLR 572, QBD.

References
D Ormandy "Condensation" (1982) February *LAG Bulletin* 16.

D Ormandy "Condensation continued" 28 *Housing Aid* 17-18.
D Ormandy "Weapons for wetness" July/August 1984 *Roof* 18.
Southwark Law Project *Management of condensation.*
J McQuillan and N Finnis "Ways of seeing dampness" May 1979 *Roof* 85.
N Martyn "Condensation dampness: the legal remedies after *Quick v Taff Ely BC*" (1985) NLJ 1202.
Tackling condensation, mould and insulation Papers presented at HCT conference 27 April 1983.
D Watkinson "Legal remedies for condensation damp in the home" (1985) November *Legal Action* 153 and (1986) April *Legal Action* 49.
Condensation in dwellings Part 1 Design guide MoPB&W, HMSO 1970.
Condensation in dwellings Part 2 Remedial measures DoE, HMSO 1971.
Condensation BRE Digest 110, 1972 edition.
The control of condensation BS 5250 HMSO 1975.
Condensation and mould growth Domestic Energy Note 4 DoE 1979.
"Dealing with condensation and mould growth" Winter 1984 *BRE News* 61.
Background notes on condensation IEHO December 1983.
Mould fungal spores – their effects on health and the control, prevention and treatment of mould growth in dwellings IEHO 1985.
Remedies for condensation and mould in traditional housing BRE (video, tape or slides).

4 Dampness

This increasingly common form of housing disrepair now affects millions of tenants. It may take the form of penetrating dampness, construction damp, rising damp or condensation (see above).

As has been shown, legal remedies for tenants suffering the effects of dampness as a result of disrepair are available both under contractual and common law rights (chapters 2 and 3) and through enforcement of statutory obligations under the Environmental Protection and Housing Acts (see chapters 5 and 6).

Those assisting tenants should consider liaison with the National Anti Dampness Campaign (c/o SCAT, address on p160). The parliamentary review of the dampness problem by the Scottish Grand Committee contains much useful information (see below).

References

Platt et al "Damp housing, mould growth and symptomatic health state" (1989) 298 BMJ 1673.

Understanding damp Tenants' Participation and Advisory Service, 1988.
Strachen "Damp housing and childhood asthma: validation of reporting of symptoms (1988) 297 BMJ 1223.
Environmental Health Standards in Housing (Sweet & Maxwell 1988) appendix 3 "Characteristics and sources of dampness".
Dampness in housing Report of the Scottish Grand Committee House of Commons paper 206i and 206ii 1983/4.
Oxley and Gabri *Dampness in buildings* (Butterworths).
Dampness North Lewisham Law Centre.
Campaigning against dampness SCAT.
Anti-dampness charter SCAT.
Dampness: one week's complaints in five local authority areas BRE, HMSO 1982.
Dampness: a tenant's guide to rehousing, rent reduction and compensation Glasgow's Anti Dampness Campaign.

5 Dangerous buildings

Not infrequently a property will be in such poor repair as to represent a danger not only to those within it but also to people using adjacent streets. Once notified of such a situation a local authority may either take urgent remedial action itself or may follow a procedure requiring the owner to remedy the dangerous condition or demolish the building (Building Act 1984 ss77-83).

No express provision is made for the removal or compensation of any tenant although rehousing may, according to the circumstances, be achieved under the HA 1985 Pt III. Tenants displaced in such circumstances would have a remedy against the landlord arising from the breach of repairing obligation which led to the dangerous condition of the property.

References

Arden and Partington *Housing Law* (Sweet & Maxwell) "Dangerous buildings".
Social Welfare Law (ed Pollard, Longman) Section C chapter 6 "Dangerous buildings" paras 6741-6750.

6 Dilapidated buildings

A property in very serious disrepair may fall within the statutory definition of "dilapidated" ie one which by reason of its ruinous or dilapidated condition is seriously detrimental to the amenities of the neighbourhood (Building Act 1984 s79).

When notified of a property in such condition the local authority for the area may require the owner either to repair/restore the property or demolish it. In default of compliance the local authority may itself undertake the necessary work.

References

Arden and Partington *Housing Law* (Sweet & Maxwell) "Dilapidated buildings".

7 Drains and sewers

Tenants may be caused serious inconvenience by the blockage, disrepair or overflow of drains as a result of landlord failure to repair or maintain them.

Local authorities have extensive powers to require owners (and occupiers) to take remedial action where a drain or sewer is prejudicial to health or a nuisance (Building Act 1984 ss21 and 59). In default, the council may itself carry out the necessary work and recover its costs thereafter.

Similarly, a local authority may by notice secure the performance of small repairs if a drain or sewer is insufficiently maintained or repaired (PHA 1961 s17).

References

Arden and Partington *Housing Law* (Sweet & Maxwell), "Drains and sewers".

David Ormandy "Drains and sewers" (1978) October *LAG Bulletin* 235.

JF Garner *Law of sewers and drains* (Shaw & Sons 1981 6th edn).

H Wilkinson *Pipes, mains, cables and sewers* (Longman 1984 4th edn).

8 Fire precautions

The powers available to require landlords to take fire precautions are abysmally poor. Although contractual and common law rights (chapter 2) will usually require a landlord to maintain an existing fire escape or stairway retained in his/her possession, they cannot be used to compel the landlord to *provide* such facilities.

The Fire Precautions Act 1971 s3 which would require fire certificates for certain houses has yet to be brought into force. The Act does however make a certificate mandatory where the property provides sleeping accommodation for staff or guests in a boarding house (s1). The term "boarding house" for these purposes was construed widely in *R v Mabbot* ((1987)

Times 4 August, CA) to cover premises such as hostels which provide overnight sleeping accommodation.

Local authorities have somewhat more extensive powers in relation to houses in multiple occupation and common lodging houses to require the provision of means of escape from fire (HA 1985 ss365-8).

Local councils also have power to require fire precautions to be taken in certain multi-storey blocks of flats, tenements and boarding houses (Building Act 1984 s72).

References

Arden and Partington *Housing Law* (Sweet & Maxwell) "Fire precautions".
David Ormandy "Fire precautions" (1979) February *LAG Bulletin* 66; August 190.
DoE Circular 12/86.
Berg v Trafford BC (1988) 20 HLR 47, CA.
Zenca and Ors v Pouyiouros (1989) September *Legal Action* 24, QBD.

9 Improvements

This book is primarily concerned with housing in need of repair rather than improvement. However in a variety of circumstances either landlord or tenant may wish to improve property in addition to or in place of carrying out repairs.

(a) Voluntary improvement

A secure *tenant* has a statutory right to carry out certain improvements subject to the consent of the landlord (HA 1985 ss97-8). Other tenants will have only such rights as are contained in their tenancy agreements.

Where the *landlord* wishes to carry out improvement to occupied property the ability to do so will be governed by the terms of letting. For circumstances in which the displacement of the tenant would be caused by the improvement work see chapter 8.

(b) Compulsory improvement

Local authorities have long had power to secure certain improvement works from the landlords of property in poor condition. The statutory process (consolidated in HA 1985 Pt VII) was initiated by the authority of its own volition in a housing action area or general improvement area (see "Area action" above) and in other cases upon receipt by the authority of written representations from a tenant.

From 1 April 1990, the compulsory improvement scheme is replaced in part by the incorporation, within the new statutory definition of unfitness, of aspects which formerly would have been addressed by HA 1985 Pt VII (repealed by Local Government and Housing Act 1989 s165(2)). Thus the failure to have sufficient heating, hot water supply or sanitary installations may render a house "unfit" and compel the local authority, on hearing of the condition of the property, to take the "most satisfactory course" of remedial action.

References
Arden and Partington *Housing Law* (Sweet & Maxwell) "Improvements".
Home improvements Office of Fair Trading.
FFF Estates Ltd v Hackney LBC [1981] QB 503.

10 Multi-occupied property

Some of the worst instances of landlord neglect and disrepair are to be found in properties subject to more than one tenancy or occupancy eg houses converted into "bedsits", hostels, hotels, and houses converted into two or more "flatlets". Although these are the most obvious types of multi-occupied property, any house or flat is in multiple occupation if it contains two or more households.

Local authorities (through EHOs) have extensive powers to control: (a) the provision of facilities in such properties (HA 1985 s352); (b) the number of occupants (HA 1985 ss354-7); and (c) the means of escape from fire (HA 1985 ss365-8).

In addition, the local authority has power to intervene where there are problems of disrepair, lack of maintenance and other unsatisfactory aspects to the state of the property because the Housing Act codes in relation to unfitness and housing in poor repair, described in chapter 6, apply to houses and flats in multiple occupation. Also, the local authority may act to enforce management regulations (HA 1985 s369) setting out the landlord's responsibilities and the work necessary to bring the property up to standard. Failure to comply may result in prosecution and the authority may do the necessary works in default and recoup its costs.

Where conditions are so poor as to represent a danger to the health, safety or welfare of the occupants, the council may impose a control order (HA 1985 ss379-400). This gives the authority the power to run the property itself and carry out the necessary work, collect the rents etc. Ultimately, the authority may compulsorily purchase the property.

References
Revised controls over houses in multiple occupation DoE Circular 5/90.
Tenants' rights in shared housing CHAR.
Arden and Partington *Housing Law* (Sweet & Maxwell) "Houses in multiple occupation".
Unsafe as houses Campaign for Bedsit Rights.
Ormandy "Standards, enforcement and improvement" (1990) May *Legal Action* 14 and (letter) *Legal Action* August 1990.
Environmental Health Standards in Housing (Sweet & Maxwell) chapter 6 "Houses in multiple occupation".
McLoughlin "Houses in multiple occupation" (1986) LS Gaz 1382.
Wandsworth LBC v Orakpo (1986) *Independent* 29 October, CA.
Wandsworth LBC v Sparling (1987) 20 HLR 169.
Webb v Ipswich BC (1989) 21 HLR 325, CA.
Hammersmith and Fulham LBC v Gill, Same v Abrahams (1989) June *Legal Action* 24.
Hammersmith and Fulham LBC v Gamble (1989) March *Legal Action* 24.

11 Neighbouring property

The effects of disrepair are often felt beyond their immediate location. The ramifications of a structure or installation out of repair may lead to injury to health or damage to neighbouring property. Indeed, one of the most common sights in areas of high density housing is the scarring effect on a number of properties of a defective WC cistern overflow in an upper-floor flat.

If the neighbouring property or building in disrepair is owned by the landlord, the tenant may be able to take action under one or more of the implied covenants contained in all letting agreements (see chapter 2):
(a) the covenant to repair common parts;
(b) the covenant of quiet enjoyment;
(c) the covenant of non-derogation from grant.
If the property is in other hands, the neighbouring tenant may involve the EHO of the local authority for the area – either on the basis that the property is a statutory nuisance (see p69) or that it is dangerous or dilapidated (see p118).

Very rarely, a neighbouring occupier may be able to secure access to the property in serious disrepair, take steps to stem the source of the problem, and recover costs incurred (see reference below). This is particularly so where a repair notice was served but not complied with (HA 1985 s196).

Regional Properties Ltd v City of London Real Property Co (1981) 257 EG 64.

12 Noise

Very substantial distress and inconvenience may be caused by noise nuisance. In modern housing this is commonly exacerbated by the lack of good insulation of party walls or between flats. Often the tenant will be able to restrain the continuation of any excessive noise by using the procedures under the EPA Pt III or by an action in private nuisance (tort). However, if the source of noise is simply normal usage of a property, the most appropriate challenge is one addressed to the landlord responsible for letting a dwelling insufficiently insulated against normal domestic noise.

Action against landlords in which tenants have successfully obtained orders for insulation work have been brought under the Control of Pollution Act 1974 s59 (now EPA s82) (*Joyce v Hackney LBC*;[1] *Lambert Flat Management v Lomas*;[2] *Rossall v Southwark LBC*[3]), under the Public Health Act 1936 s99 (now EPA s82) (*LB Southwark v Ince*[4]), and as an action in private nuisance/breach of the covenant of quiet enjoyment (*Duncan v Brent LBC*[5]). If the noise results from disrepair, eg broken floor boards, tenants can take civil proceedings.[6]

1 (1976) September *LAG Bulletin* 211.
2 [1981] 1 WLR 898.
3 (1985) unreported, noted at (1986) 8 *IEHO Housing Law Newsletter* 7.
4 (1989) 21 HLR 504, QBD.
5 (1989) March *Legal Action* 23 and June *Legal Action* 18.
6 *Guinan v Enfield LBC* (1990) June *Legal Action* 16.

13 Overcrowding

Experience suggests a degree of co-relation between properties in disrepair and those which landlords permit to become overcrowded.

Statutory limits are imposed as to the maximum number of persons permitted to occupy a dwelling and enforcement is the responsibility and duty of the local authority for the area (HA 1985 Pt X).

Overcrowding is measured by two standards and failure to comply with either or both will render the overcrowding illegal. The first of the standards is based on the number of rooms, the number of occupants and their ages. The second test is based on the size and number of rooms, the occupiers and their ages. The statutory code permits strictly limited exceptions.

Illegal overcrowding may bring to an end any Rent Act security of tenure and may lead to homelessness (and possible rehousing by the council).

Enforcement by local authorities is mandatory and may lead to the prosecution of the landlord. Overcrowding in council property is equally illegal and the code may be enforced by council tenants by a relator action with the fiat of the Attorney-General. (See *DPP v Carrick* (1985) 31 *Housing Aid* 5).

References

Arden and Partington *Housing Law* (Sweet & Maxwell) "Overcrowding".
Social Welfare Law (ed Pollard, Longman) David Ormandy Section C chapter 4 part IV, "Overcrowding".
Overcrowding Shelter Practice note 3.
David Ormandy "Overcrowding" (1973) October *LAG Bulletin* 218.
Environmental Health Standards in Housing (Sweet & Maxwell) chapter 7 "Overcrowding".

14 Refuse

Accumulations of rubbish may not only attract vermin (see below) but may also themselves constitute a danger to residents (see, eg, *Dear v Newham LBC*[1]). The former right of tenants to require a local authority to remove house refuse (PHA 1936 s72) was repealed on 6 June 1988[2] and a new code of refuse disposal is to be found in the Control of Pollution Act 1974 (see Collection and Disposal of Waste Regulations 1988[3]). This makes "collection authorities" responsible for clearing rubbish, but EHOs retain the power to require removal of "accumulations" which are a public health hazard (see chapter 5).

In multi-storey blocks of flats, difficulties may be caused if the rubbish chutes and collection bins are not regularly cleared. A tenant living in a flat adjacent to a blocked chute or overspilled collection bin may have an action in private nuisance against the landlord (see *Sillitoe v Liverpool CC*[4]).

1 (1988) 20 HLR 348, CA.
2 The Control of Pollution Act 1974 (Commencement No 19) Order 1988 SI No 818.
3 SI No 819.
4 (1988) 29 November, unreported, Liverpool County Court, HHJ Stannard.

15 Sanitary installations

Where a landlord has permitted sanitary installations to fall out of repair or proper working order the tenant may take action under contractual or common law repairing obligations (chapter 2) and if conditions have become prejudicial to health or a nuisance should involve the EHO to take action under the Public Health and Environmental Protection Acts (chapter 5).

Additional powers are given to local authorities to deal with situations where there are insufficient sanitary conveniences in a dwelling or the existing ones require replacement.

Enforcement, which is mandatory, is by notice from the council to the landlord followed, where necessary, by works in default of compliance and recovery of costs.

References

Arden and Partington *Housing Law* (Sweet & Maxwell) "Sanitary accommodation".

16 Services (gas, water and electricity)

Under the covenant implied in most tenancies by LTA 1985 s11, a landlord is required to keep in repair and proper working order the installations in the dwelling for the supply of gas, electricity and water (s11(1)(b), (c)) or, in respect of certain tenancies, the installations serving the dwelling, wherever situated (see chapter 2 p17).

However, problems commonly arise where, although the installations themselves are in good order, the landlord has caused loss of supply of the services themselves eg by failing to pay fuel bills. In these circumstances, upon receipt of a complaint from the occupiers, a local authority can make the necessary arrangements with the relevant boards to ensure reconnection of the supply. Most authorities have delegated the power to carry out this service to EHOs or tenancy relations officers. Once supply is re-established the authority can thereafter recover any necessary costs from the landlord (Local Government (Miscellaneous Provisions) Act 1976 s33).

References

WH Thomas "Gas and Electricity" (1974) August *LAG Bulletin* 190.
L Grant "Turning on the gas" (1976) September *LAG Bulletin* 209.
Letters (1976) October *LAG Bulletin* 239; December 287.
Fuel Rights Handbook SHAC, 1989.

17 Vandalism

Where disrepair results from the deliberate or negligent act of a stranger rather than from the activities of the landlord or tenant or their visitors, responsibility for repair of the damage will lie on either or neither party according to respective repairing obligations. For example, where the landlord is liable to repair the "exterior" this requires the replacement of glazing in a window smashed by the acts of a third party. Obviously, where the third party can be identified the landlord will seek redress from him/her.

In certain limited circumstances a landlord may be liable for acts of vandalism by unknown third parties which cause distress or damage to tenants. For example, the landlord of a number of adjoining properties may be liable in negligence if one property is left vacant and unsecured against vandals who destroy pipework and cause thereby flooding to the neighbouring tenanted properties (see discussion at chapter 3 p40).

References
Ward v Cannock Chase DC [1985] 3 All ER 537.
Lamb v LB Camden [1981] QB 625.
Perl (Exporters) Ltd v LB Camden [1984] QB 342.
Vandalism in London GLC Police Committee Support Unit.
Hoath "Damage Caused by Vandalism: Responsibility as between landlord and tenant" (1986) February *Legal Action* 22.
Coley v LB Camden (1983) 12 September, unreported, Bloomsbury and Marylebone County Court, but noted at *Times* 13 September.
King v Liverpool CC [1986] 1 WLR 890, CA.

18 Vermin

One of the least pleasant consequences of disrepair or of poor building design may be the incursion of vermin. These not only cause distress but also damage to personal possessions and in certain cases to the fabric of the property. Even in more modern, system-built dwellings infestation by ants or cockroaches is not uncommon (see, eg, *Hudson v Kensington and Chelsea RB*[1]).

If the landlord lets premises infested by vermin those premises may be unfit for human habitation at common law (see p12). If after a letting, a landlord negligently fails to deal with the vermin or the incursion is a nuisance for which the landlord is responsible, the tenant may have other remedies at common law (see p38).

In addition, local authorities have extensive powers to take action in case of pest infestation (Prevention of Damage by Pests Act 1949 and Public Health Act 1936 Pt II).

Premises infested with vermin are very likely to constitute a "statutory nuisance" (p69) as they are prejudicial to health. If it can be shown that the incursion or infestation is caused by the "act, default or sufferance" of the landlord, the tenant may rely on the processes of the EPA and, where necessary, prosecute the landlord using s82 (as in *White v Hackney LBC*[2] (ants)).

1 (1986) unreported, but noted at (1986) *Daily Hazard* 1; (1985) December *Legal Action* 171.
2 (1989) March *Legal Action* 24.

References

Arden and Partington *Housing Law* (Sweet & Maxwell) "Vermin".
A Spackman "The plague in all our houses" 1985 *Sunday Times* 3 November.
"Cockroach infestation on the North Peckham estate" Pitt Street Settlement (1984).
David Ormandy "Vermin, drains and garbage" (1975) June *LAG Bulletin* 152.
Bob Young "Infestation" July/August 1980 *Roof* 110.
Pesticides Action Bulletin London Pesticides Action Group.
M O'Dwyer "Pest control" (1986) June *LCF News* 10.
"Fighting the beetles and bugs" *Independent* 7 April 1990.

Chapter Eight

Displaced Tenants

1 Introduction

This chapter is concerned with the rights of tenants who occupy property in such poor condition that they eventually wish to leave or are displaced from their homes by the need to allow extensive works to be carried out, or because the premises have become uninhabitable, or because the property is beyond repair and will be redeveloped, closed or demolished.

In certain situations such tenants and other occupiers are entitled to be rehoused or financially compensated for the loss of their homes.

Before considering these forms of redress, the legal context behind the need to move from the property must be established. The most common situations are discussed below.

2 Causes of displacement

(a) Landlord willing to repair where work cannot be done with tenant in occupation

A tenant is generally under an obligation to give the landlord access to carry out repairs. Such an obligation will either be found in the express terms of the tenancy agreement or be implied into it. Indeed, at common law any right or duty to repair owed by a landlord carries with it an implied obligation on the part of the tenant to permit access so that the landlord can do the works.[1] The landlord must give reasonable notice and upon entering complete the works within a reasonable time.[2] For the proper protection of tenants this right to enter and occupy "must be limited to that which is strictly necessary in order to do the work of repair".[3]

In the *private* sector the Rent Act 1977 inserts a condition into all protected tenancies that the tenant must give the landlord not only access to the property but also "all reasonable facilities for executing therein any repairs which the landlord is entitled to execute" (s148). The Housing Act 1988 gives similar rights to the landlords of assured tenants (HA 1988 s16).

Failure to give such access will operate to suspend temporarily the landlord's repairing obligation and may put the tenant in jeopardy of possession proceedings based on the failure to comply with the implied condition.

In the *public* sector, the ordinary periodic council or housing association tenancy is subject to the implied condition that the landlord may have access to the property for the purpose of carrying out repairs.[4] Alternatively, the public sector landlord may well be able to rely on an express term of the tenancy agreement. If, ultimately, such a landlord is unable to negotiate access arrangements, possession proceedings may be commenced against a secure tenant on the basis that possession is required to enable works to be carried out and other accommodation is available to the tenant (HA 1985 Sch 2 Pt II ground 10).

Difficulties commonly arise in the private sector where the landlord is insisting on vacant possession to carry out major repairs but is unwilling to provide alternative accommodation. The parallel difficulty in the public sector arises where local authorities insist that major repair works can be carried out "around" tenants, but the tenants seek temporary rehousing. Both problems have solutions.

Private sector

If the reason that the tenant may be temporarily displaced is that the landlord is seeking to carry out repairing obligations, the landlord is under no legal duty to secure alternative accommodation for the tenant while works are in progress.[5] The justification for this is simply that the landlord is carrying out duties owed to the tenant to repair and the tenant must co-operate in this. The principle was touched on by the Court of Appeal in *Calabar Properties v Stitcher*[6] where Griffiths LJ said:

> "If in this case the landlord had sent workmen round to carry out the repairs promptly on receiving notice of the defect and the (tenant) for her own convenience had decided to move to a hotel while the repairs were carried out, she could not have claimed the cost of hotel accommodation because the landlord would not have been in breach of the repairing covenant."[7]

Real difficulties arise where the tenant has no option but to move out because of the extent of the proposed repair work. Some guidance in this area was given by the Court of Appeal in *McGreal v Wake*[8] where Donaldson MR said that the tenant was not obliged, as part of giving the landlord access, to give the landlord exclusive occupation unless *essential* for the execution of repairs. "Nor does it involve an obligation to give him access to all parts of the house at the same time unless again this is essential."[9]

The question therefore is whether it is essential for the landlord to have vacant possession in order to carry out the works.

If exclusive possession is *not* essential to enable the works to be carried out, the landlord faces a choice: either s/he pays more for getting the work done in circumstances in which the contractor can tackle only one room at a time and has to carefully protect the tenant's furniture, or s/he provides alternative accommodation for the tenant.[10]

If exclusive possession *is* essential, the tenant must move temporarily. In such circumstances the parties must carefully negotiate an agreement concerning the tenant's continued security of tenure, the duration of the works, the payment of rent and the question of expenses. Alternatively, a local authority may be willing to provide accommodation for the tenant on the basis of an undertaking from the landlord to accept a local authority nominee for the reletting of the property once repaired. Such an undertaking would be conditional as to the security and rent of the premises once repaired.

In practice, the problem appears as one of stalemate – the landlord saying that s/he is willing to carry out the repairs but that the temporary possession of the whole is essential, the tenant saying that the work can be done on a rotating, room-by-room basis. Ultimately, the issue can be resolved only in court, with proceedings perhaps brought by the tenant for a declaration as to whether the repairing covenants are being complied with.

Advisers should be wary of the private landlord using extensive repair work to recover possession from the tenant. In particular, landlords of assured tenants now have access to HA 1988 Sch 2 ground 6 which is a mandatory ground for possession where, inter alia, the landlord intends to carry out "substantial works" and the intended works "cannot reasonably be carried out without the tenant giving up *possession*". In such cases, advisers should draw attention to the fact that the tenant will usually be willing to go temporarily "out of *occupation*" but that the landlord is not providing reasonable terms, eg as to alternative accommodation. If such a case is made out, it will be virtually impossible for the landlord to establish that recovery of possession is necessary.

Public sector

The basic legal propositions discussed above also apply in the public sector. However, council tenants frequently have as little (and often less) confidence in the workmanship of council employees and sub-contractors as their counterparts in the private sector have for private contractors. It is common for local authorities and housing associations to suggest that quite substantial repair work can be done with the tenant in residence on the basis that their operatives will have careful regard to personal comfort and to the protection of the tenant's furniture and property. Tenants in the public sector remain sceptical. Yet, particularly where tenants' associations are active, much can be achieved through constructive negotiation. This may produce a detailed programme of combined repairs and improvement work leading to statutory entitlement to financial compensation and temporary rehousing in other council property (see below).

If, unusually, the landlord of a secure tenant requires vacant possession in order to do the works and the tenant declines to move, recourse may be had to HA 1985 Sch 2 ground 10. This may be satisfied where (a) the landlord intends to carry out works on the dwelling; (b) these cannot be done without obtaining possession; (c) work is intended to start within a reasonable time of obtaining possession; and (d) suitable alternative permanent accommodation is available to the tenant. The burden of proving all the elements is on the landlord.[11] Again, the tenant may defeat the operation of this ground by showing a genuine willingness to give up *occupation* and take temporary accommodation during the works. If the ground is made out, a home loss payment may become due (see below).

(b) Landlord in breach of obligation to repair where work cannot be done with tenant in occupation

Landlords in both the public and private sectors not infrequently neglect their repairing obligations (notwithstanding repeated notice of defects) to such an extent that eventually the property deteriorates into a state in which it is no longer habitable. It may be uninhabitable in the sense that conditions are so bad that the safety of the occupiers is in jeopardy or in the sense that when the landlord is finally compelled to carry out repairs (or where they are carried out in default), the works are so extensive that the tenant must move out.

In either of these circumstances the tenant may properly move into alternative accommodation and put furniture and belongings into store. The landlord will be liable to reimburse such costs as part of the compensation owed to the tenant for breach of the repairing obligation. Similar compensation is payable if the tenant remains out of occupation for longer than is strictly necessary by reason of the landlord's unreasonable delay in carrying out the repairs (see generally chapter 4 pp61-63).

If conditions have deteriorated to the extent that the local authority has served a "housing order" requiring the closure or demolition of the property, the tenant may be entitled to financial compensation and rehousing from the authority in addition to damages recovered against the landlord (see below).

(c) Landlord needs vacant possession to carry out improvement works

None of the rights to access discussed above allow the landlord to insist on exclusive possession for the purposes of carrying out *improvement* works. Nevertheless, some tenants are put under considerable pressure to move out by landlords seeking to improve their properties (often with the assistance of public funds) in order to attract higher rents or to improve capital values.[12]

In the absence of any express term in a tenancy agreement, the landlord has no right to insist upon the tenant giving vacant possession to allow improvements to be carried out.

In the *private* sector, a landlord with a statutory tenant who declines to give access for improvement works to be carried out may, in certain circumstances, apply to the county court for an order empowering him/her to enter and carry out improvement works (Rent Act 1977 s116). The improvement works must be those specified either in an application for an improvement grant or in a certificate issued by the local authority. The county court may make the order conditional upon the landlord providing alternative accommodation and may specify the maximum duration of the works. In deciding whether to make such an order, the court must have regard to all the circumstances including the age and health of the tenant, the alternative accommodation available and any disadvantage to the tenant that might result from the works (such as a higher registered rent).

If the tenant is an *assured* tenant, the landlord's otherwise qualified ability to undertake extensive improvement or other work is supplemented by the availability of mandatory possession under ground 6 (HA 1988 Sch 2). To obtain an order for possession landlords must show that (a) they intend to carry out "substantial works" to any part of the dwelling (or intend to demolish or reconstruct the whole or a substantial part); (b) the work cannot be carried out without the tenant giving up possession; (c) the landlord did not obtain the property already subject to the tenancy by purchase; and (d) the assured tenancy did not arise from succession to a Rent Act tenancy. The landlord must also show that either (e) the tenant is not willing to take an assured tenancy of whatever part of the dwelling is not being worked upon (or that such part-tenancy is not practicable) or (f) the tenant is not willing to agree some variation of the tenancy which would permit the work to be carried out (or no such variation is practicable). It follows that tenants can defeat ground 6 proceedings if they can show that it is practical for the terms of tenancy to be varied so that, for example, they move out for a short period into temporary accommodation provided by the landlord, with suitable variation as to payment of rent during that period.

In the *public* sector, in the absence of express terms, access must be negotiated with secure tenants, although ultimately possession may be sought under HA 1985 Sch 2 ground 10 (see above p131).

Tenants displaced *permanently* by improvement works carried out by local authorities or pursuant to pre-April 1990 compulsory improvement notices are entitled to statutory compensation and rehousing (see below).

3 Rehousing for displaced tenants

In certain circumstances, displaced tenants and other occupiers are entitled to be rehoused by the local housing authority either by virtue of the Land Compensation Act 1973 or pursuant to the more general provisions of the HA 1985 Pt III. In addition, local authorities are obliged to give a reasonable preference in the allocation of their available accommodation to those who are homeless or in unsatisfactory or insanitary housing (HA 1985 s22).

Advisers should consider carefully which of the two statutory routes to rehousing will produce the most suitable, speedy, good quality accommodation, having regard to the allocation policies of the local authority concerned. In order to give informed advice, recourse should be had, not just to the published summary of the authority's allocation rules (HA 1985 s106(1)), but also to the detailed rules themselves (s106(2)), copies of which can be purchased (s106(4)).

(a) Land Compensation Act 1973 s39

The rehousing aspect of the Land Compensation Act (LCA) 1973 s39[13] applies to those tenants (and other occupiers) displaced in consequence of:

(a) the acquisition of the land by an authority possessing compulsory purchase powers; or

(b) the making, or acceptance of a closing or demolition order in respect of a house or building on the land (see chapter 6 for a description of these terms); or

(c) where the land has been previously acquired by an authority possessing compulsory purchase powers or appropriated by a local authority and is for the time being held by the authority for the purposes for which it was acquired or appropriated, the carrying out of any improvement to a house or building on the land or of redevelopment on the land; or

(d) the service of an improvement notice, within the meaning of HA 1985 Pt VII, in respect of premises in which that accommodation is situated

(s39(1)).

Category (d) is repealed, with effect from 1 April 1990 by Local Government and Housing Act 1989 s194 and Sch 12.

The displacement must be from residential accommodation and the duty to provide rehousing is owed only if "suitable alternative residential accommodation" on reasonable terms is not otherwise available to the displaced person. The phrase "suitable alternative residential accommodation" is not defined by LCA 1973, but may usefully be construed in the light of decisions concerning "suitable alternative accommodation" in relation to grounds for possession under the Rent Act 1977, HA 1985 or HA 1988.[14] The rehousing obligation is owed irrespective of housing need so that both families and single persons are covered.

Where the reason for the displacement is improvement work, the obligation to rehouse permanently arises only if the displacement of the occupier is itself permanent (s39(6A)). The rehousing duty is not owed to all those displaced. It does not cover squatters or those holding temporary licences to occupy "short-life" property pending demolition or improvement (s39(3)). The displaced occupier must also have been resident at the appropriate date (usually the date of the order or notice concerned) (s39(6)).

The local authority faced with the rehousing obligation must give a preference to the displaced person in the allocation of its housing stock, but if no permanent property is immediately available for letting, temporary accommodation may be secured for the displaced person pending a full tenancy becoming available (*R v Bristol Corporation ex parte Hendy*[15]).

(b) Housing Act 1985 Pt III

Those rendered homeless by displacement from their previous accommodation are owed considerable duties by the local housing authority to which they apply for accommodation, ranging from the provision of advice and assistance to full rehousing.[16]

In the past there was the practical difficulty that tenants would not know how the local authority would respond to their application under Pt III until they became literally homeless or were within 28 days of that homelessness. This problem may now be circumvented by reference to HA 1985 s58(2A). This provides that persons shall be treated as homeless (even though they still hold a tenancy) unless the authority is satisfied that it is reasonable for them to continue in occupation. Accordingly, a tenant in very poor housing conditions need not actually wait until forced to leave before applying as "homeless" since, in order to defeat the application, the authority must be able to show that conditions have not yet deteriorated to the extent of making continued occupation unreasonable.

4 Financial compensation

The *owners* of dwellings required for redevelopment or demolition by local authorities have long enjoyed statutory rights to full compensation where councils use their extensive powers of regulation and compulsory acquisition of private housing.[17] This chapter, however, focuses on the comparatively less well explored rights of *tenants* in the private and public sectors who are required to give up their homes (permanently or temporarily) as a result of the requirements of local housing authorities. In some cases, substantial financial compensation is available to tenants and other occupiers. Depending upon the circumstances of the individual case, a tenant may be entitled to one or more of:

(a) a home loss payment;
(b) a disturbance payment;

(c) a discretionary payment;
(d) a contractual payment;
(e) a well maintained payment;
(f) help with the cost of removals;
(g) compensation for moving as a result of disrepair; and/or
(h) getting rent/community charge reduced.

These potential entitlements are considered in turn below.

(a) Home loss payments

A home loss payment is a fixed sum paid in recognition of the personal upset and distress caused to the tenant by displacement. At the time of writing, a Planning and Compensation Bill was before Parliament containing proposals to reduce the qualifying period for entitlement to home loss payments, increase amounts paid in some cases and making other amendments to home loss provisions. The following text should therefore be read subject to the changes this legislation may produce. The proposals in the Bill are to take effect retrospectively from 16 November 1990.[18]

The amount to which people are entitled by way of home loss payment depends on the date of their displacement. A table showing the amounts is set out in Appendix 8.

The conditions of entitlement are set out in LCA 1973 s29[19] and can be broadly summarised as follows:

(a) the tenant must have been in occupation of the property as an only or main residence for at least five years before the displacement (or one year if the displacement is on or after 16 November 1990[20]); and
(b) the displaced tenant must have been in occupation by virtue of a legal interest or right (this includes a contractual tenancy, a statutory tenancy, restricted contracts and service occupancies[21]); and
(c) the displacement must have been in consequence of *one* of five prescribed circumstances, namely:
    (i) the compulsory purchase of the landlord's interest (or agreed sale by the landlord to an authority intending to exercise compulsory purchase powers[22]);
    (ii) the making of a demolition, closing or clearance order or other housing order[23] or undertaking, or service (prior to 1 April 1990[24]) of a statutory compulsory improvement notice;
    (iii) the *improvement* of the dwelling or *redevelopment* of the land by a registered housing association;
    (iv) the *improvement* of the dwelling or *redevelopment* of the land by a local authority having compulsory purchase powers, where the authority appropriated or acquired the property and is holding it for the purpose for which it was originally appropriated or acquired;[25]

(v) the making of an order for possession against a secure tenant on ground 10 (see p131) or 10A of HA 1985 Sch 2.[26]

For displacement occuring after 13 May 1980 the time limit for claiming the home loss payment is the statutory limitation period of six years.[27] For displacement prior to that date the time limit was six months (LCA 1973 s32(1)). Claims must be made in writing to the responsible authority[28] and must be accompanied by such information as the authority may reasonably require. The authority to which the claim is made must make a payment within three months of the date of claim.[29]

The forum for litigation concerning disputed entitlement is the local county court, where an action should be commenced by the tenant for statutory debt.

Joint tenants will have the home loss payment divided between them.[30]

The five-year/one-year rule

There may occasionally be difficulty in showing that a tenant has been in occupation for the full period. For the purpose of satisfying the qualifying period the occupier at the time of displacement may add, to his/her own period as a tenant, any time during which s/he was resident but another person was then tenant (for example where the present occupier is the statutory successor to an earlier tenant).[31] Similarly, a resident can add together periods of tenancy during which s/he occupied other rooms in the same house.[32] Also, a claimant will not usually be prevented from achieving the five-year period by reason of short temporary absences.

Unfit council housing

It is now clear that no entitlement accrues to a council tenant of unfit property whose landlord is the local housing authority *and* condition (c)(ii) above is relied on, since councils cannot serve housing orders etc on themselves (*R v Cardiff CC ex parte Cross*[33]). Council tenants may be entitled to payments if action is taken under one of the other circumstances in LCA 1973 s29. It is also important to note that the definition of a housing order does not include a prohibition order made in respect of unfit property under what was the PHA 1936 s94(2) and is now EPA s82(3) (see p87).

The meaning of "improvement" of the dwelling

"Improvement" for these purposes is defined to include the "alteration and enlargement" of the dwelling.[34] Whether an activity carried out by the landlord is one of "improvement" will be a question of fact in each case. Where the landlord, authority or association is undertaking the modernisation or upgrading of an older property the position is reasonably clear and payment should be made. Problems arise however where the reason for requiring vacant possession is the carrying out of extensive *repair* work. The present Government has made it clear that in such circumstances the tenant will have to rely on his/her rights under landlord and tenant law (if any) rather than on the statutory right to compensation.[35] It will therefore be for secure tenants and their advisers to ensure that the process of compulsory consultation with public landlords (under HA 1985 s105) results in plans for at least an element of modernisation in the repair programme so as to entitle the tenant to a home loss payment. The Department of Environment has declined to prepare amending legislation or to carry out a review, restating the view that "major repairs which do not result in improvement to property are part of the normal maintenance which any owner would undertake" and "anyone displaced solely for that reason is not eligible."[36]

The meaning of "redevelopment" of the land

"Redevelopment" has its ordinary meaning, and is extended by statute to include change of use of the land in question.[37] The process of redevelopment need not be in its final stages for the entitlement to accrue, for example a tenant required to move so that the first stage of redevelopment can take place, ie clearance of the site, is entitled even though redevelopment does not proceed thereafter.[38] "Redevelopment" includes demolition of unfit council property,[38a] but not the transfer of such unfit property from public to private ownership.[39]

A local authority may be "redeveloping" land for the purposes of (c)(iv) above even if it is simply clearing the site with the intention of selling it to a private enterprise to redevelop.[40] Depending on the circumstances of the individual case, "redevelopment" may even be made out where the landlord's immediate intention is simply to demolish the property and fence and grass-over the site.[41] In such cases, the landlord may in any event be required to make a home loss payment as a result of taking possession proceedings under HA 1985 Sch 2 ground 10 or 10A (see above).

Compulsory displacement

If the tenant simply leaves the property voluntarily, no entitlement to a home loss payment arises. The test of whether the tenant is displaced, or has otherwise left voluntarily, is an objective one. There will be sufficient displacement in respect of a tenant if "he or she is told to go or that he or she will have to go"[42] and that statement is not countermanded.[43] It may also be sufficient to show that the conduct of the landlord authority has been such as to lead the tenant to believe that s/he has no alternative but to leave, so that the improvement, redevelopment etc can be carried out.[44] The authority cannot escape liability by showing that the tenants were already actively seeking alternative accommodation (eg by applying for a transfer) at the date that the relevant action was taken. In such cases, the tenants rehoused are "displaced" by the development just as much as those who had taken no preliminary steps.[45]

(b) Disturbance payments

Disturbance payments are intended to compensate financially the displaced tenant for the actual expenses associated with the need to move.

The amount of the disturbance payment will accordingly vary in every case and is to be assessed as "the reasonable expenses of the person entitled, in removing from the land from which he is displaced".[46] The forum for disputes as to the *amount* of a disturbance payment is the Lands Tribunal.[47] Disputed *entitlement* may be determined in a civil action or proceedings for judicial review.

The conditions of entitlement for a disturbance payment are set out in LCA 1973 s37(2) and are broadly as follows:

(a) the claimant was in lawful possession immediately prior to displacement (see "Key dates" below); and
(b) the claimant must not have a statutory entitlement to compensation under another enactment in respect of the same displacement; and
(c) the displacement must result from one of the prescribed causes, namely:
    (i) any acquisition (whether by agreement or by compulsory purchase order) of land by an authority having compulsory purchase powers;
    (ii) the making of a housing order[48] or acceptance of an undertaking in respect of the property or service (before 1 April 1990[49]) of a compulsory improvement notice;
    (iii) the improvement of the dwelling or redevelopment of the land by a registered housing association;
    (iv) the redevelopment of the land or improvement of the dwelling by a local authority landlord having compulsory purchase powers, which has acquired or appropriated the property.

The claimant need not have been in occupation of the property for any minimum period, save that s/he must have been in *lawful* possession on or before the key date (see below). There is no statutory time limit within which claims must be made.

The overlap with home loss payments

Disturbance and home loss payments are entirely separate entitlements. The former are directed at compensating any lawful occupier for the cost of removing, the latter at recognising the loss of a home for a long-standing resident.

In many cases there will be an entitlement to both payments. The prohibition on overlapping payments contained in LCA 1973 s37(2)(b) (see above) does not apply to home loss payments as they are paid under the same enactment as disturbance payments.

Displacement from "land"

Disturbance payments are concerned with displacement from "land". It is not yet settled whether the definition of "land" for these purposes definitively incorporates short-term tenancies or other short-term interests such as licences.[50] However, many cases have proceeded to the higher courts on the assumption, probably correct, that short-term tenants and others are covered. There seems to be no statutory reason why lodgers and other short-term licensees should be prevented from receiving a payment.[51]

Compulsory displacement

As with home loss payments, the displacement must be consequent upon the action of the authority/housing association and not simply the voluntary removal or transfer by the tenant.

The key date

The tenant must have been in possession on one of the four key dates:

(a) where the property was compulsorily purchased, the date when the notice of the compulsory purchase order was first published or prepared in draft;

(b) where specific legislation provided for the compulsory purchase of the particular land, the date when the Bill was published;

(c) where displacement arises from a housing order etc, the date when the order was made;

(d) where the land was acquired by agreement, the date the agreement was made

(LCA 1973 s37(3)).

It is the last of these key dates which will be important to tenants of local authorities which are redeveloping land originally acquired by agreement many years previously from private owners. Is it necessary for the tenant to show that s/he was in possession when the council *first* acquired the property by agreement for housing purposes, possibly decades earlier? It had long been thought that the relevant date for these purposes was the date that the council recovered the present tenant's tenancy, by agreement or notice to quit (cases up to and including *Newey v Liverpool CC*[52]) and that accordingly all tenants were entitled. However, a more recent authority[53] is specifically to the contrary and the point must await final determination by the Court of Appeal. Pending such determination, a county court judge hearing a dispute as to entitlement to a disturbance payment must choose which of the two conflicting authorities is to be preferred. It can be expected that most will prefer the latter decision as it gave specific consideration to the former and did not follow it.[54]

Improvement or redevelopment

The same principles and definitions of the words "redevelopment" and "improvement" apply as for home loss payments (see above).

The amount

As noted above, the "reasonable costs associated with removing" will vary according to the individual circumstances of each case. The provision covers "not only the immediate expenses of the physical transfer of furniture and fittings but also the reasonable expenses which can be shown to flow from and be incurred as a natural and direct consequence of the necessity to remove from the old house and set up in the new".[55] The intention is that all the associated costs of displacement should be borne by the authority and not by the affected tenant. In the usual case the payments should cover the following items:

(a) the removal contractor's expenses;
(b) the cost of altering or purchasing new soft furnishings and other moveable fittings;
(c) money lost through the forced sale of immovable fittings;
(d) disconnection and reconnection costs for telephone, cooker, plumbed-in washing machine and other installations;
(e) the redirection of mail;
(f) the refitting of alarms etc;
(g) extra travel expenses of the tenant;
(h) any new school uniforms for children; and
(i) the special cost of adapting premises for a disabled tenant[56] etc.

In *Nolan v Sheffield MDC*[57] the tenant succeeded in recovering, in addition to the costs of those items mentioned above, costs of redecorating the new house (ie paint, wallpaper, filler etc) and compensation for items lost or destroyed during the removal itself. Similarly, in *O'Grady v Westminster CC*[58] the tenant further recovered compensation for the costs of disconnecting and reconnecting a tumble drier and television aerial, as well as sums for additional carpeting and curtaining.

Given the scale of present-day costs associated with moving home, disturbance payments can be expected to be considerably higher than in the past.

It is regrettable that so many local authorities continue to obscure their liability by maintaining fixed-scale disturbance payments for their tenants (£150, £200 etc to be paid "in every case"). Authorities have been reminded that although payments based on such scales are administratively convenient, they cannot remove the tenant's right to an individual assessment of entitlement and to full payment based thereon.[59] Fixed rates are only of assistance to the small minority of tenants who have expenses falling below the amount of the fixed rate. Tenants with claims exceeding the scale of a particular authority should always submit a full claim for the amount of their total expenses. In November 1980 one London law centre was forced to initiate High Court proceedings to persuade a local authority to depart from its practice of fixed disturbance payments and instead to meet full home loss and statutory disturbance payments.[60]

Interest is payable from the date of displacement until the date on which payment is made LCA 1973 s37(6)).

Disturbance payments and rehousing

The entitlement to a disturbance payment is not affected by the question of how the tenant is rehoused, for example by being offered council accommodation. Indeed a tenant moving into the private sector as a result of displacement may recover such costs as survey fees and solicitors' costs.[61]

Home loss and disturbance payments for "temporary" removal

The entitlement to a home loss or disturbance payment may arise whether the removal of the tenant caused by redevelopment is temporary or permanent. However in the case of persons displaced in consequence of improvement work or the service of statutory improvement notices or closing orders or other housing orders and undertakings the displacement must be permanent.[62] Difficult questions as to entitlement arise where tenants are told they may return to their homes once extensive work of modernisation or improvement is complete. Where dwellings have been completely gutted or reconstructed internally, it may well be that the returning tenant finds that the "home" no longer exists in its previous form. In such cases tenants will contend that they have been "permanently displaced" from their original dwelling. Local authority responses to claims in these cases are known to vary. The High Court in *Casale v Islington LBC*[63] has held that permanent displacement will arise even though the occupier returns to take up residence, if the works are "so radical and far-reaching as to cause the original dwelling to lose its identity".

(c) Discretionary home loss and disturbance payments

Where the tenant or other occupier is displaced from property covered by LCA 1973 s37(1) but does not satisfy the other statutory conditions for entitlement to a disturbance payment (see above) the authority nonetheless has a discretion to make a payment corresponding to a disturbance payment.[64] The relevant circular indicates that it is hoped that "authorities will make full and appropriate use" of the power to make discretionary awards.[65] If an authority resolves to make a discretionary payment, it then has no discretion as to the amount. This is to be fixed by the same principles of assessment as apply to mandatory disturbance payments with a right of appeal to the Lands Tribunal if the amount cannot be agreed.[66]

Discretionary home loss payments are also available. These may be made (a) where a landlord could have launched proceedings for possession under HA 1985 Sch 2 ground 10 (see above p131) or could have applied for redevelopment consent related to ground 10A but the tenant is persuaded to give up possession voluntarily to permit the scheme of redevelopment or substantial works to go ahead;[67] and (b) for displacements on or after 16 November 1990, where the occupier cannot meet the one-year qualifying period.[67a] In the former case the award will be the same as a home loss payment. In the latter, an amount not exceeding the maximum home loss payment will be set by the authority.

(d) Contractual payments

Even if there is no entitlement to a statutory home loss or disturbance payment, and the authority declines to make a discretionary payment, the tenant may nevertheless have an entitlement to compensation as a result of an express contractual term in the tenancy agreement. Such a term may be relied on even if the tenant falls well short of qualifying under one of the statutory schemes.[68]

(e) Well maintained payments

The provisions of HA 1985 giving rise to well maintained payments were repealed from 1 April 1990, and accordingly payments cannot be made in respect of orders served etc after that date (Local Government and Housing Act 1989 Sch 9 para 76). For displacements before that date, well maintained payments are substantial payments intended to compensate occupiers required to vacate dwellings which have been declared unfit by an acquiring housing authority but which are nevertheless maintained internally or externally or both in good condition.[69] Thus tenants occupying a house declared unfit by virtue of the landlord's neglect of external repairs, will obtain compensation if they themselves have maintained the interior of their part in good condition. In determining whether a dwelling is well maintained, factors (other than repair) which have led to the declaration of unfitness are ignored. The amount of a well maintained payment is found by multiplying the rateable value of the well maintained dwelling by 14. If the payment is in respect of the internal condition only, the payment is reduced by 50 per cent. The maximum payment is a sum representing the difference between the site value of the land and the full compulsory purchase value of the dwelling. Tenants must be able to show that the entitlement accrues to the dwelling by reason of conditions attributable to a material extent to work carried out by them at their own expense. It is intended that landlords should be informed when a well maintained payment is made to a tenant rather than to themselves as owners. The conditions of entitlement and the procedures for claiming, vary slightly according to the statutory background of the exercise of the local authorities' powers.[70]

(f) Removal expenses

Those entitled to disturbance payments will receive assistance with the cost of removals as part of their compensation (see above). However there are alternative sources of financial assistance to those moving home who are not covered by the disturbance payments scheme.

Homeless persons
Local housing authorities have a duty towards certain homeless persons to take reasonable care of their property and possessions.[71] Where appropriate this will extend to include the undertaking of removal of these possessions from one dwelling to another.[72]

Council tenants
Tenants moving out of local authority or new town accommodation either into alternative council accommodation or into the private sector may seek a discretionary payment towards the cost of removal from their local authority.[73]

Assured tenants
An assured tenant, required to move as a result of proceedings brought under HA 1988 Sch 2 ground 6 or 9, is entitled to the "reasonable expenses likely to be incurred" in moving, from the landlord (HA 1988 s11).

(g) Compensation for displacement caused by repairs work (see generally pp128-131 above)

Financial compensation for displacement caused by the need to allow major repairs to be undertaken has always been a matter fraught with difficulty. Since home loss and disturbance payments do not cover the situation where displacement arises from the simple need to carry out repairs, any entitlement is to be found, if at all, only in landlord and tenant law. Where temporary vacant possession is needed by a landlord who is proposing to carry out his/her repairing obligations, the entitlement of the tenant will turn upon the terms of the tenancy agreement, if any, or subsequent oral agreement between the parties. Where a tenant is forced to move out by conditions arising from the landlord's *neglect* of repairs, the cost thereof may be recovered as part of an action for breach of the repairing covenant.[74]

(h) Getting the rent/community charge reduced

For the tenant forced to move by poor conditions, some immediate financial assistance may be available through a reduction in the rent or community charge. Those with a registered fair rent may apply to the rent officer for a *rent* reduction before they move.[75] In respect of past liability for *rates*, the occupier may apply to the local valuation officer for the valuation list to show the rateable value as nil.[76] If a property becomes uninhabitable and tenants move temporarily, this may have the effect of replacing their liability for personal community charge with the landlord's liability for the standard charge (see generally Ward and Zebedee *Guide to the Community Charge*).

5 Help from a solicitor

A solicitor may assist a person with matters concerning their entitlement to, or assessment of, any of the payments mentioned above under the green form scheme. In the event that the matter is not resolved by agreement, legal aid is available for proceedings in the Lands Tribunal, the county court and the High Court.

Solicitors' fees in drawing up an assessment of a disturbance payment are a reasonable expense recoverable as part of the disturbance payment itself.

6 Help from an ombudsman

The commissioners for local administration (or "ombudsmen") have been called upon frequently by tenants to investigate claims of maladministration in respect of failure to pay home loss or disturbance payments. A successful complainant may well find that the ombudsman is prepared to "advise" the local authority to make an ex gratia payment equivalent to the sum to which the claimant would have been entitled. A useful discussion of investigations by ombudsmen into the administration of home loss payment claims is given in Harlow and Rawlings *Law and Administration* (Weidenfeld and Nicolson 1984).

7 Further reading

Several useful guides are available for tenants and others faced with compulsory displacement:

Tenants' claims for compensation and remedies Hackney Law Centre.
Is your home under a compulsory purchase order? These are your rights to compensation Newham Rights Centre.
Land compensation – your rights explained 1: Your home and compulsory purchase Department of Environment 1983 (3rd edn).
Guide for residents on compulsory purchase orders Small Heath Law Centre, Birmingham.
"A new home at what price?: A guide to rehousing and compensation" 39 *Community Action* 24-25.

1 *Saner v Bilton* (1878) 7 Ch D 815.
2 *Granada Theatres v Freehold Investment (Leytonstone)* [1959] 1 WLR 570.
3 *McGreal v Wake* (1984) 269 EG 1254 per Donaldson MR at p1257.
4 *Smith v Bradford MC* (1982) 44 P&CR 171, CA per Donaldson LJ.
5 *Green v Eales* (1841) 2 QB 225.
6 [1983] 3 All ER 759, CA.
7 Ibid p769.
8 N3.
9 Ibid p1257.
10 Ibid.
11 *Wansbeck DC v Morley* (1987) 20 HLR 247, CA.

12 See *Taken for granted* Paddington Federation of Private Tenants.
13 As amended by Housing (Consequential Provisions) Act 1985 Sch 2 para 24(4).
14 See generally Arden and Partington *Housing Law* (Sweet & Maxwell).
15 [1974] 1 All ER 1047, CA and *R v East Hertfordshire DC ex p Smith* (1990) *Independent* 4 April, CA.
16 See generally Arden *Homeless Persons: The Housing Act 1985 Part III* (LAG, 3rd edn, July 1988).
17 See, eg, Corfield and Carnwath *Compulsory acquisition and compensation* (Sweet & Maxwell 1978) or *Encyclopedia of compulsory purchase law* (Sweet & Maxwell).
18 Planning and Compensation Bill 1990 clause 47(9).
19 As substantially amended by Housing (Consequential Provisions) Act 1985 Sch 2 para 24.
20 Planning and Compensation Bill 1990 clause 47.
21 LCA 1973 s29(4).
22 Ibid s29(6).
23 Ibid s29(7) (as amended by Housing (Consequential Provisions) Act 1985 Sch 2 para 24) for the definitions.
24 The provision for compensation to follow service of improvement notices is repealed by Local Government and Housing Act 1989 Sch 12 Pt II.
25 For the situation where a local authority is no longer holding land for the same purpose see *GLC v Holmes* (1985) 18 HLR 131, CA.
26 Inserted by Housing and Planning Act 1986 s9(3).
27 LCA 1973 s32(1) as amended by Local Government and Planning Act 1980 s114 and LCA 1973 s32(7).
28 As to which authority is responsible for making the payment, see LCA 1973 s29(1) as amended by HA 1974 s130(1) and Sch 13.
29 LCA 1973 s32(2).
30 Ibid s32(6).
31 Ibid s32(3).
32 Ibid s32(5).
33 (1983) 6 HLR 1, CA.
34 LCA 1973 s29(7A) as amended by HA 1974 s130 and Sch 13.
35 Wyn Roberts MP, Standing Committee B, Housing and Building Control Bill, *Hansard* 24 November 1983 cols 889-890
36 Report to council meeting by Lambeth Housing Committee 25 January 1984.
37 N34.
38 *Follows v The Peabody Trust* (1983) 10 HLR 65, CA.
38a *R v Corby DC ex p McLean* [1975] 2 All ER 568.
39 *R v Cardiff CC ex p Cross* n33.
40 *GLC v Holmes* n25.
41 *Bulgar v Knowsley BC* (1989) June *Legal Action* 25.
42 *Caplan v GLC* (1980) 5 HLR 104, CA.
43 *Armstrong v GLC* (1980) November *LAG Bulletin* 269.
44 See *Follows v The Peabody Trust* n38.
45 *Bulgar v Knowsley BC* n41.
46 LCA 1973 s38(1).
47 Ibid s38(4) and see "How to use the Lands Tribunal" 40 *Community Action* 33.
48 LCA 1973 s37(9).
49 Local Government and Housing Act 1989 Sch 12 Pt II.
50 See *Newey v Liverpool CC* (1982) 14 HLR 73.
51 See Denyer-Green "The statutory disturbance payment" (1980) JPEL 726.
52 N50.
53 *R v Islington LBC ex p Knight* [1984] 1 All ER 154.
54 As in *Bulgar v Knowsley BC* n41. See also McLeod "Home loss payments and disturbance payments: a purposive approach to interpretation" (1986) LS Gaz 1375.
55 *Glasgow Corp v Anderson* 1976 SLT 225.
56 LCA 1973 s38(3).
57 (1979) P&CR 741, Lands Tr. See also *Sylvester v Solon Housing Association* (1978) 246 EG 665, Lands Tr; *Roberts v GLC* (1975) 3 LTC case 6; and *Cole v Southwark LB* (1979) 251 EG 477, Lands Tr.

58 (1983) 266 EG 227, Lands Tr, applying *Goss v Paddington Churches Housing Association* (1981) 261 EG 373.
59 See Tunney "Disturbance payments roulette" (1978) *Roof* 133.
60 *Ex p Sonola* (1980) November, unreported; the law centre was North Kensington Law Centre. See also *Home loss – whose gain?* Handsworth Law Centre 1978.
61 *Harvey v Crawley DC* [1957] 1 QB 485; and see *Sim v Aberdeen CDC* (1981) 258 EG 451; (1984) P&CR 278, Ct of Session.
62 LCA 1973 ss29(3A) and 37(3A) as amended by HA 1974 Sch 13 paras 38(2) and 39(3).
63 (1985) 18 HLR 146.
64 LCA 1973 s37(5).
65 DoE Circ 73/1973 para 28.
66 *Gozra v Hackney LBC* (1988) 21 HLR 1; (1988) 46 EG 87, CA.
67 Housing and Planning Act 1986 s9(4) inserting LCA 1973 s32(7B).
67a LCA 1973 s29(2) as amended by the Planning and Compensation Bill 1990.
68 *Borg v Southwark LBC* (1987) June *Legal Action* 19, CA.
69 HA 1985 s586 and Sch 23 paras 1–3, 7 and 8.
70 See generally Arden and Partington *Housing Law* (Sweet & Maxwell) chapter 23.
71 HA 1985 s70.
72 DoE Code of Guidance 2nd edn para 8.4.
73 HA 1985 ss26 and 30.
74 See *Calabar Properties v Stitcher* n6.
75 Rent Act 1977 s67(3).
76 *Black v Oliver* [1971] 1 QB 870, applied to a displaced tenant in *Udechuku v Lambeth LBC* (1982) 262 EG 1309; Rating Appeals 291, Lands Tr. Reductions can be backdated for up to six years. See *Sheffield MBC* cases noted at 61 *Community Action* 8–9. See also chapter 4 n24 above.

Appendix One

Defective Premises Act 1972 s4

Landlord's duty of care in virtue of obligation or right to repair premises demised

4.—(1) Where premises are let under a tenancy which puts on the landlord an obligation to the tenant for the maintenance or repair of the premises, the landlord owes to all persons who might reasonably be expected to be affected by defects in the state of the premises a duty to take such care as is reasonable in all the circumstances to see that they are reasonably safe from personal injury or from damage to their property caused by a relevant defect.

(2) The said duty is owed if the landlord knows (whether as the result of being notified by the tenant or otherwise) or if he ought in all the circumstances to have known of the relevant defect.

(3) In this section "relevant defect" means a defect in the state of the premises existing at or after the material time and arising from, or continuing because of, an act or omission by the landlord which constitutes or would if he had had notice of the defect, have constituted a failure by him to carry out his obligation to the tenant for the maintenance or repair of the premises; and for the purposes of the foregoing provision "the material time" means–

(a) where the tenancy commenced before this Act, the commencement of this Act; and

(b) in all other cases, the earliest of the following times, that is to say–

(i) the time when the tenancy commences;

(ii) the time when the tenancy agreement is entered into;

(iii) the time when possession is taken of the premises in contemplation of the letting.

(4) Where premises are let under a tenancy which expressly or impliedly gives the landlord the right to enter the premises to carry out any description of maintenance or repair of the premises, then, as from the time when he first is, or by notice or otherwise can put himself, in a position to exercise the right and so long as he is or can put himself in that position, he shall be treated for the purposes of subsections (1) to (3) above (but for no other purpose) as if he were under an obligation to the tenant for that description of maintenance or repair of the premises; but the landlord shall not owe the tenant any duty by virtue of this subsection in respect of any defect in the state of the premises arising from, or continuing because of, a failure to carry out an obligation expressly imposed on the tenant by the tenancy.

(5) For the purposes of this section obligations imposed or rights given by any enactment in virtue of a tenancy shall be treated as imposed or given by the tenancy.

(6) This section applies to a right of occupation given by contract or any enactment and not amounting to a tenancy as if the right were a tenancy, and "tenancy" and cognate expressions shall be construed accordingly.

Appendix Two

Housing Act 1985 s606

606.—(1) The proper officer of the local housing authority shall make a report in writing to the authority whenever he is of the opinion–

(a) that a [dwelling-house or house in multiple occupation] in their district is unfit for human habitation, or

(b) that an area in their district should be dealt with as a clearance area;

and the authority shall take into consideration as soon as may be any such report made to them.

(2) If a complaint in writing that a [dwelling-house or house in multiple occupation] is unfit for human habitation, or that an area should be dealt with as a clearance area, is made to the proper officer of the local housing authority by–

(a) a justice of the peace having jurisdiction in any part of their district, or

(b) a parish or community council for a parish or community within their district,

the officer shall forthwith inspect the house or area and make a report to the authority stating the facts of the case and whether in his opinion the [dwelling-house or house in multiple occupation] is unfit for human habitation or the area should be dealt with as a clearance area.

(3) The absence of a complaint under subsection (2) does not excuse the proper officer of the authority from inspecting a [dwelling-house or house in multiple occupation] or area or making a report on it under subsection (1).

Amendment: the words in square brackets were substituted by the Local Government and Housing Act 1989 Sch 9 para 86.

Appendix Three

Environmental Protection Act 1990 ss79-82*

Statutory nuisances and inspections therefor

79.—(1) Subject to subsections (2) to (6) below, the following matters constitute "statutory nuisances" for the purposes of this Part, that is to say—
(a) any premises in such a state as to be predjudicial to health or a nuisance;
(b) smoke emitted from premises so as to be predjudicial to health or a nuisance;
(c) fumes or gases emitted from premises so as to be predjudicial to health or a nuisance;
(d) any dust, steam, smell or other effluvia arising on industrial, trade or business premises and being prejudicial to health or a nuisance;
(e) any accumulation or deposit which is prejudicial to health or a nuisance;
(f) any animal kept in such a place or manner as to be prejudicial to health or a nuisance;
(g) noise emitted from premises so as to be prejudicial to health or a nuisance;
(h) any other matter declared by any enactment to be a statutory nuisance;
and it shall be the duty of every local authority to cause its area to be inspected from time to time to detect any statutory nuisances which ought to be dealt with under section 80 below and, where a complaint of a statutory nuisance is made to it by a person living within its area, to take such steps as are reasonably practicable to investigate the complaint.

. . .

Summary proceedings for statutory nuisances

80.—(1) Where a local authority is satisified that a statutory nuisance exists, or is likely to occur or recur, in the area of the authority, the local authority shall serve a notice ("an abatement notice") imposing all or any of the following requirements—
(a) requiring the abatement of the nuisance or prohibiting or restricting its occurence or recurrence;
(b) requiring the execution of such works, and the taking of such other steps, as may be necessary for any of those purposes,

---

* Reproduced in part only

and the notice shall specify the time or times within which the requirements of the notice are to be complied with.

(2) The abatement notice shall be served—

(a) except in a case falling within paragraph (b) or (c) below, on the person responsible for the nuisance;

(b) where the nuisance arises from any defect of a structural character, on the owner of the premises;

(c) where the person responsible for the nuisance cannot be found or the nuisance has not yet occurred, on the owner or occupier of the premises.

(3) The person served with the notice may appeal against the notice to a magistrates' court within the period of twenty-one days beginning with the date on which he was served with the notice.

(4) If a person on whom an abatement notice is served, without reasonable excuse, contravenes or fails to comply with any requirement or prohibition imposed by the notice, he shall be guilty of an offence.

(5) Except in a case falling within subsection (6) below, a person who commits an offence under subsection (4) above shall be liable on summary conviction to a fine not exceeding level 5 on the standard scale together with a further fine of an amount equal to one-tenth of that level for each day on which the offence continues after the conviction.

(6) A person who commits an offence under subsection (4) above on industrial, trade or business premises shall be liable on summary conviction to a fine not exceeding £20,000.

(7) Subject to subsection (8) below, in any proceedings for an offence under subsection (4) above in respect of a statutory nuisance it shall be a defence to prove that the best practicable means were used to prevent, or to counteract the effects of, the nuisance.

(8) The defence under subsection (7) above is not available—

(a) in the case of a nuisance falling within paragraph (a), (d), (e), (f) or (g) of section 79(1) above except where the nuisance arises on industrial, trade or business premises;

(b) in the case of a nuisance falling within paragraph (b) of section 79(1) above except where the smoke is emitted from a chimney; and

(c) in the case of a nuisance falling within paragraph (c) or (h) of section 79(1) above.

(9) In proceedings for an offence under subsection (4) above in respect of a statutory nuisance falling within paragraph (g) of section 79(1) above where the offence consists in contravening requirements imposed by virtue of subsection (1)(a) above it shall be a defence to prove—

(a) that the alleged offence was covered by a notice served under section 60 or a consent given under section 61 or 65 of the Control of Pollution Act 1974 (construction sites, etc); or

(b) where the alleged offence was committed at a time when the premises were subject to a notice under section 66 of that Act (noise reduction notice), that the level of noise emitted from the premises at that time was not such as to constitute a contravention of the notice under that section; or

(c) where the alleged offence was committed at a time when the premises were not subject to a notice under section 66 of that Act, and when a level fixed under section 67 of that Act (new buildings liable to abatement order) applied to the premises, that the level of noise emitted from the premises at that time did not exceed that level.

(10) Paragraphs (b) and (c) of subsection (9) above apply whether or not the relevant notice was subject to appeal at the time when the offence was alleged to have been committed.

Supplementary provisions

81.—(1) Where more than one person is responsible for a statutory nuisance section 80 above shall apply to each of those persons whether or not what any one of them is responsible for would by itself amount to a nuisance.

(2) Where a statutory nuisance which exists or has occurred within the area of a local authority, or which has affected any part of that area, appears to the local authority to be wholly or partly caused by some act or default committed or taking place outside the area, the local authority may act under section 80 above as if the act or default were wholly within that area, except that any appeal shall be heard by a magistrates' court having jurisdiction where the act or default is alleged to have taken place.

(3) Where an abatement notice has not been complied with the local authority may, whether or not they take proceedings for an offence under section 80(4) above, abate the nuisance and do whatever may be necessary in execution of the notice.

(4) Any expenses reasonably incurred by a local authority in abating, or preventing the recurrence of, a statutory nuisance under subsection (3) above may be recovered by them from the person by whose act or default the nuisance was caused and, if that person is the owner of the premises, from any person who is for the time being the owner thereof; and the court may apportion the expenses between persons by whose acts or defaults the nuisance is caused in such manner as the court considers fair and reasonable.

(5) If a local authority is of opinion that proceedings for an offence under section 80(4) above would afford an inadequate remedy in the case of any statutory nuisance, they may, subject to subsection (6) below, take proceedings in the High Court for the purpose of securing the abatement, prohibition or restriction of the nuisance, and the proceedings shall be maintainable notwithstanding the local authority have suffered no damage from the nuisance.

(6) In any proceedings under subsection (5) above in respect of a nuisance falling within paragraph (g) of section 79(1) above, it shall be a defence to prove that the noise was authorised by a notice under section 60 or a consent under section 61 (construction sites) of the Control of Pollution Act 1974.

(7) The further supplementary provisions in Schedule 3 to this Act shall have effect.

Summary proceedings by persons aggrieved by statutory nuisances

82.—(1) A magistrates' court may act under this section on a complaint made by any person on the ground that he is aggrieved by the existence of a statutory nuisance.

(2) If the magistrates' court is satisfied that the alleged nuisance exists, or that

although abated it is likely to recur on the same premises, the court shall make an order for either or both of the following purposes—

(a) requiring the defendant to abate the nuisance, within a time specified in the order, and to execute any works necessary for that purpose;

(b) prohibiting a recurrence of the nuisance, and requiring the defendant, within a time specified in the order, to execute any works necessary to prevent the recurrence;

and may also impose on the defendant a fine not exceeding level 5 on the standard scale.

(3) If the magistrates' court is satisfied that the alleged nuisance exists and is such as, in the opinion of the court, to render premises unfit for human habitation, an order under subsection (2) above may prohibit the use of the premises for human habitation until the premises are, to the satisfaction of the court, rendered fit for that purpose.

(4) Proceedings for an order under subsection (2) above shall be brought—

(a) except in a case falling within paragraph (b) or (c) below, against the person responsible for the nuisance;

(b) where the nuisance arises from any defect of a structural character, against the owner of the premises;

(c) where the person responsible for the nuisance cannot be found, against the owner or occupier of the premises.

(5) Where more than one person is responsible for a statutory nuisance, subsection (1) to (4) above shall apply to each of those persons whether or not what any one of them is responsible for would by itself amount to a nuisance.

(6) Before instituting proceedings for an order under subsection (2) above against any person, the person aggrieved by the nuisance shall give to that person such notice in writing of his intention to bring the proceedings as is applicable to proceedings in respect of a nuisance of that description and the notice shall specify the matter complained of.

(7) The notice of the bringing of proceedings in respect of a statutory nuisance required by subsection (6) above which is applicable is—

(a) in the case of a nuisance falling within paragraph (g) of section 79(1) above, not less than three days' notice; and

(b) in the case of a nuisance of any other description, not less than twenty-one days' notice;

but the Secretary of State may, by order, provide that this subsection shall have effect as if such period as is specified in the order were the minimum period of notice applicable to any description of statutory nuisance specified in the order.

(8) A person who, without reasonable excuse, contravenes any requirement or prohibition imposed by an order under subsection (2) above shall be guilty of an offence and liable on summary conviction to a fine not exceeding level 5 on the standard scale together with a further fine of an amount equal to one-tenth of that level for each day on which the offence continues after the conviction.

(9) Subject to subsection (10) below, in any proceedings for an offence under subsection (8) above in respect of a statutory nuisance it shall be a defence to prove that the best practicable means were used to prevent, or to counteract the effects of, the nuisance.

(10) The defence under subsection (9) above is not available—

(a) in the case of a nuisance falling within paragraph (a), (d), (e), (f) or (g) of section 79(1) above except where the nuisance arises on industrial, trade or business premises;

(b) in the case of a nuisance falling within paragraph (b) of section 79(1) above except where the smoke is emitted from a chimney;

(c) in the case of a nuisance falling within paragraph (c) or (h) of section 79(1) above; and

(d) in the case of a nuisance which is such as to render the premises unfit for human habitation.

(11) If a person is convicted of an offence under subsection (8) above, a magistrates' court may, after giving the local authority in whose area the nuisance has ocurred an opportunity of being heard, direct the authority to do anything which the person convicted was required to do by the order to which the conviction relates.

(12) Where on the hearing of proceedings for an order under subsection (2) above it is proved that the alleged nuisance existed at the date of the making of the complaint, then, whether or not at the date of the hearing it still exists or is likely to recur, the court shall order the defendant (or defendants in such proportions as appears fair and reasonable) to pay to the person bringing the proceedings such amount as the court considers reasonably sufficient to compensate him for any expenses properly incurred by him in the proceedings.

(13) If it appears to the magistrates' court that neither the person responsible for the nuisance nor the owner or occupier of the premises can be found the court may, after giving the local authority in whose area the nuisance has occurred an opportunity of being heard, direct the authority to do anything which the court would have ordered that person to do.

Appendix Four

Landlord and Tenant Act 1985 ss8 and 11-17

Implied terms as to fitness for human habitation

8.—(1) In a contract to which this section applies for the letting of a house for human habitation there is implied, notwithstanding any stipulation to the contrary–

(*a*) a condition that the house is fit for human habitation at the commencement of the tenancy, and

(*b*) an undertaking that the house will be kept by the landlord fit for human habitation during the tenancy.

(2) The landlord, or a person authorised by him in writing, may at reasonable times of the day, on giving 24 hours' notice in writing to the tenant or occupier, enter premises to which this section applies for the purpose of viewing their state and condition.

(3) This section applies to a contract if–

(*a*) the rent does not exceed the figure applicable in accordance with subsection (4), and

(*b*) the letting is not on such terms as to the tenant's responsibility as are mentioned in subsection (5).

(4) The rent limit for the application of this section is shown by the following Table, by reference to the date of making of the contract and the situation of the premises:

TABLE

Date of making of contract	*Rent limit*
Before 31st July 1923.	In London: £40. Elsewhere: £26 or £16 (see Note 1).
On or after 31st July 1923 and before 6th July 1957.	In London: £40. Elsewhere: £26.
On or after 6th July 1957.	In London: £80. Elsewhere: £52.

NOTES

1. The applicable figure for contracts made before 31st July 1923 is £26 in the case of premises situated in a borough or urban district which at the date of the contract had according to the last published census a population of 50,000 or more. In the case of a house situated elsewhere, the figure is £16.

2. The references to "London" are, in relation to contracts made before 1st April 1965, to the administrative county of London and, in relation to contracts made on or after that date, to Greater London exclusive of the outer London boroughs.

(5) This section does not apply where a house is let for a term of three years or more (the lease not being determinable at the option of either party before the expiration of three years) upon terms that the tenant puts the premises into a condition reasonably fit for human habitation.

(6) In this section "house" includes–

(*a*) a part of a house, and

(*b*) any yard, garden, outhouses and appurtenances belonging to the house or usually enjoyed with it.

Repairing obligations in short leases

11.—(1) In a lease to which this section applies (as to which, see sections 13 and 14) there is implied a covenant by the lessor–

(a) to keep in repair the structure and exterior of the dwelling-house (including drains, gutters and external pipes),

(b) to keep in repair and proper working order the installations in the dwelling-house for the supply of water, gas and electricity and for sanitation (including basins, sinks, baths and sanitary conveniences, but not other fixtures, fittings and appliances for making use of the supply of water, gas or electricity), and

(c) to keep in repair and proper working order the installations in the dwelling-house for space heating and heating water.

[(1A) If a lease to which this section applies is a lease of a dwelling-house which forms part only of a building, then, subject to subsection (1B), the covenant implied by subsection (1) shall have effect as if–

(a) the reference in paragraph (a) of that subsection to the dwelling-house included a reference to any part of the building in which the lessor has an estate or interest; and

(b) any reference in paragraphs (b) and (c) of that subsection to an installation in the dwelling-house included a reference to an installation which, directly or indirectly, serves the dwelling-house and which either–

  (i) forms part of any part of the building in which the lessor has an estate or interest; or

  (ii) is owned by the lessor or under his control.

(1B) Nothing in subsection (1A) shall be construed as requiring the lessor to carry out any works or repairs unless the disrepair (or failure to maintain in working order) is such as to affect the lessee's enjoyment of the dwelling-house or of any common parts, as defined in section 60(1) of the Landlord and Tenant Act 1987, which the lessee, as such, is entitled to use.]

(2) The covenant implied by subsection (1) ("the lessor's repairing covenant") shall not be construed as requiring the lessor–

(a) to carry out works or repairs for which the lessee is liable by virtue of his duty to use the premises in a tenant-like manner, or would be so liable but for an express covenant on his part,

(b) to rebuild or reinstate the premises in the case of destruction or damage by fire, or by tempest, flood or other inevitable accident, or

(c) to keep in repair or maintain anything which the lessee is entitled to remove from the dwelling-house.

(3) In determining the standard of repair required by the lessor's repairing covenant, regard shall be had to the age, character and prospective life of the dwelling-house and the locality in which it is situated.

[(3A) In any case where–

(a) the lessor's repairing covenant has effect as mentioned in subsection (1A), and

(b) in order to comply with the covenant the lessor needs to carry out works or repairs otherwise than in, or to an installation in, the dwelling-house, and

(c) the lessor does not have a sufficient right in the part of the building or the installation concerned to enable him to carry out the required works or repairs,

then, in any proceedings relating to a failure to comply with the lessor's repairing covenant, so far as it requires the lessor to carry out the works or repairs in question, it shall be a defence for the lessor to prove that he used all reasonable endeavours to obtain, but was unable to obtain, such rights as would be adequate to enable him to carry out the works or repairs.]

(4) A covenant by the lessee for the repair of the premises is of no effect so far as it relates to the matters mentioned in subsection (1)(a) to (c), except so far as it imposes on the lessee any of the requirements mentioned in subsection (2)(a) or (c).

(5) The reference in subsection (4) to a covenant by the lessee for the repair of the premises includes a covenant—

(*a*) to put in repair or deliver up in repair,

(*b*) to paint, point or render,

(*c*) to pay money in lieu of repairs by the lessee, or

(*d*) to pay money on account of repairs by the lessor.

(6) In a lease in which the lessor's repairing covenant is implied there is also implied a covenant by the lessee that the lessor, or any person authorised by him in writing, may at reasonable times of the day and on giving 24 hours' notice in writing to the occupier, enter the premises comprised in the lease for the purpose of viewing their condition and state of repair.

Restriction on contracting out of s11

12.—(1) A covenant or agreement, whether contained in a lease to which section 11 applies or in an agreement collateral to such a lease, is void in so far as it purports–

(a) to exclude or limit the obligations of the lessor or the immunities of the lessee under that section, or

(b) to authorise any forfeiture or impose on the lessee any penalty, disability or obligation in the event of his enforcing or relying upon those obligations or immunities,

unless the inclusion of the provision was authorised by the county court.

(2) The county court may, by order made with the consent of the parties, authorise the inclusion in a lease, or in an agreement collateral to a lease, of provisions excluding or modifying in relation to the lease, the provisions of section 11 with

respect to the repairing obligations of the parties if it appears to the court that it is reasonable to do so, having regard to all the circumstances of the case, including the other terms and conditions of the lease.

Leases to which s11 applies: general rule

13.—(1) Section 11 (repairing obligations) applies to a lease of a dwelling-house granted on or after 24th October 1961 for a term of less than seven years.

(2) In determining whether a lease is one to which section 11 applies–

(a) any part of the term which falls before the grant shall be left out of account and the lease shall be treated as a lease for a term commencing with the grant,

(b) a lease which is determinable at the option of the lessor before the expiration of seven years from the commencement of the term shall be treated as a lease for a term of less than seven years, and

(c) a lease (other than a lease to which paragraph (b) applies) shall not be treated as a lease for a term of less than seven years if it confers on the lessee an option for renewal for a term which, together with the original term, amounts to seven years or more.

(3) This section has effect subject to–

section 14 (leases to which section 11 applies: exceptions), and

section 32(2) (provisions not applying to tenancies within Part II of the Landlord and Tenant Act 1954).

Leases to which s11 applies: exceptions

14.—(1) Section 11 (repairing obligations) does not apply to a new lease granted to an existing tenant, or to a former tenant still in possession, if the previous lease was not a lease to which section 11 applied (and, in the case of a lease granted before 24th October 1961, would not have been if it had been granted on or after that date).

(2) In subsection (1)–

"existing tenant" means a person who is when, or immediately before, the new lease is granted, the lessee under another lease of the dwelling-house;

"former tenant still in possession" means a person who–

(a) was the lessee under another lease of the dwelling-house which terminated at some time before the new lease was granted, and

(b) between the termination of that other lease and the grant of the new lease was continuously in possession of the dwelling-house or of the rents and profits of the dwelling-house; and

"the previous lease" means the other lease referred to in the above definitions.

(3) Section 11 does not apply to a lease of a dwelling-house which is a tenancy of an agricultural holding within the meaning of the [Agricultural Holdings Act 1986].

(4) Section 11 does not apply to a lease granted on or after 3rd October 1980 to–

a local authority,
a new town corporation,
an urban development corporation,
the Development Board for Rural Wales,
a registered housing association,

a co-operative housing association, or
an educational institution or other body specified, or of a class specified, by regulations under section 8 of the Rent Act 1977 or paragraph 8 of Schedule 1 to the Housing Act 1988 (bodies making student lettings)
[a housing action trust established under Part III of the Housing Act 1988].

(5) Section 11 does not apply to a lease granted on or after 3rd October 1980 to–
(a) Her Majesty in right of the Crown (unless the lease is under the management of the Crown Estate Commissioners), or
(b) a government department or a person holding in trust for Her Majesty for the purposes of a government department.

Jurisdiction of county court

15. The county court has jurisdiction to make a declaration that section 11 (repairing obligations) applies, or does not apply, to a lease–
(a) whatever the net annual value of the property in question, and
(b) notwithstanding that no other relief is sought than a declaration.

Meaning of "lease" and related expressions

16. In sections 11 to 15 (repairing obligations in short leases)–
(a) "lease" does not include a mortgage term;
(b) "lease of a dwelling-house" means a lease by which a building or part of a building is let wholly or mainly as a private residence, and "dwelling-house" means that building or part of a building;
(c) "lessee" and "lessor" mean, respectively, the person for the time being entitled to the term of a lease and to the reversion expectant on it.

Specific performance of landlord's repairing obligations

17.—(1) In proceedings in which a tenant of a dwelling alleges a breach on the part of his landlord of a repairing covenant relating to any part of the premises in which the dwelling is comprised, the court may order specific performance of the covenant whether or not the breach relates to a part of the premises let to the tenant and notwithstanding any equitable rule restricting the scope of the remedy, whether on the basis of a lack of mutuality or otherwise.

(2) In this section–
(a) "tenant" includes a statutory tenant,
(b) in relation to a statutory tenant the reference to the premises let to him is to the premises of which he is a statutory tenant,
(c) "landlord", in relation to a tenant, includes any person against whom the tenant has a right to enforce a repairing covenant, and
(d) "repairing covenant" means a covenant to repair, maintain, renew, construct or replace any property.

Appendix Five

Some Useful Addresses

1 **AMA** – Association of Metropolitan Authorities, 35 Great Smith Street, London SW1P 3BJ Tel 071–222 8100.
2 BRE – Building Research Establishment, Garston, Watford, Herts WD2 7JR Tel 0923–664848.
3 CHAR – Campaign for the Single Homeless, 5 Cromer Street, London WC1 Tel 071–833 2071.
4 DoE – Department of the Environment, Publications Sales Unit, Building 1, Victoria Road South, Ruislip, Middlesex HA4 0NZ.
5 Health and Housing Group, 120 Wilton Road, London SW1 1JZ Tel 071–233 7780.
6 IEHO – Institution of Environmental Health Officers, Chadwick House, Rushworth Street, London SE1 0QT Tel 071–928 6006.
7 LAG – Legal Action Group, 242 Pentonville Road, London N1 9UN Tel 071–833 2931.
8 LCF – Law Centres Federation, Duchess House, 18–19 Warren Street, London W1P 5EB Tel 071–387 8570.
9 London Hazards Centre, Headland House, 308 Gray's Inn Road, London WC1X 8DS Tel 071–837 5605.
10 RIBA – Royal Institute of British Architects, 66 Portland Place, London W1N 4AD Tel 071–580 5533.
11 SCAT – Services to Community Action and Trades Unions, 1 Sidney Street, Sheffield S1 4RG Tel 0742–727484.
12 SHAC – The London Housing Aid Centre, 189A Old Brompton Road, London SW5 0AR Tel 071–373 7276.
13 Shelter, 88 Old Street, London EC1V 9HU Tel 071–253 0202.

Appendix Six

Tables of Damages Awards for Disrepair

L = landlord T = tenant LA = local authority CCJ = county court judge

Table One: Court of Appeal (since Calabar v Stitcher)

Calabar Properties Ltd v Stitcher 28 July 1983

Top-floor flat; 99-year lease. Severe penetrating damp; L said condensation. 5 years before T driven to leave by conditions. Official Referee awarded (a) £4,606 (being cost of redecoration plus 10% for supervision and VAT, less one third for betterment) and (b) £3,000 general damages for disappointment, discomfort and loss of enjoyment. On appeal, T sought (c) rates, rent and other running costs paid while flat uninhabitable and (d) loss of capital value/notional loss of rental income from sub-letting.

Held: (c) not recoverable. T could instead recover costs of reasonable alternative accommodation but these had to be pleaded. (d) not recoverable. Flat was taken and used as a home by T not for commercial re-sale or letting. As to (a) there should have been no deduction for betterment (but this was not appealed).

Award: £7,606 upheld.

McGreal v Wake 3 February 1984

Old house. Rent £7pw. Rising damp. Wet rot. Decayed and open-jointed brickwork. Cracked and sagging ceilings in most rooms. LA repair notice served. No action. LA did work in default. T out of occupation 15 weeks in temporary tenancy (rent £10pw).

Held: remitted to CCJ to assess damages for (a) cost of redecorating (b) cost of removal and storage of furniture and alternative accommodation and (c) general damages for having to live in an "unrepaired house for some months after it should have been repaired".

Award: (to be assessed).

Bradley v Chorley Borough Council 27 February 1985

House was rewired. Damage to decorations. L declined to make good decorations.

Held: "repair" includes making good decorations.

Award: £220 ("virtually agreed").

Taylor v Knowsley Borough Council 21 March 1985

Flat. £15pw rent. Single, young, male T in arrears. No hot water (5 months). One ceiling light unusable (3 months). Small leak from bathroom ceiling (8 months). CCJ awarded £100 for loss of hot water and ceiling light, £59 for leak. Total award included £68 special damages for cost of baths.

Held: young, single, male T with relatives in neighbourhood allowing him to use their bathroom. General damages "not so clearly low" that appeal court should intervene.

Award: £159.

Minchburn v Peck 2 November 1987

Flat; 99-year lease. Penetrating damp (roof leaks) over 2 years. Cracking to wallplaster (from settlement) over 4 years. CCJ awarded £800 general and £250 special damages.

Held: general damages could be reduced for T's failure to press complaint of disrepair earlier.

Award: £700 general (reduced from £800); £250 special damages.

Lubren v Lambeth London Borough Council 12 November 1987

Basement and ground-floor LA maisonette. Penetrating damp. Defective windows and guttering. Disrepair reported 1979, which by 1984, was "appalling". CCJ awarded (a) special damages of £500, (b) general damages of average of £800 per annum for first 5 years, plus (c) £500 per annum for period in temporary accommodation while work under way.

Held: award too high in respect of earlier period if assessed separately; too low in respect of later period if assessed separately. Taken as averages the awards could be upheld. General damages for stay in temporary accommodation follow from L's repeated delay in completing work.

Award: £4,500.

Sturolson & Co v Mauroux 25 January 1988

T had lived in flat for 24 years. L in breach of covenant to repair and supply hot water and heating. L brought possession proceedings for arrears of rent; T pleaded set-off and counterclaim. CCJ awarded £1,345 for diminution of value to the premises and £4,550 for inconvenience, discomfort and injury to health.

Held: CCJ not constrained in assesement of damages by actual rent payable for premises. Registration of fair rent which takes into account disrepair, does not compensate T for breach of repairing covenant.

Award: £5,895 + £1,250 interest.

PRs of Chiodi v Demarney 7 June 1988

One-bedroom top-floor flat. £8pw rent. Penetrating damp (holes in roof). Fallen ceilings. Broken water heater. No repairs from 1980. T, single female aged 32. CCJ said "quite intolerable" conditions. CCJ awarded (a) general damages at £30pw for 3½ years, (b) special damages for furniture, clothing etc, (c) special damages for ill health.

Held: award for general damages at very top end of the range. CCJ did not err by not taking level of actual rent as prima facie measure for assessment.

Award: (a) £5,460; (b) £4,657; (c) £1,500.

Davies v Peterson 12 October 1988

House. At least 12 months' disrepair. CCJ awarded £858 including element of £250 for general damages for inconvenience.

Held: £250 in respect of 12 months' disrepair "little more than nominal". General damages element should have been at least £1,000.

Award: £1,000 general damages; £608 special damages.

Sella House Ltd v Mears 16 November 1988

Third-floor flat; 65-yr lease. Common parts not maintained. CCJ said "dingy and some window ledges filthy". Awarded £1,250 for loss of amenity over 7 years (less £570 for T's contribution from breach of repairing covenant).

Held: general damages award neither so high nor so low as to call for appeal court to intervene.

Award: £1,250 general damages (less deduction).

Table Two: High Court (since Calabar v Stitcher)

Finch v Manchester City Council 10 October 1986
Manchester District Registry

Severe disrepair and dampness throughout flat over several years. Whole family affected by ill health. One child died.

Award: £14,000 (by consent).

Mira and Others v Aylmer Square Investments 17 January 1989
HHJ John Newey QC (Official Referee)

Three blocks of flats. Action for breach of covenants of quiet enjoyment and nuisance and negligence caused by L's construction works on site. Direct effect on upper-floor tenants (falling ceilings etc).

Held: long lessees who would have sub-let are entitled to damages for loss of income from sub-letting; others, damages for inconvenience etc.

Award: £539,000 (by consent).

Loria v Hammer 31 July 1989
Mr John Lindsay QC (sitting as deputy High Court judge)

House converted to 5 flats. Damp penetration as a result of faults to water tank, asphalt roofing and guttering. T suffered 5 months' inconvenience before moving to other accommodation and arranging for remedial works to be done.

Held: L liable for the defects. T entitled to organise the works herself as L failed to respond to notice.

Award: £14,472 cost of repair work; £1,709 expenses of storage and accommodation; £900 distress and inconvenience over 5 months.

Table Three: County Courts (since Calabar v Stitcher)

Kearns v Liverpool City Council 22 February 1985
Liverpool County Court, HHJ Stannard

First-floor maisonette. Rent £17pw. T plus 9 children. Disrepair 1982–84. Gaps in windows. Broken glazing. Glass blown out. Defective WC. Rewired but failure to "make good" disturbed plaster and decorations.

Award: £1,000 general damages; £350 special damages.

Yorston and Yorston v Crewfield Ltd and Festal International Ltd 19 April 1985
Clerkenwell County Court, HHJ Krikler

Top-floor, one-bedroom flat. Long lease. Leaking roof. Dry rot to roof timbers. Inspection holes bored in ceilings for treatment. No repair. Falling plaster. Inconvenience over 22 months. No hot water for 2 months.

Award: £1,750 general damages; £500 special damages (cost of redecoration).

Hubble v Lambeth London Borough Council 28 October 1985
Wandsworth County Court

Dampness caused by defective guttering and downpipes. Dangerous wiring. Poor plasterwork and windows. Some rotten floor joists.

Award: £4,000 (including £1,660 special damages) by consent.

Fraser v Hopewood Properties 29 October 1985
West London County Court, HHJ Parker

Top-floor flat. Penetrating damp around windows. Work done but took 3½ years to complete. Smallest bedroom uninhabitable.

Award: £2,000 general damages; £2,250 cost of redecoration; £200 other special damages.

Downie v Lambeth London Borough Council 3 June 1986
Wandsworth County Court, HHJ White

Three-bedroom house. Extensive damp. Leaking roof. No repairs nor maintenance for 5 years. "Appalling" condition.

Award: £4,000 general damages; £451 special damages; £230 interest.

Meah v Tower Hamlets London Borough Council 14 August 1986
Bow County Court, Mr Registrar Platt

Flat. T and 3 children. 3½-year period of damp penetration through windows. Kitchen infested with beetles.

Award: £1,750 general damages; £1,534 special damages.

Savory v Southwark London Borough Council 3 October 1986
Lambeth County Court

Two-bedroom flat. Dampness. Disrepair stretching over 2 to 3 years.

Award: £4,000 (including £800 special damages) by consent.

McDermott v Southwark London Borough Council 5 November 1986
Lambeth County Court, HHJ Pearce

House. Roof leaked. Defective wiring. Damp penetration. All but 2 rooms affected. T and 5 children. 3 periods for award (a) 1981–83, (b) 7 months in 1983 in temporary accommodation, (c) 1983–85.

Award: period (a) = £4,200 general damages; £2,000 special damages (£1,600 for damage to possessions £400 for extra fuel costs): period (b) = £820 agreed payment by L: period (c) = £1,900 general damages and £257 special damages (£245 for extra fuel costs and £12 for damaged property)- implementing local arbitration award.

Moodie v Hackney London Borough Council 6 February 1987
Shoreditch County Court, HHJ Clapham

Three-bedroom maisonette. £25pw rent. T and 4 children. Rainwater penetration initially through windows (1980–85), thereafter through concrete panels.

Award: £2,200 general damages for 1980–85; £375 general damages from 1985 to trial; £250 for ill health; £20 other special damages.

Felix v Karachristos 4 March 1987
Bloomsbury County Court, HHJ Dobry

One-bedroom flat. Warped and rotted windows. Damp walls and ceilings. Rainwater penetration. Faulty water heater. Inconvenience over 4½-year period.

Award: £5,000 general damages; £375 interest.

Zone Properties v Painter 13 April 1987
Edmonton County Court, HHJ Tibber

Top-floor flat. Leaking roof from 1981. LA served repair notice. No work until 1983. Works took 6 months.

Award: £2,000 for general damages (separate award for special damages).

Savage and Savage v Harscott Ltd 11 June 1987
Lambeth County Court, HHJ Macnair

Ground-floor flat. Rising damp. Dry rot. L inserted DPC. Ts moved out for 3 months during work. Mess left behind. General damages sought for dampness, overcrowding in temporary accommodation with relatives and work of cleaning up. Special damages claimed for cost of cleaning and redecoration.

Award: £3,000 general damages; £747 special damages; plus interest.

Abdullah, Kesteris and Elliot v South Tyneside Borough Council 22 July 1987
South Shields County Court, HHJ Paling

Flats. Condensation. Plaster deterioration. Rusted and distorted metal window frames. One T with leaking roof. Period of claim 6 years in each case.

Award: A = £150 (including £100 for windows); K = £350 (including £200 for windows); E = £1,200 (including £800 for leaking roof).

Rees v Davies (undated) 1987
Swansea County Court

Old house. Complaints from T since 1980. Repair notices from LA since 1981. Roof leaked. One ceiling fell. Penetrating and rising damp. Uneven and rotten timbers. 4-page list of defects. 4 years of "inconvenience and hardship".

Award: £4,000 general damages; £398 special damages; plus interest.

Ireland v Sheffield City Council 2 September 1987
Sheffield County Court, HHJ Henham

House. Gross disrepair. Damp. Water penetration. Independent EHO said "unfit" from outset of tenancy. Claim for maximum of 6 years.

Award: £7,200 (£5,000 in general damages; £2,200 rent arrears written off) by consent.

Weller v Lewisham London Borough Council 18 January 1988
Bromley County Court

End of terrace house. Rising damp. Condensation. Independent EHO said whole house "unfit".

Award: £6,250 (including £1,107 special damages) by consent.

Kinch v Lambeth London Borough Council 15 March 1988
Wandsworth County Court, Mr Recorder Russell

House. LA served informal repair notice (1980) and unfitness notice (1986). Problems with roof, window frames, guttering, chimneystack. Claim for 6-year period plus 6 months from issue of proceedings to completion of work.

Award: £7,000 general damages; £551 special damages; £449 interest by consent.

Pursey v Acrochoice Investments Ltd 11 October 1988
Willesden County Court, HHJ Krikler

T aged 73. House in very bad disrepair. Tenant for 41 years. Forced by L to move to better quality, temporary accommodation for work to be carried out. No effort to start work. L attempted quick sale with vacant possession.

Award: £4,500 general damages (£500 for each month in temporary accommodation).

McManus v Landfarm Properties Ltd 20 March 1989
Liverpool County Court, HHJ Stannard

Serious disrepair. No action by L. T did work in default after 2½ years of poor conditions.

Award: £1,000 general damages; £2,225 interim award towards full cost of reasonable works.

Staves v Leeds CC 24 November 1989
Leeds County Court, HHJ Coles

Ts occupied 'No-Fines' concrete house. Acute condensation dampness. Perished plaster and mould growth. L aware of situation since 1984.

Award: £5,406 general damages.

Lewisham LBC v All-Aziz 10 January 1990
Bromley County Court

Counterclaim for disrepair in arrears possession proceedings. Ts and 5 children. Leaking and sagging roof, gaps between roof and walls, defective guttering, crumbling plaster and severe dampness. Disrepair for over 8 years.

Award: £9,500 general damages; £3,000 personal injury (respiratory ailments etc); £500 special damages.

Thompson v Birmingham CC 11 July 1990
Birmingham County Court, HHJ Gosling

Old terraced house. Extensive penetrating damp caused by failure of DPC. Several ineffective repairs. Problems for over 3½ years.

Award: £3,028 general damages (184 weeks at £17 pw); £1,200 cost of redecoration; £150 special damages.

Battersea Freehold and Leasehold Property Co Ltd v Norman
Inworth Property Co Ltd v Presslee 3 August 1990
Lambeth County Court, HHJ Macnair

Adjoining properties, owned by 2 separate but associated companies. Purchased 1982. Almost no repairs or maintenance since. Actions for possession. Counterclaims for extensive disrepair.

Award: £5,000 plus interest to each T and mandatory injunctions for considerable work.

Bygraves v Southwark LBC 20 September 1990
Lambeth County Court, Recorder Dohmann QC

T and 1 child. Flat. Severe damp. Child contracted serious and acute asthma. T settled claim for general and special damages for disrepair for herself (£3,500), but proceeded with claim for child under DPA 1972 s4.

Award: £4,000 ill health, pain and suffering over 4 years; £5,000 disruption to schooling and possible psychological consequences up to age 18; £3,000 inconvenience, discomfort and distress over $3\frac{1}{2}$ years.

Brent LBC v Roberts 9 October 1990
Willesden County Court, HHJ Lowe

Counterclaim in arrears possession action. Cockroach infestation over 4-year period. No effective action taken by council.

Award: £6,250 (less £5,000 set-off against arrears of rent).

Appendix Seven

Precedents

This appendix contains precedent documentation for a routine disrepair case in which the tenant:
(a) brings an action for damages in the county court (see chapter 4); and
(b) complains to a magistrate under HA 1985 s606 (see p101); and
(c) brings proceedings under EPA s82 (see p77).

It is assumed that before launching the proceedings, the tenant's advisers have (as appropriate):
(1) taken a detailed statement of facts from the client;
(2) instructed an independent EHO/surveyor to inspect and report;
(3) sought medical reports and evidence;
(4) had the premises professionally photographed;
(5) set the client gathering receipts etc for items of special damage; and
(6) sent a "letter before action" to the landlords.

Anna Tennant lives with her four-year-old son in a two-bedroom council flat on the fourth (top) floor of a council block. She has been the tenant for three years. Throughout the tenancy the premises have been damp. There are damp patches on the ceilings of the small bedroom and kitchen and rainwater penetration around the windows. There are numerous other defects. Her rent is £35.00 per week and is covered by housing benefit.

She has complained frequently to the council's estate officer, reported the defects at the neighbourhood housing office and called in the council's Environmental Health Officer. She has also seen her councillor. With only limited (and largely "botched") repair work having been undertaken, and her son in declining health, she has turned to the Rainbow Community Law Centre. Its letter addressed to the Director of Housing has received no reply. Its letter to the Legal Department has received only an acknowledgement.

I THE CIVIL ACTION

I.1 Particulars of Claim (could be adapted for use as a counterclaim)

IN THE ANYTOWN COUNTY COURT Case No: 90/7273

BETWEEN:

Anna Tennant Plaintiff

and

Anytown District Council Defendants

PARTICULARS OF CLAIM

1. In or about January 1987 the Plaintiff was granted a secure tenancy of 17 Tower House, Moors Estate, Anytown ("the premises") by the Defendants. The premises consist of a two-bedroom flat and have at all material times been occupied by the Plaintiff and her son Jeremy who was born on 3 December 1986.
2. It is an express term[1] of the tenancy that the Defendants will keep in repair the structural parts of the premises.
3. Further and in the alternative, it is an implied term[2] of the said tenancy that the Defendants will keep in repair the structure and exterior of the dwelling and keep in repair and proper working order the installations therein for the supply of water, gas and electricity and for sanitation, space heating and heating water.
4. Further and in the further alternative, the Defendants owe a duty[3] to take reasonable care that the Plaintiff and her son are reasonably safe from injury or damage to their property.
5. Yet further and in the alternative, it is an express term[1] of the tenancy that the Defendants will keep in repair the common parts of the building containing the premises.
6. Yet further and in the further alternative, it is an implied term[4] of the said tenancy that the Defendants shall not derogate from their grant and more particularly that they shall ensure that the parts retained in their possession and control remain reasonably safe and do not cause damage to the Plaintiff or the premises.
7. The Defendants have throughout the period of the tenancy been in breach of the terms duties and obligations aforementioned.

Particulars

(i) Some two months after the commencement of the tenancy a damp patch (approximately 2 feet in diameter) formed on the ceiling in the small bedroom. It is intermittently wet and dry and has discoloured the ceiling paper. Plaster in the area is cracked and since December 1988 rainwater has dripped from the cracks in periods of heavy rain.

(ii) In March 1989 a patch similar to that described above developed on the kitchen ceiling. The area is covered during winter months with black mould which the Plaintiff is forced to clear regularly with a disinfectant wipe.

(iii) From the outset of the tenancy there has been a half-inch gap above the window frame of the main window in the living room.

(iv) In or about April 1988 a crack developed around the window frame of the window in the main bedroom. The plaster around the said window is loose and crumbling.

(v) The inner sills to both the aforementioned windows are rotted by reason of the accumulation of water upon them.

(vi) From the outset of the tenancy the sole gas fire provided in the living room at the premises has operated only to approximately two-thirds capacity even when switched full on.

(vii) The wallplaster to the external kitchen wall immediately below the window is cracked and since in or about November 1988 has crumbled and flaked upon contact.

(viii) The parapet wall to the walkway balcony immediately opposite the front door of the premises has throughout the tenancy had three of its upper row of bricks missing.

(ix) The window glazing to the common stairwell providing access to the premises has been broken on two occasions. In 1988 the Defendants replaced the same after a delay of eight months. In 1989, after the glass was again broken, the Defendants replaced the same after six months.

(x) In or about September 1989 a patch of damp began to develop on the wall of the premises immediately above the front door as a result of overflows from the roof guttering above.

(xi) From the outset of the tenancy, the pull-cord switch to the bathroom ceiling light has operated intermittently and the electrical socket provided in the hallway of the premises emits a spark when used.

8. The matters complained of in paragraph 8 above are known to the Defendants.

Particulars

(i) On occasions too numerous to particularise (but no less frequently than six times each year throughout the tenancy) the Plaintiff has reported the defects by telephone and in person to the Defendants at their Neighbourhood Housing Office.

(ii) On occasions too numerous to particularise Estate Officers, workmen and other persons employed by the Defendants have visited the premises for the purpose of inspection.

(iii) Without prejudice to the generality of the foregoing the Plaintiff has been visited at the premises by two successive Estate Officers (Ms Jenkinson and Mr Peters) in or about April 1987 and June 1988 respectively and both were shown the defects in the premises at the dates of their visits.

(iv) In or about July 1989 an Environmental Health Officer in the employ of the Defendants visited the premises and inspected the state thereof.

(v) In or about September 1989 the Plaintiff reported the aforementioned defects to one Desmond Haines who is a councillor of the Defendant authority.

9. By reason of the aforementioned breaches of terms, obligations and duties the Plaintiff and her son have suffered loss, damage, injury, distress and inconvenience.

Particulars[5]

(i) For the duration of the tenancy the premises have been damp and unsightly and each winter have carried a pervading smell of dampness.

(ii) Decorations, carpets and soft furnishings provided at the premises by the Plaintiff have been ruined by dampness and/or mould growth.

(iii) The Plaintiff has expended additional monies on heating the premises as a result of the dampness of the premises.

(iv) Clothing kept in the premises by the Plaintiff and her son has to be repeatedly washed and/or replaced as a result of permeation by damp odour and the effect of mould.

(v) For the duration of the tenancy, the Plaintiff and her son have suffered from repeated colds and influenza and her son has developed an upper respiratory tract infection.

(vi) For six weeks in the winter of 1988/89 the Plaintiff was forced by conditions in the premises to leave and stay with her own mother. She paid her mother £20 weekly for expenses during that stay.

(vii) For the duration of the tenancy the Plaintiff has suffered stress as a result both of the defects particularised above and the dangerous state of the premises. Further stress has resulted from the failure of remedial work carried out by the Defendants in or about May 1988 and the failure of the Defendants to respond to complaints thereafter.

(viii) From the winter of 1987/88 and during each successive winter the premises have been infested with insects most particularly in the kitchen area which has caused additional stress and inconvenience to the Plaintiff and caused her to incur additional expenditure through the cost of eating out.

10. The Plaintiff claims interest pursuant to the provisions of section 69 of the County Courts Act 1984 at the rate of 15% or such other rate as the court may think fit.

AND THE PLAINTIFF CLAIMS

1. An order for specific performance to remedy the defects set out at paragraph 7 above.
2. Damages limited to £5,000.[6]
3. Interest at the rate of 15%.
4. Costs.

Dated this 3rd day of April 1990

Rainbow Community Law Centre
Rainbow High Street
Anytown
Solicitors for the Plaintiff

To: The Registrar and
the Defendant

Notes

1 Plead any relevant express term in the tenancy agreement.
2 Relying on LTA 1985 s11 (see p18).
3 Relying on DPA 1972 s4 (see p43).
4 Plead appropriate implied term (see pp12-30).
5 For the pleading of damages see pp60-64.
6 May be raised to £10,000 in 1990/91.

I.2 The application for an injunction (see p58)

IN THE ANYTOWN COUNTY COURT Case No: 90/7273

BETWEEN:

Anna Tennant Plaintiff

and

Anytown District Council Defendants

NOTICE OF APPLICATION

TAKE NOTICE that the Plaintiff intends to apply to a Judge of the Court sitting at the Court Offices, Court Street, Anytown on the 9th day of April 1990 at 10.30 o'clock in the forenoon for an order by way of interlocutory injunction in the following terms:

1. That on or before Monday 7th May 1990 the Defendants do:

(a) repair the roof immediately above the premises let to the Plaintiff to prevent the ingress of rainwater

(b) seal the gaps and cracks around the windows to the main bedroom and main living room of the premises

(c) overhaul and repair or replace the fixed gas fire in the main living room of the premises

(d) clear, clean and repair the roof guttering immediately above the front door of the premises.

2. That the Defendants do pay the costs of and incidental to this application in any event.

AND TAKE NOTICE that the grounds of the Plaintiff's application are set out in her affidavit served herewith.

Dated this 5th day of April 1990

Rainbow Community Law Centre
Rainbow High Street
Anytown
Solicitors for the Plaintiff

To: The Chief Clerk
and the Defendant

I.3 The draft order (see p56)

IN THE ANYTOWN COUNTY COURT Case No: 90/7273

BETWEEN:

Anna Tennant Plaintiff

and

Anytown District Council Defendants

ORDER

Before His Honour Judge Right sitting at Anytown on Monday the 9th day of April 1990

UPON HEARING the solicitor for the Plaintiff and the Defendant and
UPON READING the Plaintiff's affidavit sworn on the 5th day of April 1990

AND UPON the Plaintiff undertaking by her solicitor to abide by any order that this Court may make for the payment of damages in case this Court shall hereafter find that the Defendants have sustained any loss or damage by reason of this Order

IT IS ORDERED THAT on or before Monday 7th May 1990 the Defendants do:

(a) repair the roof immediately above the premises let to the Plaintiff to prevent the ingress of rainwater
(b) seal the gaps and cracks around the windows to the main bedroom and main living room of the premises
(c) overhaul and repair or replace the fixed gas fire in the main living room of the premises
(d) clear, clean and repair the guttering to the roof of the premises immediately above the front door.

IT IS FURTHER ORDERED that the Defendants should pay the costs of and incidental to this hearing in any event.

DATED this 9th day of April 1990

To the Mayor and Burgesses of the Anytown District Council, Council Offices, Anytown.

TAKE NOTICE that unless you obey the directions contained in this order you will be guilty of contempt of court and will be liable to be committed to prison.

Judge Right

II THE COMPLAINT

II.1 The complaint to the magistrate (see p101)

IN THE ANYTOWN MAGISTRATES' COURT

To: Thomas Hardy being a Justice of the Peace for the Anytownshire County area.

THE complainant one Anna Tennant complains that the property occupied by her at 17 Tower House, Moors Estate, Anytown being a dwelling-house within the area of the Anytown District Council is unfit for human habitation having regard to the matters set out in Housing Act 1985 section 604 as amended.

The complainant applies to you as Justice of the Peace for the area that you do cause complaint to be made to the said District Council in writing as provided by Housing Act 1985 section 606(2) requiring them to carry out an inspection of the said premises and to make a report stating the facts of the case and to make a finding as to whether, in the opinion of that council, the dwelling is unfit for human habitation.

Dated this 10th day of April 1990

Rainbow Community Law Centre
Rainbow High Street
Anytown
Solicitors for the Complainant.

II.2 Draft complaint by magistrate (see p101)

IN THE ANYTOWN MAGISTRATES' COURT

To: The Proper Officer of the Anytown District Council
Council Offices
Anytown

I, Thomas Hardy being an appointed JUSTICE OF THE PEACE for the area of Anytownshire County, do hereby make complaint to you in the terms of section 606(2) Housing Act 1985 that the premises at 17 Tower House, Moors Estate, within the area of your Council are unfit for human habitation and that I call for an inspection and report to be made in the terms of that provision.

Dated this 11th day of April 1990

Signed

Thomas Hardy
JP

III THE EPA PROCEEDINGS

III.1 The initial information

IN THE ANYTOWN MAGISTRATES' COURT

Dated this 12th day of February 1991

Defendant: The Anytown District Council

Address: Council Offices, Anytown.

Alleged offence: That on this 12th day of February 1991 a statutory nuisance as defined by section 79(1)(a) Environmental Protection Act 1990 exists at 17 Tower House, Moors Estate, Anytown and continues to exist and that the nuisance (particulars of which are given in the attached statement) is the responsibility of the Anytown District Council and in so far as it results from structural defects is their responsibility as owners.

The Information of: Anna Tennant who being a person aggrieved for the purposes of section 82 of the said Act complains that the defendant is responsible for the said nuisance, has given the required notice to bring these proceedings and asks that the accused be summoned to answer this information.

Address: Solicitor
Rainbow Community Law Centre
Rainbow High Street
Anytown

Taken before me this 12th day of February 1991

....

Justice of the Peace/Clerk to the Justices

III.2 Further information laid in magistrates' court

IN THE ANYTOWN MAGISTRATES' COURT

Dated this 12th day of April 1991

Accused: The Anytown District Council

Address: Council Offices, Anytown.

Alleged Offence: That contrary to section 82(8) of the Environmental Protection Act 1990 you have without reasonable excuse failed to comply with an order made by this court on 8th March 1991 requiring you to abate a statutory nuisance at 17 Tower House, Moors Estate, Anytown.

The Information of: Anna Tennant who being a person aggrieved for the purposes of section 82(1) of the said Act alleges that the accused committed the alleged offence and applies that the accused by summons do answer this information.

Address: Solicitor
Rainbow Community Law Centre
Rainbow High Street
Anytown

Taken before me this 12th day of April 1991

....

Justice of the Peace/Clerk to the Justices

III.3 Draft summons

IN THE ANYTOWN MAGISTRATES' COURT

To the accused: The Mayor and Burgesses of the Anytown District Council

Of: Council Offices, Anytown

You are hereby summoned to appear on 6th May 1991 at 10.00am before the Magistrates' Court at Court House, Rainbow Street, Anytown to answer the information (of which particulars are given in the attached schedule).

Alleged Offence: that you have without reasonable excuse failed to comply with an order made under s82(2) Environmental Protection Act 1990 by this court on 8th March 1991 requiring you to abate a statutory nuisance at 17 Tower House, Moors Estate, Anytown as defined by section 79(1)(a) of the said Act.

The Prosecutor is: Solicitor, Rainbow Community Law Centre, Rainbow High Street, Anytown.

Dated this 12th day of April 1991

....

Justice of the Peace/Clerk to the Justices

Appendix Eight

Amount of Home Loss Payment

Displacement on or after 16 November 1990:

(a) where the displaced person is a freeholder or leaseholder with more than three years unexpired on the lease — 10% of the market value of that interest (subject to a maximum of £15,000 and a minimum of £1,500);

(b) other occupiers — a sum of £1,500.[1]

Displacement between 1 April 1990 and 15 November 1990:

the amount is a fixed sum of £1,500.[2]

Displacement between 16 January 1989 and 31 March 1990:

an amount equal to 10 times the rateable value subject to a maximum of £1,500 and a minimum of £1,200.[3]

Displacement between 1 April 1973 and 15 January 1989:

an amount equal to three times the rateable value subject to a maximum of £1,500 and a minimum of £150.[4]

1 Land Compensation Act 1973 s30 as amended.
2 Local Government Finance (Repeals, Savings and Consequential Amendments) Order 1990 SI No 776 Sch 3 para 19.
3 Home Loss Payments Order 1989 SI No 24.
4 Land Compensation Act 1973 s30(1).

Index

ABATEMENT NOTICE, 73–75, 78
ACCESS
  EHOs', premises to, 73
  landlords', premises to, 15, 17, 18, 28, 29–30, 44, 128, 129
ACCOMMODATION
  alternative, 62, 63, 64, 102, 129, 130, 131, 132, 133
  furnished, 12, 13
  residential, 133
  short-life, 100, 134
  temporary, 15, 62, 100, 102, 129, 130, 131, 134
  unfurnished, 10, 12, 13
APPEALS, 74, 85, 94, 96, 98, 100, 105
ARCHITECT
  liability (statutory) of, 42, 43
  liability (tortious) of, 36, 115
AREA ACTION, 111–113
  clearance area, 15, 96, 99, 111, 112
  general improvement area, 111, 120
  group repair scheme, 96, 101
  housing action area, 111, 120
  renewal area, 73, 104, 112
ASBESTOS, 113
ATTORNEY-GENERAL, 124

BOARDING-HOUSE, 119, 120
  common, 120
BUILDER
  liability (contractual) of, 35
  liability (statutory) of, 42, 43
  liability (tortious) of, 35, 36, 37, 115
BUILDING
  dangerous, 69, 100, 118, 122
  dilapidated, 26, 118, 122

CARE
  breach of duty of *see* REMEDIES
CAUTION, 54, 98
CAVEAT EMPTOR, 9–10
CHARGE
  service, 52
CIRCULAR
  DoE, of, 92, 94, 96, 99, 112, 141
CLEARANCE AREA, 15, 96, 99, 111, 112
CLEARANCE ORDER, 135
CLOSING ORDER, 96, 99–100, 102, 131, 133, 135, 141
COMMITTAL
  contempt, for, 58, 59
COMMON PARTS
  repair of, 11, 15, 16–18, 27, 39, 41–42, 59, 73, 104, 106, 122
COMMUNITY CHARGE, 143
COMPENSATION, 64, 84, 99, 102, 103, 116, 143
  displaced tenants, to, 100, 102, 112, 130, 131, 132, 134–143
    contractual payment, 135, 142

COMPENSATION—*cont*
discretionary payment, 135, 141
disturbance payment, 134, 138–141
home loss payment, 131, 134, 135–137
removal expenses, 62, 63, 135, 140, 142–143
well maintained payment, 112, 135, 142
order, 79, 84, 99, 105
COMPLAINT
laying of, 78
COMPULSORY PURCHASE, 99, 111, 112, 121, 133, 134, 135, 138, 139
order, 99, 138, 139
CONDENSATION, 5, 21, 39, 45, 71, 80, 114–117
dampness, 117
EPA 1990 s82 and, 115
LTA 1985 s11 and, 114
CONTRACT
breach of *see* REMEDIES
restricted *see* RESTRICTED CONTRACT
unfair terms, 11, 13
CONTRACT OF LETTING *see* TENANCY AGREEMENT
CONTROL ORDER, 121
COSTS, 74, 80, 85, 86
COUNTERCLAIM, 50, 52, 53, 55
COUNTER-NOTICE, 75
COVENANT
breach of *see* REMEDIES
quiet enjoyment, for, 16, 122, 123
CROWN TENANCY, 27

DAMAGE
property to, caused by defect, 35, 36, 38, 41
DAMAGES, 49, 52, 53, 60–64, 84, 131, 160–166
assessment of, 61
general, 61–62
lessee unable to re-sell, 62
tenant in occupation, 61–62
tenant moved out, 62
tenant unable to sub-let, 62
interim, 60
liquidated, 53
special, 63
DAMPNESS, 4, 5, 13, 26, 63, 71, 75, 93, 117
DANGEROUS BUILDING *see* BUILDING
DECLARATION, 28, 60, 86, 112, 130
DEFAULT
repair, in, 50, 51, 52, 60, 64, 74, 75, 98, 99, 102, 105, 106, 119, 121, 125
DEFECT
design, 5, 11, 19, 21, 42
latent, 35, 36, 38
'relevant', 45–46
structural, 23, 36, 74, 80, 82, 114
DEFECTIVE PREMISES
DPA 1972, 42–46
'relevant defect', 45–46
DEMOLITION, 5, 99–100, 102, 111, 118, 119, 131, 132, 137
order, 96, 99–100, 102, 131, 133, 135
DoE
circular *see* CIRCULAR
DEROGATION
grant, from, 122
DESIGN DEFECT *see* DEFECT
DEVELOPER
liability (tortious) of, 35, 37, 115
DILAPIDATED BUILDING *see* BUILDING
DISCOMFORT, 71, 72, 73, 91, 106, 130

DISPLACEMENT
causes of, 128–131
compulsory, 137, 139
private tenants of, 128, 129, 132
public sector tenants of, 129, 130, 132
temporary, 141, 143
DISREPAIR
fit house in, 105
notice of, to be given to landlord *see* NOTICE
'serious', 94, 95, 112
substantial, 91, 104–105
DISTRICT LAND REGISTRY, 54, 98
pending land action, 60
DISTURBANCE PAYMENT, 134, 138–141
discretionary, 141
home loss payment and, 138
key date for, 139
DRAINS, 12, 119
DWELLING-HOUSE, 22, 24, 93, 106

ECONOMIC LOSS *see* LOSS
ENGINEER
liability (tortious) of, 36
EHO, 29, 113, 121, 122, 125
access to premises *see* ACCESS
EPA powers and, 71, 73, 76–79, 81, 115, 124
HA powers and, 92, 103
ESTATE ACTION PROGRAMME, 1

FIRE PRECAUTIONS, 119–120, 121
FLATS, 13, 23, 70, 93, 96, 99, 106
block of, 5, 17, 18, 41, 54, 70, 99, 104, 106, 120, 124
council, 13
multiple occupation, in, 93, 96, 106, 121
unfurnished, 13
FREEHOLDER, 97, 104
FURNISHED ACCOMMODATION, 12, 13
FURNITURE
storage of, 63, 131

GENERAL IMPROVEMENT AREA, 111, 120
GROUP REPAIR SCHEME, 96, 101

HABITATION
human, unfit for *see* UNFIT
HEALTH
prejudicial to, 69–71, 113, 115, 124
HOME LOSS PAYMENT, 131, 134, 135–137, 138, 141, 182
discretionary, 141
disturbance payment and, 138
HOMELESS, 100, 123, 133, 134, 143
HOSTEL, 120, 121
HOUSE
definition of, 93[7], 106
HOUSE IN MULTIPLE OCCUPATION, 93, 96, 104, 106, 120, 121
HOUSING
unfit *see* UNFIT
HOUSING ACTION AREA, 111, 120
HOUSING ACTION TRUST, 103
HOUSING ASSOCIATION, 84, 130
registered, 135, 138
tenancy *see* TENANCY
HOUSING BENEFIT, 51
HOUSING ORDER, 135, 136, 138, 139, 141
HOUSING STOCK, 134
decline of, 1–6, 91
HUMAN HABITATION
unfit for *see* UNFIT

IMPROVEMENT, 83, 97, 120–121, 131–132, 135, 138, 141
compulsory, 120–121
grant, 98, 132
order, 132, 133, 135, 138, 141
redevelopment, or, 136–137, 139

IMPROVEMENT—*cont*
repair, or, 19, 63, 83, 120–121, 136
voluntary, 120
INFORMATION
laying of, 78, 79, 80, 81, 82, 84, 85, 86
INJUNCTION, 45, 59, 75 *and see* SPECIFIC PERFORMANCE
interim/interlocutory, 56–58
mandamus, 101
mandatory, 57, 59
Mareva, 60
INJURY
personal *see* PERSONAL INJURY
INSTALLATION
repair of, 18, 22, 24–25, 94, 121, 124, 125
INSULATION, 83, 114–115
sound, 123
INTEREST, 64, 98, 106, 140

JUDICIAL REVIEW, 77, 85, 96, 100, 101, 138

KEY DATE
disturbance payment, for, 139

LAND, 70, 138–139
LAND CHARGE, 54, 98
local, 105
pending land action, 60
LANDLORD
access to premises *see* ACCESS
identity of, 50, 54
liability (contractual) of, 12, 13, 16, 18, 28, 34, 37, 50, 53, 58, 63, 116 *and see* TENANCY AGREEMENT
liability (statutory) of, 18, 41–46, 58, 114, 116, 125
visitors etc, to, 42, 43, 78
liability (tortious) of, 18, 34, 36–41, 58, 114–115
visitors etc, to, 34, 45
LANDS TRIBUNAL, 138, 141, 144
LEASE
long, 14, 15, 27, 37
LEASEHOLDER, 62, 97, 104
LEGAL AID, 55, 56, 79, 85, 144
ABWOR, 85
emergency, 56
green form, 49, 79, 81, 144
statutory charge, 55
LIABILITY *see* LANDLORD, BUILDER etc
exclusion of, 11, 13, 15, 17, 18, 42, 46, 51
immunity from, 10, 12, 34, 36, 37, 38, 39, 43
LICENCE, 13, 134, 139
LICENSEE, 43, 46, 78, 97, 104
LIMITATION, 41, 55–56
contract, in, 41, 55
personal injury, 41, 55
statutory, 56, 136, 138
tortious, 5, 41, 55
LOCAL AUTHORITY
liability (tortious) of, 35, 37
mobilisation of, 100
particular duty of, 26, 38, 83
statutory duty of, 42, 73, 74, 77, 86, 92, 95, 101, 102, 103, 106, 112, 121, 123, 125
statutory power of, 92, 98, 101, 104, 105, 106, 112, 118, 119, 120, 121, 126, 141
tenant of *see* TENANT
LODGER, 139
LOSS
economic, caused by defect, 36, 47[28]

MAGISTRATE
complaint of, 101, 103
MAINTENANCE
repair or, 19
MAKING GOOD
repairs, after, 19, 63, 104

MANAGER
appointment of, 54
MANDAMUS, 101
MAREVA
injunction, 60
MITIGATION
loss, of, 51, 64
MORTGAGEE, 97, 99, 104
MULTI-OCCUPATION, 93, 96, 106, 121

NEGLIGENCE, 21, 25, 34–41
damage to property and, 35, 36, 38, 41
economic loss and, 36, 47[28]
personal injury and, 35, 36, 38, 39, 41
NEIGHBOURING PROPERTY, 17, 72, 73, 118, 122, 124
NOTICE *and see* ORDER
abatement, 73, 74, 75, 78
disrepair of, to be given to landlord, 12, 16, 17, 26, 27, 28–29, 44–45, 49, 50
intention to prosecute, of, 78, 79, 80
'nine-day', 75
NUISANCE
noise, 72, 73, 123
order, 74, 75, 78, 82–84, 86
private, 39, 72, 124
public, 72
recurring, 74, 75–76
statutory, 69–73, 74, 75, 76, 77, 78, 79, 81, 82, 86
'person aggrieved', 78, 79

OCCUPANCY
service, 135
OCCUPIER, 74, 76–77, 79, 96, 98, 99, 104, 112, 133, 136, 138
agricultural, 105
displaced, 134
OCCUPIER—*cont*
liability (statutory) of, OLA 1957, 41
service, 135
OFFICIAL REFEREE, 55, 164
OMBUDSMAN, 64, 76, 77, 101, 116, 144
ORDER
breach of *see* REMEDIES
clearance, 135
closing, 96, 99–100, 102, 131, 133, 135, 141
compensation, 79, 84, 99, 105
compulsory purchase, 99, 138, 139
control, 121
costs, 78, 80, 82, 85
demolition, 96, 99–100, 102, 131, 133, 135
housing, 131, 135, 136, 138, 139, 141
improvement, 132, 133, 135, 138, 141
nuisance, 74, 75, 78, 82–84, 86
prohibiting occupation, 83, 87
prohibition, 76, 136
OVERCROWDING, 121, 123

PAYMENT *and see* COMPENSATION
court, into, 60
well maintained, 112, 135, 142
PERSON AGGRIEVED, 85, 98, 100
statutory nuisance, by, 78, 79
PERSONAL INJURY
defect, caused by, 35, 36, 39, 41
POSSESSION PROCEEDINGS, 52, 55, 129, 130, 131, 132, 135, 137, 141, 143
PREMISES
definition of, 70, 106
PROHIBITION ORDER, 75, 136
PROOF
burden of, 41, 82, 86

PROPERTY
neighbouring, 17, 72, 73, 118, 122, 124

QUIET ENJOYMENT
covenant of, 16, 122, 123

RATES
reduction in, 54, 143
'REASONABLE EXPENSE'
repairing unfit housing, of, 15, 96
'REASONABLE TIME'
repairs, for, 26, 49, 50, 55, 75, 103, 128
RECEIVER
appointment of, 54
REDECORATION
repairs, after, 19, 63, 104
REDEVELOPMENT, 91, 135, 137, 138, 139
improvement or, 137, 139
REFUSE, 124
REHOUSING
displaced tenants, of, 81, 86, 100, 102, 108, 118, 123, 132–134, 141
RELATOR
action, 123
'RELEVANT DEFECT', 45–46
REMEDIES
contract, breach of, for, 13, 16, 18, 28, 53
court proceedings, 39, 55–64, 77–86
damages *see* DAMAGES
declaration, 60
direct action, 50–54
duty of care, breach of, for, 18, 39, 46
express covenant, breach of, for, 12
implied covenant, breach of, for, 13, 16, 18, 28, 122

REMEDIES—*cont*
injunction, 45, 59, 75
interim/interlocutory, 56–58
mandamus, 101
mandatory, 57, 59
Mareva, 60
manager, appointment of, 54
orders, breach of, for, 59–60
payment, court into, 60
rates, reduction in, 54, 143
receiver, appointment of, 54
rent
reduction in, 53, 103, 143
strike, 52
use of, to pay for repairs, 50–51, 103
withholding of, 52, 103
sequestration, 60
set-off against rent, 52–53, 103
specific performance, 28, 57, 58–59
REMOVAL
costs of, 62, 63, 140, 142–143
RENEWAL
area, 104, 112
repair or, 11, 19, 21
RENT
low rent
lettings at, 14
reduction in, 53, 103, 143
registered, 27, 53, 62, 103, 132
set-off against, 52–53, 103
strike, 52
use of, to pay for repairs, 50–51, 103
withholding of, 52, 103
REPAIR
basic, 18
common parts, of *see* COMMON PARTS
default, in *see* DEFAULT
improvement or, 19–22, 63, 83, 120, 136

REPAIR—*cont*
installations, of *see* INSTALLATIONS
'keep in repair', 11, 18, 22
maintenance or, 19
major work, 19–21
notice, 96, 102, 104, 122
patch, 20, 21–22, 82, 83, 86, 100, 102
'reasonable expense' of, 15, 96
renewal or, 11, 19, 21
structural, 10, 12, 13, 17, 18, 19, 23, 28, 73, 114
'structure and exterior', of, 17, 18, 19, 23–24
substantial, 104, 130, 132
REPORT
expert, 49, 55, 56, 79, 81, 85, 115
medical, 50, 79, 85
RESTRICTED CONTRACT, 105, 106, 135

SCOTLAND, 14
SERVICE CHARGE, 52
SERVICES
installations and, 24, 84, 124, 125
SET-OFF, 52–53, 103
SEWERS, 12, 119
SPECIFIC PERFORMANCE, 28, 57, 58–59
SQUATTER, 78, 134
SUB-LETTING, 62
SUB-TENANT, 59
SUMMONS, 79, 80, 84
witness, 79
SURVEYOR
expert report by, 56, 81

TENANCY *and see* TENANT
agricultural, 27
assured, 30, 43, 52, 128, 130, 132, 143
business, 27, 36
TENANCY—*cont*
contractual, 104, 135
council, 77, 136, 143
Crown, of, 27
housing association, 11, 51, 53, 76, 78, 129
post-14/1/1989, 17, 24, 27
pre-24/10/1961, 28
pre-1974, 45
protected, 30, 43, 128
secure, 11, 51, 53, 120, 129, 130, 136, 137
short-term, 139
statutory, 30, 59, 103, 104, 106, 132, 135
TENANCY AGREEMENT, 9
basic repairs and, 18
caveat emptor and, 9–10
common parts, repair of, and, 16–18
express terms, 10–12, 15, 17, 18, 26, 43, 51, 128, 129, 131, 142, 143
breach of *see* REMEDIES
furnished premises, 12, 13
implied terms, 12–30, 43, 122, 128
breach of *see* REMEDIES
low-rent lettings, 14
tenant's duty to repair, 11, 28
Unfair Contract Terms Act and, 11, 13
unfurnished premises, 10, 12, 13
variation of, 11, 103, 132
TENANT *and see* TENANCY
direct action by, 50–54, 77
disabled, 140
joint, 136
liability (contractual) of, 10, 11, 28, 58, 59, 60, 125
local authority, of, 11, 27, 51, 53, 54, 64, 65, 77, 78, 83, 103–104, 123, 129, 130, 132, 136, 143

TENANT—*cont*
occupying, 104–105
private, 64, 76, 78, 128, 129, 132
rent strike by, 52
sub-tenant, 59
TENANTS' ASSOCIATION, 64
unincorporated, 55
TIME LIMIT
home loss payment claim, for, 136
issue of proceedings, for, 41, 55
repairs, for, 26, 73

UNDERTAKING
landlord, of, 58, 62, 96, 99, 135, 138, 141
UNFIT
housing
definition of, 13, 15, 92–95
nuisance order and, 74, 86
UNFIT—*cont*
human habitation, for, 10, 12–15, 42, 86, 91, 92–95, 100, 106, 121, 126, 136, 142
UNFURNISHED ACCOMMODATION, 10, 12, 13

VALUATION OFFICER, 54, 143
VANDALISM, 40, 125
VARIATION
tenancy of, 11, 103, 132
VERMIN, 5, 12, 13, 15, 38, 93, 114, 124, 126

WELL MAINTAINED PAYMENT, 112, 142
WITNESS SUMMONS, 79
WORKS IN DEFAULT, 50, 51, 52, 60, 64, 74, 75, 98, 99, 102, 105, 106, 119, 121, 125

Other LAG Law and Practice Guides

The Emergency Procedures Handbook

second edition Dowell, Forbes, Hall, Olley and Wyld

In five main sections — relationship breakdown, children, housing, police station emergencies and debt crises — this *Handbook* provides time-saving precedents and checklists for taking instructions when situations demand immediate action.

Fully up-to-date, all the legislative changes that have been made since the 1986 edition was published have been taken into account.

It was said of the first edition:

> ". . . written with less experienced advisers in mind . . . [it] will concentrate your mind and organise your efforts . . . buy it" — *Roof*

> "This is a book that can confidently be recommended to the busy practitioner" — *Solicitors Journal*

September 1989 456pp **£19.00**

Defending Possession Proceedings

second edition Luba, Madge and McConnell

Completely revised and updated to take into account the Housing Act 1988, this edition of LAG's best selling guide to procedure and tactics is for advisers of public and private sector tenants, *and* mortgagors.

The authors consider the position of diverse tenants, licensees, service occupiers, mortgagors, rental purchasers, squatters and short life occupiers, and explain housing benefit, problems arising on relationship breakdown, rights under homelessness legislation, bailiffs and legal aid.

Of the first edition it was said:

> "A splendid manual . . . I can unreservedly recommend this book" — *Law Centres News*

> ". . . cannot be praised too highly . . . the authors are to be congratulated" — *Roof*

April 1989 347pp **£17.00**

Homeless Persons: The Housing Act 1985 Part III

third edition Arden

A third edition of LAG's popular guide to the homeless persons legislation, as consolidated by the Housing Act 1985 and amended by the Housing and Planning Act 1986.

Homeless Persons has been revised to cover the 1985 and 1986 legislation and the case-law. With an expanded index and comprehensive tables of statutes and cases, *Homeless Persons* reproduces the text of the Housing Act 1985 Part III, as amended, the Local Authority Agreement on local connection, the statutory instruments on the resolution of such disputes and the Code of Guidance.

Written by Andrew Arden, a practising barrister and well-known specialist in housing law, this LAG guide will be an indispensible addition to any housing practitioner's library.

July 1988 240pp **£12.00**

Arden and Partington on Quiet Enjoyment

third edition Carrott and Hunter

Tenants' remedies for illegal eviction and harassment by landlords are expertly and concisely explained in *Quiet Enjoyment*. The book covers all the law, both civil and criminal, relevant to this complex and technical area, and the full text of the Protection from Eviction Act 1977, as amended, is reproduced in an appendix.

Completely up-to-date, this third edition is a revision by two practising barristers who specialise in housing law. It takes into account the amendments made to the Protection from Eviction Act 1977, and the new tenancies and new tort of unlawful eviction created by the Housing Act 1988.

Essentially a practical guide, *Quiet Enjoyment* includes forms and precedents, and gives detailed descriptions of the steps for obtaining an injunction and how to complete the forms used in civil proceedings.

"This lucidly written book deserves a wide audience."

— *Solicitors Journal* (on the 2nd edition)

March 1990 135pp **£11.00**

Action on Racial Harassment: Legal Remedies and Local Authorities
Forbes

Written by a solicitor who has specialised in the field, the book explores the wide-ranging powers of local authorities that can be utilised to combat racial harassment, not only on council housing estates, but also in the streets, in schools and social services accommodation.

Action on Racial Harassment is for councillors, local authority officers, solicitors, advisers and community organisations — and for victims of harassment themselves. It covers civil and criminal proceedings including court procedure, concentrating particularly on the rules of evidence and their implications for the interviewing of witnesses and the collection of evidence.

In conclusion, Duncan Forbes makes a series of recommendations for the improvement of local authority practices and for changes in the law, which, if implemented, could go a long way towards the eradication of this evil in our society.

The book is comprehensively tabled and indexed and the appendices include model tenancy agreements and precedents for court documents.

May 1988 355pp **£10.00**

Police Powers: a practitioner's guide
second edition Levenson and Fairweather

This book, written by two solicitors, is for the practitioner and gives practical, step-by-step guidance to the legislation and common law. It is the successor to the authors' highly acclaimed *Practitioner's Guide to the Police and Criminal Evidence Act 1984* and updates their earlier book.

Police Powers covers the considerable case-law that has grown up since the passing of the Police and Criminal Evidence Act and also covers police powers under the legislation relating to terrorism, drug trafficking, serious fraud, customs and excise, confiscation of proceeds of crime and interception of communications. A very useful chapter deals with the exclusion of confessions and other evidence, while the police complaints procedure and remedies for abuse of police powers are also considered.

"A thorough perusal of this book is mandatory" — *New Law Journal*

"Lucid and helpful" — *Criminal Law Review*

"A whole chapter on remedies . . . takes the work further than any other" — *Justice of the Peace* (on the first edition)

December 1990 580pp **£26.00**

Using Civil Legal Aid: the 1989 scheme

second edition Hansen

Using Civil Legal Aid is LAG's guide to the legal aid scheme. It examines the green form scheme, assistance by way of representation, the legal aid certificate, emergency applications, family proceedings, costs and the statutory charge.

The 1988 Act and 1989 Regulations are reproduced in appendices, and the book is well indexed and cross-referenced.

In the *Law Society's Gazette*, it was said of the first edition.

> "It ought to be at the elbow of all legal aid practitioners . . . being admirably clear, concise and comprehensive . . . It ought also to be bought by every CAB and related advice agency."

April 1989 325pp **£15.00**

Claim in Time: time limits in social security law

second edition Partington

Professor Martin Partington has updated his highly acclaimed book on the time limit rules in social security law.

Claim in Time considers all the relevant changes in the rules resulting from the new Claims and Payments Regulations and Adjudication Regulations. The book examines the time limits for payment of national insurance contributions, deals with housing benefit and provides detailed analysis of the commissioners' case-law on "good cause" for late claim.

The book is an indispensable aid to all who advise on social security. Of the first edition, it was said:

> ". . . thoroughly and clearly written . . . of most use to the welfare rights specialist" — *Journal of Social Welfare Law*

> ". . . a valuable reference work for those advising or representing claimants in appeals against adverse decisions, dealing with the issues often raised in relation to the various pensions and benefits and the different contexts in which difficulties arise" — *Paul Burgess, then of the Manchester Welfare Rights Service*

April 1989 120pp **£8.50**

Practice and Procedure in Industrial Tribunals: A Guide to Unfair Dismissal and Redundancy

Clayton

This book comprises the series of articles by Richard Clayton first published in LAG's monthly journal, *Legal Action.* The full texts of the Industrial Tribunals and Employment Appeal Tribunal Rules of Procedure are included, with comprehensive tables and index.

Detailed guidance and practical advice on tactics are provided for the employment law adviser, from first application through to the substantive hearing, costs, reviews and enforcement, to appeals.

October 1986 142pp **£7.50**

Immigration Emergency Procedures

Fransman and Webb

Immigration Emergency Procedures is a complete guide to dealing with the range of immigration emergencies which require immediate action to prevent a client's removal from the UK and/or to secure release from detention.

Additional appendices include official forms used by the immigration authorities which an adviser is likely to encounter, client questionnaire, visa requirements, charts indicating the administrative structure of the immigration authorities (with useful telephone numbers) and appeals and time limits, relevant organisations and bibliography. The Immigration Act 1971, as amended, is also provided.

"a useful and practical book" — *Solicitors Journal*

"this is a book to be recommended" — *SCOLAG*

March 1986 198pp **£11.00**

All titles available from: LAG, 242 Pentonville Road, London N1 9UN, tel 071-833 2931.

Prices include postage and packing. Please send cash with orders, making cheques payable to: Legal Action Group.